10. 23-72

Democracy, Militarism, and Nationalism
in Argentina, 1930–1966

Latin American Monographs, No. 25
Institute of Latin American Studies
The University of Texas at Austin

Democracy, Militarism, and Nationalism in Argentina, 1930–1966

AN INTERPRETATION

By MARVIN GOLDWERT

PUBLISHED FOR THE INSTITUTE OF LATIN AMERICAN STUDIES
BY THE UNIVERSITY OF TEXAS PRESS, AUSTIN AND LONDON

Library of Congress Cataloging in Publication Data

Goldwert, Marvin.
  Democracy, militarism, and nationalism in Argentina,
1930–1966.

  (Latin American monographs, no. 25)
  Bibliography: p.
  1. Argentine Republic—Armed Forces—Political
activity. 2. Argentine Republic—Politics and
government—1910–   I. Texas. University at
Austin. Institute of Latin American Studies.
II. Title. III. Series: Latin American mono-
graphs (Austin, Tex.) no. 25.
F2849.G58   320.9′82′06   76-37843
ISBN 0-292-71500-5

Composition by G&S Typesetters, Austin
Printing by Capital Printing Company, Austin
Binding by Universal Bookbindery, Inc., San Antonio

1717974

To My Mother and Father

CONTENTS

PREFACE

Argentina is a land of endless promise and never-ending frustration. It is a nation with seemingly all the preconditions for stable democracy. It is inhabited by a homogeneous, slowly growing population that, in general, eats well from the produce of its fertile soil. The majority of the people have a caloric intake well above the minimum considered necessary for the maintenance of health. In contrast to other Latin American nations, Argentina has not been confronted with the problem of integrating and economically elevating a large Indian population. Her middle class is the largest in Latin America, comprising from 40 to 50 per cent of the population of approximately 24 million, and roughly 90 per cent of that population is categorized as being effectively literate.[1] The nation has a democratic tradition, and, prior to 1930, was governed mainly by civilians. Its people are fervently nationalistic, but it is a nationalism that extends over the entire range of political emotions, dividing instead of uniting.

Until 1930, Argentina was one of the great hopes for stable democracy in Latin America. Argentines themselves believed in the great destiny of their nation, in its mission to become the leading Latin American country in wealth, power, and culture. But the revolution of 1930 unleashed the scourges of modern militarism and chronic instability in the land. Between 1930 and 1966 the Argentine armed forces, or factions thereof, have overthrown the government five times: in 1930, when General José F. Uriburu deposed the constitutional regime of Hipólito Yrigoyen; in 1943, when President Ramón Castillo was over-

[1] Argentina Census, mid-1968, reports total population as 23,707,000 and literacy as 91.4 per cent.

thrown in a military coup which paved the way for the rise of Colonel Juan D. Perón; in September, 1955, when the dictator Perón was himself ousted; in March, 1962, when President Arturo Frondizi, the first elected chief executive after Perón, was toppled; and finally, on June 26, 1966, when, after thirty-two months in office, President Arturo Illía was unseated.

For more than four decades militarism has been the central problem in Argentine political life. This volume is an interpretation of the rise, growth, and development of militarism in Argentina from 1930 to 1966. An attempt is made to explain the tortuous course of Argentine militarism through an integrating hypothesis. The army is viewed as a power factor, torn by a permanent dichotomy of values that rendered it incapable of bringing social order and modernization to Argentina. At first frustrated by incompetent politicians (1916 to 1943), the army was later driven by Perón into an uneasy alliance with labor (1943 to 1955) and during this time it set out on a fruitless quest to reconcile social order and traditionalism with modernization under authoritarian military rule. Since 1955, when Perón was overthrown, a deeply divided army has struggled to contain the lusty remnants of its own dictatorial creation. In 1966 and 1970, the army, dedicated to staunch anti-Peronism, again seized the state and revived the dream of reconciling social order and modernization through military rule.

Although militarism is today the central problem in Argentine political life, it is also the fever that suggests deeper maladies in the body politic. In this interpretation, an attempt is made to relate developments in the military to the larger political, social, and economic developments in Argentine history. An effort has been made to view the army, and factions thereof, as integral parts of the whole political spectrum during all the periods treated. Inasmuch as the army defines its nationalist missions in terms of prevailing historical trends, and since the army's power is always relative to the strength of other social institutions, it is hoped that this broadly based approach will serve to illuminate the problem of militarism in Argentina.

The research for this volume was carried out during the years 1959 to 1961 under the Argentine Nationalism Project financed by the Rockefeller Foundation at the University of Pennsylvania. The author wishes to express his appreciation to Professor Arthur P. Whitaker, supervisor of the project, for aid and encouragement, and thanks also go to Professors Ricardo Caillet-Bois, José Luis Romero, and Gino Germani, consultants to the project in Argentina, who aided me in my research in that country. Professor Thomas F. McGann, at The University of Texas, has always been very liberal with helpful advice and encouragement. Thanks are also due to Professor Robert Alexander, of Rutgers University, for opening his vast files of interviews to me. The completion of this volume was made possible by a summer grant from La Salle College in 1966. Finally, my parents contributed the great spiritual support without which this volume could never have been completed.

INTRODUCTION
Approach, Hypotheses, and Terminology

Militarism is the central theme of this interpretation. The period from 1930 to 1966 has been chosen because it brackets the major themes of a continuous historical process: the rise and growth of Argentine militarism, and the fruitless quest of the army to reconcile its conflicting drives for social order and modernization. Actually, the process began in 1916 when the Argentine army had become fully professionalized and supported the democratic transference of power from the landed-commercial oligarchy to the Radical party representatives of the middle class. However, the vaunted democracy and stability in Argentina during the years 1916 to 1930 proved an illusion.

What took place during this period of Radical rule was the replacement of an oligarchical form of presidentialism by a popular version of that same form of government. Nearly all political power was still lodged in a presidency that overshadowed the legislature, the courts, and the provincial administrations. With the Radicals in control of the almighty presidency, constant war was waged within the institutional structure of the state against political enemies. The necessary political consensus was absent; there was no agreement of political parties on how power was to be used and how it was to be transferred. Political hate, destined to become a permanent feature of Argentine life, developed between the oligarchy and the middle class. For the oligarchy, the Radicals were the hated representatives of the upstart immigrants and the "illiterate" masses. For the Radical middle class, the oligarchy was a corrupt, cosmopolitan elite that must be driven from its provincial bulwarks. This despite the fact that it was an enlightened sector of the oligarchy that had passed in 1912 the Sáenz Peña Law decreeing secret manhood suffrage. It was the passage of this law that enabled the Radicals to come to power four years later.

While popular presidentialism under the Radicals sought to expand its power, one institution escaped its control. This was the army, which had undergone professionalization in the years from 1880 to 1916. During this period, the army had gained autonomy in vital professional matters, including the control of promotions, and consequently able officers could rise in the profession and gain military prestige apart from that bestowed by the presidency. The army now had the leadership as well as the guns to define political change, should presidentialism falter.

It did falter in 1930. A major pitfall of presidentialism was that it led to the personalization of the state. Hence, when in the years 1928 to 1930 senility gripped the Radical president, Hipólito Yrigoyen, economic depression swept the land and the state was shaken to its foundations. It was then that the leaders of the professional army, Lieutenant General José F. Uriburu and General Augustín P. Justo, began to conspire to overthrow the government. They were encouraged by the oligarchy's willingness to sacrifice Argentina's fragile tradition of civilian rule by accepting the political leadership of the generals.

The military coup which overthrew Yrigoyen in 1930 marks the rise of modern militarism in Argentina. And yet most of the army officer-corps, middle-class, nationalistic, and pro-Radical, did not participate in the coup. It was minority factions of the Argentine army that toppled the Radicals at a time when that party showed signs of moving leftward into the areas of economic nationalism and social welfare. This trend toward using the state as an instrument for economic liberation and amelioration represented an adaptation of democracy to changing social conditions similar to that occurring in other nations at the time. There were indications that the Radical party, the majority party of the nation, would evolve into a broadly based political organization, capable of responding to nationalistic stirrings and dynamic social changes. Commitments to political democracy, economic nationalism, social welfare, and an independent foreign policy, all of these characterized this nascent Radical nationalism. But in 1930

Radical nationalism failed as the vehicle of army nationalism and Argentina moved instead to the right.

From the eclipse of Radical nationalism in 1930, to the rise of Perón in the years 1943 to 1946, dominant factions of the armed forces represented two competing nationalisms of the Argentine elites. To describe this nationalist dichotomy, this interpretation adapts two categories developed by European historians: "liberal nationalism" and "integral nationalism."[1] Both of these elitist nationalist traditions were deeply rooted in Argentine soil and history.

Liberal nationalism, signifying a belief in cooperation between nations, a free flow of ideas and goods between countries, and an emphasis on personal liberties within the state, is given larger meaning in the Argentine context. In the twentieth-century Argentina, liberal nationalism represents a conservative adaptation of the nineteenth-century oligarchical traditions of such leaders as Bartolomé Mitre and Domingo Sarmiento. Liberal nationalism, or conservatism, has supported: the constitutional forms, if not the substance, of republican-democratic institutions; the free interplay of economic forces within the state and between nations; and close cooperation with the western democracies. Liberal nationalism is identified with the "democratic," civilianist tradition in the Argentine army, represented by such generals as Julio A. Roca and Agustín P. Justo.

After a brief interlude of integral nationalist dictatorship in 1930–1931 under Lieutenant General Uriburu, the liberal nationalist faction led by General Justo won control of the army for more than a decade. This period of corrupt pseudodemocracy under the restored landed-commercial oligarchy and their political allies became known as the Infamous Decade (1932–1943), and it witnessed electoral fraud, governmental corruption, and a free field for foreign investment in Argentina. During this decade, nationalistic army officers lost all faith in the professional politicians. And yet, enraged by the "sell-out" of the nation to foreign interests in league with the oligarchy and the Justista faction, army officers found no outlet for their nationalism in

[1] Louis L. Snyder, *The Meaning of Nationalism*, pp. 116–117. The author wisely suggests that the adjective-modified categories of nationalism be used in describing its many specific manifestations.

the Radical party either. Divided in tactics, rent by feuds over leadership, excluded from power by corruption, Radicalism again proved inept as the civilian vehicle for army nationalism. Betrayed by the oligarchy, frustrated by the Radical middle class, army officers turned to integral nationalism as a political weapon.

The military coup of 1943 marked the victory of integral over liberal nationalism within the army and within the political arena. "Integral nationalism," writes Louis L. Snyder, "rejected sympathy for and cooperation with other nations, promoted jingoism, militarism, and imperialism, and opposed all liberties when they interfered with the aims of the state."[2] In twentieth-century Argentina, integral nationalism represents a modern adaptation of the nativist, dictatorial tradition of the nineteenth-century *caudillo*, Juan Manuel de Rosas. Integral nationalism has continually favored: the authoritarian state and military rule over the constitutional forms and personal liberties of western democracy; economic nationalism and protectionism; and sometimes expansionism. Integral nationalism is identified with the authoritarian, militarist tradition in the Argentine army, represented by such officers as José F. Uriburu, the leaders of the revolution of 1943, and Juan D. Perón.

With the rise of Colonel Perón in the years 1943 to 1946, the military dictatorship of the integral nationalists began to evolve into majoritarian dictatorship. The Perón dictatorship (1946–1955) represented the popularization of integral nationalism. Integral nationalism had previously drawn its support from the army, fascistoid elites, and some members of the clergy. Popular integral nationalism, or Peronism, maintained by an alliance of the army and captive labor unions, represented a dictatorial synthesis of many of the conflicting drives in Argentine political life.

For the army, Peronism bridged the sharp dichotomy which underlay the seeming opportunism of that institution's political positions. Since 1880, the army, or dominant factions thereof, has been aligned in turn with the oligarchy (1880–1916), with the middle-class Radicals (1916–1930), with fascistoid elites (1930–1931), with the

[2] *Ibid.*

oligarchy and conservative allies (1932–1943), with fascistoid elites (1943–1946), with Peronist labor (1946–1955), and finally, since 1955 with conservative elites against the Peronist masses. The tortuous course of Argentine militarism is, in part, explained by a basic dichotomy of institutional values. As the sociologist José Luis de Imaz has written, the army in Argentina represents a power factor with permanent objectives and values.[3] It is a major thesis of this interpretation that the Argentine army is at once a traditional and a modern institution, and that it is torn by these conflicting values. On the one hand, the Argentine army officer has been inculcated with respect for tradition, a simple patriotism, a gentlemanly Catholicism, and a desire for social order. On the other hand, he has been driven by a modern nationalism derived from his technical-military functions. This nationalism calls for autarchy, industrialization, and technical modernization to build the economic base of a strong war machine. Yet, such modernization inevitably carries in its wake social changes that collide with and erode traditional values. How to reconcile his traditional value structure with the requirements and effects of modernization, has been one of the fundamental dilemmas of the Argentine army officer.

For many army officers, Peronism offered a way out of this dilemma. It promised to bridge the traditional-modern dichotomy through the controlled popularization of an integral nationalist military revolution. So long as the army stood as a pillar of the Perón regime, military fears that modernization and industrialization would produce a revolutionary proletariat were restrained. Furthermore, the *descamisados* ("the shirtless masses") provided much of the voting strength that sanctioned the nationalistic Peronist programs so dear to the army. Viewed from this standpoint, Peronism initially represented the means by which army officers could have their cake, in the way of nationalistic modernization, and still eat it in peace, with the masses organized in captive unions tied to an authoritarian state.

But Peronism changed after 1951. By that year, Perón could no longer buy the support of both pillars of the regime—the army and labor. His economic policies had undermined the exchange-earning

[3] José Luis de Imaz, "Los que mandan: Las fuerzas armadas en Argentina," *América Latina* 7, no. 4 (October–December, 1964): 40.

power of the agrarian sector, and inflation and deterioration began to set in. During the period from 1952 to 1955, he moved towards a totalitarianism that violated both the traditional and the modern values of the army. From 1952 to 1955, economic weakness forced him into a rapprochement with the United States that was climaxed by a hated contract with Standard Oil in 1955. Perón had thus betrayed the modern side of army nationalism. Moreover, this betrayal came on the heels of a program to indoctrinate the whole institution with Peronist ideals that threatened the traditional value-structure of the military. The program sought to inculcate the idea of loyalty to the state as the leading value on all levels of the military, superseding loyalty to institution and to historic fatherland. In addition, Perón launched an attack on the church in 1954, giving proof of his totalitarian intentions and of his desire to bend all traditional institutions—army, church, and even family—to his will. And finally, facing intense opposition that had been aroused by an abortive naval uprising in June, 1955, Perón threatened to arm and unleash the *descamisado* horde. This threat to organize and arm labor-militias was the very nightmare of the military, for it challenged the institution's traditional control over the other organized forces of the state.

The drive towards totalitarianism sparked an alliance between a small sector of the army officer-corps, the conservative navy, and the air force, which overthrew Perón in the Liberating Revolution of September, 1955. But after Perón was gone, Argentina remained, in the words of Dr. Arthur P. Whitaker, "a haunted house."[4] After 1955 the army that created Peronism sought to bottle it up, and even to destroy it. Seemingly polarized forever, the army and Peronist labor clashed as the most powerful power factors in a fragmented society characterized by opportunistic civilian elites, a deeply divided middle class, and a politically marooned mass. Each day brought military crises or even coups as the armed forces tried to check the lusty remnants of Peronism. Only recently has the military, under President Alejandro Agustín Lanusse, attempted to reconcile its positions with those of the Peronists in the interest of stable democracy in Argentina.

4 Arthur P. Whitaker, *Argentina*, p. 151.

Democracy, Militarism, and Nationalism
in Argentina, 1930–1966

PART I
DEMOCRACY AND THE RISE OF
MODERN MILITARISM, 1880-1930

When, in 1930, factions of the army over-
threw the regime of Hipólito Yrigoyen, it marked the emergence of
modern militarism in Argentina. Modern Argentine militarism is distinguished from previous military intervention in politics by the fact
that since 1930 professional army officers rather than civilian politicians
have exercised revolutionary leadership. Prior to 1930, the army, or
factions thereof, had served as the necessary instruments of force in
attempts by civilian political leaders to overthrow the constituted authorities. With the revolution of 1930, army officers themselves began
to initiate, plan, and lead military conspiracies. Furthermore, rebel army
leaders began to aspire to rule Argentina in the aftermath of military
revolution.

The army officers who came to prominence and power in the revolution of 1930 were leaders of The New Army. Beginning in the late
nineteenth century, the military establishment had undergone professionalization—that is, the formation of a technically trained officer

corps comprised of paid career-men dedicated solely to professional matters. This process necessitated the establishment of academies for advanced training in modern methods and weaponry and the adoption of promotion criteria based on merit rather than on political favoritism. Paradoxically, professionalization, with its emphasis on strict subordination to civilian authority and dedication to military matters, was a necessary precondition for modern militarism. With professionalization, control of military advancement was gradually removed from the presidency and vested in the officer corps. The army possessed guns and a ready-made revolutionary organization, and it became the only state institution in which leadership, prestige, and potential power could be maintained and acquired apart from presidential favor.

Having gained semi-autonomy in professional matters and with its own built-in prestige system, the army was prepared to provide not only the requisite force, but also the leadership to define political all institutions to totter.

change. The expansion of the army's influence in politics in Argentina was facilitated by two major conditions. First, the lack of a basic political consensus on how power was to be used and how it was to be transferred. Second, the pervasiveness of presidential government and the weakness of other institutions. This led to the personalization of government and parties so that the failures of one individual could cause

The two themes are interrelated. When in 1916 the Radical leader, Hipólito Yrigoyen, became president of Argentina, he sought to reestablish presidentialism by popular sanction. This effort included assaults on both the professional autonomy of the army and on the provincial bulwarks of the oligarchy. Leaders of the army responded by professional protestation that was later converted into political action as conservative politicians beckoned the military men into the political arena. Hence, neither the Radicals nor the liberal nationalist oligarchy adhered to the tradition of an apolitical army. When in 1930 the popular presidentialism of the Radicals was profoundly shaken by the senility of President Yrigoyen, professional army officers, guided but no longer controlled by power-seeking politicians of the right, seized the state and became leaders of the nation.

In order to understand the rise of modern militarism in Argentina, it is necessary to relate developments within the professional army—as the major repository of the organized force of the state—to larger political and social processes. As the political scientist K. H. Silvert has stated, the "armed forces can never be divorced from the societies in which they develop, their influence and their power being always relative to that displayed by other social institutions in terms of the values of the time." The subordination of the military establishment to civilian rule may be a generally accepted value in Argentine society, "but that value depends for its maintenance on how much it is believed by all groups (not only by the military but also by those who are tempted to manipulate the military), as well as on the amount of power other political groups display. It is obvious that if political parties lose themselves in functionalism and in irrationality, the military gains power without the purchase of a single new rifle. And conversely, a complex and healthy set of democratic institutions creates a system of checks within which the armed forces can remain most legitimately professional."[1] Therefore, in order to trace the rise of militarism in Argentina it is valuable to examine the army within the general setting of the nation's institutional, political, and social developments from 1880 to 1930.

[1] K. H. Silvert, "The Military: A Handbook for Their Control," in *Letters and Reports Written for the American Universities Field Staff, 1955–1958*, p. 3.

1. Developments within the Army Related to Institutional, Political, and Social Developments

The professional Argentine army was a creation of nineteenth-century liberal nationalism. Both Bartolomé Mitre and Domingo F. Sarmiento, the first statesmen to rule Argentina after the legal unification of the nation in 1861, envisaged a professional army as part of the larger liberal nationalist program of education, immigration, and economic development through foreign investment; that is, the army was to establish conditions necessary for stable democracy under civilian rule. In the short run, this goal required a modern, well-trained military establishment capable of taming the gaucho militias of rebellious provincial *caudillos*. As part of his lifelong crusade against the authoritarian, gauchesque tradition personified by the deposed dictator Juan Manuel de Rosas, Sarmiento began the trend toward military professionalization by establishing the Colegio Militar (1870) and the Escuela Naval (1872), the officers' training schools of present-day Argentina.[1]

[1] For a description of the military thought and reforms of Domingo F. Sarmiento, see Augusto G. Rodríguez, *Sarmiento militar*, especially pp. 344–346.

When the long-standing conflict between the port and the provinces was ended in 1880 with the federalization of the city of Buenos Aires, the national army began to play a new role in pacified Argentina. During the years from 1880 to 1916, the army served as the pretorian guard of the all-powerful presidents who represented the landed oligarchy. Although a powerful chief executive was characteristic of all previous administrations, presidentialism was first fully established during the regime of President Julio A. Roca (1880–1886). Granted extensive powers, including control of the armed forces, under the constitution of 1853, Roca was able to bend all other institutions to his will. As a strong head of state and leader of the only powerful political party, Partido Autonomista Nacional (PAN), Roca instituted the *unicato*, the one-man rule of the president. Using the threat of intervention by an army that was equipped with the recently acquired Remington rifle and capable of swift transport by newly constructed railroads, Roca transformed the once powerful provincial governors into docile instruments of the president. Through the Ministry of the Interior, charged with electoral supervision, and the provincial governors, Roca controlled elections to the Congress. Thus it was that the provinces, the legislature, the courts, and the armed forces were all subordinated to the *unicato*.[2]

Presidentialism based on force and electoral fraud was not full-fledged democracy, and the ruling liberal nationalist oligarchy recognized this fact. However, they viewed the *unicato* as a kind of tutelary democracy by which an enlightened elite, dedicated to progress along positivistic lines, would control the nation until the development of conditions necessary for full-fledged democracy.[3] A significant aspect

---

[2] The conversion of the national army into a presidential pretorian guard is described in A. Belín Sarmiento, *Una república muerta*, pp. 19–21. On the army and the development of presidentialism under Roca, see Ataúlfo Pérez Aznar, "El ejército de línea" in his "Esquema de las fuerzas políticas actuantes hasta 1890," *Revista de Historia*, no. 1 (1957): 48–49; and José Nicolás Matienzo, "La revolución de 1890 en la historia constitucional," in his *Nuevos temas políticos e históricos*, pp. 287–289.

[3] The ideology and values of the landed oligarchy are analyzed in Thomas F. McGann, *Argentina, the United States, and the Inter-American System, 1880–1914*, chaps. 2–5.

of the oligarchy's program for the development of Argentina was the continuation of military professionalization. During the more than three decades of tutelary democracy, The Old Army, an ill-equipped force of impressed soldiers led by amateur officers, was converted into The New Army, a conscript army with modern arms and a professional officer-corps.

The driving force behind military professionalization in this period was General Julio A. Roca, who twice served as president and who became the dominant influence in the army officer-corps during the late nineteenth and early twentieth centuries. Roca's protegé, General Pablo R. Riccheri, is revered today as a major figure in the organization of The New Army, and the movement for military professionalization. In 1884, during his first administration, Roca converted the Argentine general staff from a simple bureau for the transmission of orders into one of the major institutions for the preparation of the nation for war.[4] During the 1890's, Riccheri headed an armaments commission in Europe and made successful large-scale purchases of modern German weaponry for the Argentine army. These developments led to the creation of a war academy to train general staff officers in new military methods and weaponry. In 1899, Roca, then in his second term (1898–1904), engaged the first German training mission to Argentina to organize such an academy on the Prussian model, thereby inaugurating a forty-year period of service collaboration between the two nations. On January 29, 1900, the Escuela Superior de Guerra was created by general order of the Ministry of War.[5]

One year later, the famous Law No. 4,031, sponsored by Minister of War Riccheri, was passed and established obligatory military service in Argentina.[6] This law of conscription, generally referred to as the

---

[4] Círculo Militar, *Monografía histórica del estado mayor*, pp. 60–62.

[5] Riccheri's contributions to military modernization are described in Círculo Militar, *Teniente General D. Pablo Riccheri*, pp. 15–18. For the organization of the Escuela Superior de Guerra, see "Escuela Superior de Guerra," *Revista Universitaria* 6, no. 61 (1935): 135–138.

[6] The actual operation of the obligatory military-service act is described in detail in George Marvin, "Universal Military Service in Argentina," *World's Week* 33 (1916–1917): 381–392.

nationalization of the military establishment, marked the passage of the *enganchado* ("impressed soldier") into history. Both professionalization and nationalization were intended to fulfill the liberal nationalist goal of a conscript army led by professional officers subordinate to civilian rule in a democracy. But, as has been stated, these developments were in fact essential preconditions for the rise of modern militarism in Argentina.

Professionalization heightened the corporate consciousness of the officer corps, especially the determination of the military to acquire and maintain autonomy on vital matters such as promotion. By 1910, the criteria for promotion had changed from political favoritism to seniority and particularly to the mastery of the techniques of modern warfare.[7] A related development was the shift in control of promotions from the presidency to the professional army, represented by a Comisión Informativa de Calificación comprised of commanders of army divisions headed by the highest ranking general.[8] This meant that able officers could rise in the profession and acquire military prestige and influence apart from that bestowed by the president. In other words, a peacetime military establishment had become the first state institution to escape the shadow of presidentialism.

Nationalization, since it required the expansion of the officer corps to meet the needs of a conscript army, made the institution more responsive to social and political changes in Argentina. The expansion of the corps came at a time when the adoptions of professional standards and of obligatory retirement laws were compelling senior officers, tied by personal allegiances to Roca and the oligarchy, to leave the army. Their highly trained successors were drawn from Argentina's growing middle class and were largely of immigrant origin. More than twenty years elapsed between the beginning of Roca's first administration (1880) and the end of his second (1904). During this period, the transformation of the armed forces coincided with massive immigration, largely

---

[7] Enrique Pavón Pereyra, *Perón, 1895–1942*, p. 43.

[8] Augusto A. Maligne, "El ejército en octubre de 1910," *Revista de Derecho, Historia y Letras* 39 (1911): 408–409.

from Spain and Italy. In the first Argentine census of 1869 the population numbered 1,830,214. By 1909, the figures had risen to 6,805,684, and 2,531,853 of these were foreigners.[9]

The middle and lower classes, largely of immigrant origin, soon began to clamor for a voice in governing Argentina and for an end to tutelary democracy. Their first attempt to topple the oligarchical *unicato* came in 1890 with a revolt against the regime of Miguel Juárez Celman by the Unión Cívica. Significantly, the civilian leaders of this movement received their military support from a secret lodge of junior officers known as the Logia de Los 33. This lodge reflected the first breach between the ambitious, highly trained junior officers, drawn from the new middle class, and the older Roquista generals who had risen in the profession through political favoritism.[10] Although the revolt failed to unseat the oligarchy, it led to the formation of the Radical party in 1892. For more than two decades this party would seek to regenerate republican-democracy through effective suffrage and honest elections.

As the officer corps of the professionalized army was opened to the socially aspiring sons of Argentina's new middle class, there occurred a decided shift in political sympathy from the oligarchy to the Radical movement. By 1912, virtually all of the high ranks of the officer corps were occupied by young men, drawn mainly from the new middle class.[11] In the years from 1900 to 1912, Hipólito Yrigoyen, leader of the Radical movement, had propagandized intensively for the support of junior officers. When General Julio A. Roca finally retired, Yrigoyen established political connections with such influential Roquista generals as Edmundo Racedo, governor of Entre Ríos, and Riccheri. From the politico-military standpoint, the stage was set by 1912 for a peaceful transference of power from the oligarchy to the Radicals. When the famous Roque Sáenz Peña Law assuring the secrecy of the ballot was

[9] Jorge Abelardo Ramos, *Historia política del ejército argentino*, pp. 53–56.

[10] Juan Balestra, *El noventa: Una evolución política argentina*, pp. 132–133; also see, Adolfo Buezas, *Las fuerzas armadas ante la alternativa: Pueblo o imperialismo*, pp. 9–10.

[11] Maligne, "El ejército en 1910," p. 563.

passed in 1912, most of the middle-class army officers had come to see in Radicalism the great national movement of the day.[12]

Prior to the election of 1916, growing Radical sympathy in the officer corps was bolstered by fear of revolution in the event of Yrigoyen's defeat through fraud. For almost three decades, the nation had lived with the threat and the developing reality of Radical revolution. Even those officers who did not share the Radical sympathies of their colleagues were in no mood to disrupt a peaceful transference of power. And so it was that in 1916, in the first honest national elections in Argentine history, Hipólito Yrigoyen became president of the nation with the blessing of most army officers.[13]

Radical party victory in 1916 meant that tutelary democracy had become popular. This, however, by no means reversed the institutional imbalance which presidentialism had come to represent. Under Hipólito Yrigoyen, the oligarchical *unicato* was replaced by popular presidentialism. In his attitudes toward his own Radical party as well as toward Congress and other institutions of state, Yrigoyen displayed a curious commingling of democratic precepts and personalistic authoritarianism: as the personification of the popular will at last made manifest, his words and his actions were not to be questioned by men or institutions. To the mystical Yrigoyen, a recluse whose austere manner of living endeared him to the masses, the election of 1916 was a popular mandate to complete the revolution by smashing the oligarchical crust that had formed around institutions.

This policy of continued revolution through popular, messianic presidentialism could hardly be expected to convert the conservative politicians of the oligarchy into a loyal opposition. Political strife in Argentina was thus raised to the intensity of a holy war. Control of the Senate remained with the conservatives throughout Yrigoyen's administration, and that body thwarted many of his measures. At the outset of his term, eleven of the fourteen provincial governments were ruled by conservative cliques that had been elected by fraud. From 1916 to

---

[12] Ramos, *Historia política del ejército argentino*, pp. 55–56.
[13] Roberto Etchepareborda, "Aspectos políticos de la crisis de 1930," *Revista de Historia*, no. 3 (1958): 14.

1922, Yrigoyen ordered twenty provincial interventions, far more than those executed by any previous administration. Of the fourteen provinces, only Santa Fe, which he had controlled since 1912, was spared.[14] Radical revolution was thus continued within the framework of Argentine institutions. Subjected to such pressure, the conservatives, their power waning, represented a seemingly permanent minority and an opposition not averse to the use of force to gain control of the presidency or the government.

Yrigoyen's effort to restore the *unicato*, albeit by popular sanction, was extended to the military establishment although that institution had been acquiring control of its own affairs. During revolts in 1890, 1893, and 1905, the Radicals had built up in the officer corps a backlog of sympathizers whose careers had suffered owing to their participation in those unsuccessful upheavals. To reward these officers, to provide historical sanction for Radical revolts against the constituted authorities, and to convert the armed forces into part of his personalized political machine, Yrigoyen used the officer corps as a source of patronage. Dead and retired fighters for the Radical cause were raised in rank in order to enlarge their, or their families', pensions. For the active members, promotions and citations of merit, granted with little regard for military regulations and law, rewarded past services and promised further benefits for future support.[15] Popular presidentialism and military professionalism thus collided during the first Yrigoyen administration.

To oppose Yrigoyen's military policy, a group of discontented officers formed a secret lodge in 1921, the Logia de San Martín. The number of lodge members probably was never more than 188 out of an officer corps of about 1,600,[16] but the lodge was to play an important role in shaping Argentine history down to the revolution of

[14] Ernesto Palacio, *Historia de la Argentina, 1515–1938*, p. 596; Ismael Bucich Escobar, *Historia de los presidentes argentinos*, pp. 477–479.

[15] Juan V. Orona, "Una logia poco conocida y la revolución del 6 de septiembre," *Revista de Historia*, no. 3 (1958): 73–74. An editorial entitled "En el ejército" in *La Nación*, September 17, 1921, p. 4, declared that political influence in the Radical party had become the "open sesame" for military advancement.

[16] Exposé of the lodge in *Ultima Hora*, December 9, 1828, p. 5.

1930. By 1922 the lodge had gained control of the directorate of the Círculo Militar, the officers' club.[17] Through this institution, it could voice protests and exert pressure on the government in behalf of "the army."

When in 1922 Yrigoyen's hand-picked successor, Marcelo T. de Alvear, was elected to the presidency, the lodge sought to influence the selection of his minister of war. Yrigoyen, in an effort to perpetuate his control of that ministry, was attempting to impose the appointment of his close friend, General Luis J. Dellepiane. The lodge countered by backing its own candidate, General Agustín P. Justo. President Alvear, bent on proving he was no mere creature of Yrigoyen, chose Justo.[18]

The appointment of Justo marked still another stage in the military establishment's encroachment on presidentialism: an organized faction of the army had influenced the selection of the minister of war. This event also had other important political repercussions. It represented the first step in Alvear's rebellion against Yrigoyen, and so foreshadowed the split in the Radical party in 1924 into the Radical Personalists (followers of Yrigoyen) and the Radical Antipersonalists (supporters of Alvear). Henceforth, the Radical Personalists will be referred to as Radicals, and the Radical Antipersonalists as Antipersonalists. When the appointment of Justo was made known in 1922, cries of "Treason! Treason!" swept the plenary committee of the Radical party.[19]

The controversy which swirled around the appointment also caused stirrings within the military establishment. Professional divisions were arising within the officer corps, which would later take on political overtones. Each of the three major aspirants for minister of war had established a reputation for professional achievement. Justo was an able officer and an engineer, who from 1915 to 1922 had served as one of the most popular directors of the Colegio Militar. His word was law to seven graduating classes.[20] Dellepiane, having won fame first as the officer who did most to develop the engineering division

[17] Orona, "Una logia poco conocida y la revolución," pp. 77–78.
[18] *Ibid.*, pp. 78–79.
[19] Manuel Gálvez, *Vida de Hipólito Yrigoyen: El hombre de misterio*, p. 380.
[20] Bucich Escobar, *Historia de los presidentes argentinos*, pp. 589–590.

of the army,[21] had gained Yrigoyen's support by strong leadership in bringing order to Buenos Aires during the Tragic Week of January 1919. Given virtually complete authority over the city during that bloody period of labor strife and panic, Dellepiane had restored both order to the city and authority to the civilians. The third minister of war candidate was Lieutenant General José F. Uriburu, the most distinguished officer in the Argentine army.[22] Having risen to prominence as a cavalry officer, Uriburu was identified with two major army developments. During his youth he had been a member of a group known as the Young Turks who, schooled in the techniques of scientific war, fought to batter down resistance of The Old Army to scientific methods.[23] Later, after receiving advanced training with the Uhlan Guards in Berlin in 1908, Uriburu became the leader of the Germanophiles in The New Army. In 1910, he was named director of the Escuela Superior de Guerra, the center of German influence in the Argentine army.[24]

Professionalism had enabled all three of these officers to advance in a peacetime army, and to maintain their positions under all kinds of political conditions. As the army became increasingly politicized, their military leadership would be translated into political power. Justo's career as a political leader dates from his tenure as minister of war under Alvear (1922–1928). Given encouragement and strong financial backing by the Alvear administration, he executed a sweeping program of military modernization which benefited officers and conscripts alike.[25] This program won him broad support on every level of the army.

21 *Quien es quien en la Argentina: Biografías contemporáneas*, p. 203.
22 For further information on Uriburu's candidacy for the ministry of war, see Palacio, *Historia de la Argentina*, pp. 610–611.
23 Emilio Kinkelín, "La personalidad militar del Teniente General Uriburu," *La Nación*, May 3, 1932, p. 4.
24 Enrique J. Spangenberg Leguizamón, *Los responsables: El ejército y la Unión Cívica Radical ante la democracia argentina*, pp. 65–66. On Uriburu's leadership of the military Germanophiles during World War I, see Percy A. Martin, *Latin America and the War*, pp. 185–186.
25 Vicente de Pascal, "Argentina's Man of Destiny?" *Inter-American Monthly* 1 (1942): p. 15.

It also gained him the hostility of the two other aspirants for the minister of war appointment. On March 24, 1924, General Dellepiane, assigned to the innocuous post of adviser to the section on international boundaries in the foreign relations ministry, fought a bloody but indecisive duel with Minister of War Justo. The duel resulted from Dellepiane's charges of corruption in Justo's program of military modernization.[26] Although the referee, Uriburu, then serving as inspector general of the army, stepped in to halt the duel after both officers had suffered minor wounds, he was no friend of the minister of war. Relations between Justo and Uriburu had always been impersonal and formal. By 1926 the two had become enemies as a result of bureaucratic differences and a contest for power within the institutional framework of the army. Appointed to the newly created post of inspector general in 1923, Uriburu claimed that he was responsible directly to the president and not to the minister of war. The judge-advocate of the armed forces, Dr. Carlos Risso Domínguez, ruled against Uriburu's position.[27] In 1926, after further disagreement with Justo on military matters, Uriburu requested to be relieved from his post.[28]

With the approach of the presidential elections of 1928, the Justo-Uriburu rivalry took on ideological overtones. The anti-Yrigoyen group within the officer corps had tasted real power during the Alvear regime. Looking to the future, these officers were unwilling to relinquish such power and were determined to resist Yrigoyen's reelection in 1928. As early as 1924, there were well-founded rumors of a military coup in the event of Alvear's death and an attempt to transfer power to Yrigoyen's aide, Vice-President Elpidio González. As the presidential elections of 1928 drew closer, rumors were circulated of military rebellion should Yrigoyen be elected. The two officers generally acknowledged as possible leaders of such a revolt were General Agustín P. Justo and Lieutenant General José F. Uriburu.[29]

[26] *Ibid.*, pp. 15–16.
[27] Spangenberg Leguizamón, *Los responsables*, p. 69.
[28] Carlos Ibarguren, *La historia que he vivido*, p. 363.
[29] Félix Luna, *Hipólito Yrigoyen: El templario de la libertad*, I, 459–461, in *Hipólito Yrigoyen: Pueblo y gobierno.*

General Justo's dynamic term as minister of war had won him broad support in the officer corps of the army. As the Logia de San Martín's candidate for the post, he had spared no effort to fulfill that secret military organization's demands for professionalism and military modernization. The success of the lodge, along with Justo's ambitions, swept it into politics as the organized faction of the minister of war. After 1924, the Logia de San Martín was sworn to propagandize for military revolt in the event of Yrigoyen's election.[30] By 1928, Justo's office had become, in the words of Manuel Gálvez, "a telephone center for anti-Radical politics."[31] It was the Radical Personalist faction, the followers of Yrigoyen, against whom the Justista conspiracy was directed. The 1924 schism in the Radical party had endured, and by 1928 the Antipersonalist supporters of Alvear were moving towards an alliance with the conservative politicians of the oligarchy. Justo would later leave the army to become the leader of this alliance of liberal nationalists and Antipersonalists. In 1928, however, his political ambitions were temporarily thwarted by Alvear, who would brook no interference with the democratic processes. On February 21, 1928, General Justo, acting on the advice of Alvear, wrote a letter to the leading newspapers of Buenos Aires eschewing ambitions for the role of military dictator. Such rumors, he added, were either the work of sick souls or a political maneuver to discredit him.[32]

If Justo represented the shrewd military conspirator working with the traditional liberal nationalist forces of Argentina, rumors of Uriburu's projected uprising told quite another story. Uriburu was planning a military revolt to be executed without civilian participation and without commitments to any politician or political party. The armed forces alone would rule in the aftermath, with Uriburu installed as military dictator.[33]

Uriburu's conspiracy reflected the rise of integral nationalism that took place during the 1920s within the Argentine army and the political arena at large. This trend was in part inspired by developments

30 Atilio E. Cattáneo, *Entre rejas-memorias*, pp. 3–4.
31 Gálvez, *Vida de Hipólito Yrigoyen*, p. 393.
32 Text of Justo's letter in *La Nación*, February 21, 1928, p. 1.
33 Spangenberg Leguizamón, *Los responsables*, pp. 219–220.

in Europe where fascists and integral nationalists were calling upon military strongmen to rescue their countries from parliamentarians and the democratic-republican system. Italy provided an influential example of a regimented state, organized along corporate lines for internal order and external power, being led down the path to "military glory" by a dictator. In 1925, only six years after the organization of his Fascio di Combatimento in Milan, Benito Mussolini became dictator of Italy. In Spain two years before, a military dictatorship had been established by General Miguel Primo de Rivera, of Catalonia, whose movement was directed against the rampant corruption of the professional politicians. By 1924 Charles Maurrás and León Daudet, leaders of Action Française, were calling upon the French to follow the Italian example of authoritarian rule dedicated to empire and glory. As early as 1923, Adolf Hitler, head of the German National-Socialist Labor party, led an unsuccessful putsch, and, after serving only eight months of a five-year prison term, was set free and began to reorganize his forces.

The integral nationalism that emerged in Argentina in the 1920s drew its inspiration both from exotic intellectual currents such as Italian fascism and Action Française and from the indigenous authoritarian tradition of Juan Manuel de Rosas. It appealed mainly to four elements in Argentine society: disillusioned intellectuals; the *niños bien* ("sons of provincial landed oligarchs," often under financial duress); rebels from the conservative political ranks of the oligarchy, who wanted elitism legitimized by force; and members of the armed forces, especially young army officers. Although these elements would form a number of integral nationalist organizations in the 1930s, they were never united into a single political grouping or party. The extremist proponents of discipline and unity in society were never able to subject themselves to one leader or one organization.[34]

For the Argentine integral nationalists the 1920s were years of ideological development, rather than of organization. In 1923, Leopoldo Lugones, a poet who had run the gamut of political doctrines prior to his conversion to integral nationalism, delivered a series of

[34] Ibarguren, *La historia que he vivido*, p. 463.

lectures, in the Teatro Coliseo of Buenos Aires. In these lectures, sponsored by the Liga Patriótica Argentina (a direct-action organization formed to combat strikes during the Tragic Week of 1919), Lugones called upon the integral nationalists to exalt the Fatherland to the point of mysticism against the dual menace of internal subversion by radical foreigners and the external threat of communism. One year later, Lugones, speaking at the Lima centennial of the battle of Ayacucho, declared the arrival "for the good of the world, [of] the hour of the sword."[35] Lugones was calling for the military heroes to restore an authoritarianism indigenous to Argentina. As the last formal hierarchy in the nation, only the army could impose the discipline necessary to combat radicalism and the demagoguery of the professional politician. This demagoguery resulted from the imposition of an alien political system on the nation—the republican-democracy that had been imported as a part of a reaction against the authoritarian, gauchesque tradition of Juan Manuel de Rosas.

With the establishment in 1926 of *La Voz Nacional* by Roberto de Laférrere, integral nationalism had its first voice in the Argentine press. This newspaper was an outspoken critic of individualistic demoliberalism. It considered the republican-democratic system with its political parties a synthetic structure that stifled the national will. Only corporate representation, a system of direct socio-economic representation ordered by dictatorial discipline, could release the vital forces of the nation.[36] In 1928 a group of young Argentine journalists, among them Julio and Rodolfo Irazusta, Ernesto Palacio, and Juan E. Carulla, resigned from the conservative newspaper *La Fronda*, to establish the integral nationalist organ *La Nueva República*. Shortly thereafter, *La Fronda*, edited by Francisco Uriburu (no relation to Lieutenant General José F. Uriburu), also took on an integral nationalist orientation.[37]

Further support for the integral nationalist movement came from the prominent historian and essayist Carlos Ibarguren, who has left the most systematic account of its early ideas. Ibarguren indicates that the young integral nationalists aimed at giving theoretical sophistication

---

[35] Oscar Troncoso, *Los nacionalistas argentinos*, pp. 39–40.
[36] Alfredo Palacios, *En defensa de los instituciones libres*, pp. 49–50.
[37] Troncoso, *Los nacionalistas argentinos*, p. 45.

to the rudimentary concepts of the Liga Patriótica Argentina, an organization advocating the direct use of violence to maintain "the great Argentine family" against leftist movements tending to foment socioeconomic strife.[38] In their struggle against the demoliberal system, the integral nationalists added to the mystical exaltation of the state a concept of the nation as an integral organism superior to the liberties of the individual and to the interests of parties and classes. In their view, Argentina's power and historic leadership in Latin America would be fostered by an all-powerful state, capable of harmonizing internal conflicts. This concept led many integral nationalists to favor corporate representation under authoritarian leadership. By the same token, the movement was directed against the traditional political parties and the professional politicians, whose conquest of the state through elections open to the masses on a geographical basis enabled them to rule in line with narrow individual and class interests.[39]

It should be noted that integral nationalists like Lugones, Ibarguren, and the Irazusta brothers were also to become identified with the cult of the gaucho and the revisionist school of history that sought to reverse unfavorable historical judgments of dictator Juan Manuel de Rosas. Integral nationalism was, above all, a nativist and elitist movement against the nineteenth-century imports of liberal nationalism—republican-democracy, the immigrant, and foreign capital. In the works of integral nationalist historians, the crude xenophobia of the Liga Patriótica Argentina became the sentimentalized and heroic depiction of the gaucho, the indigenous Argentine, glorified over the immigrant.

On the action level, the integral nationalists called for revolution by the army, the last of the hierarchies and the only apolitical repository of patriotism.[40] Many army officers, including Lieutenant General José F. Uriburu, already deeply influenced by the dictatorship of Primo de Rivera in Spain, were attracted by this integral national doctrine. In addition, the integral national doctrine appealed to Uriburu, the man-

[38] Liga Patriótica Argentina, *Cuarto congreso nacionalista de la Liga Patriótica Argentina, sesiones del 19, 20 y 21 de mayo de 1923*, pp. 28–29.

[39] Ibarguren, *La historia que he vivido*, pp. 464–465.

[40] Palacio, *Historia de la Argentina*, p. 618; Juan E. Carulla, *Valor etico de la revolución del 6 de septiembre de 1930*, pp. 34, 36.

of-action whose philosophical leanings were towards Carlyle's cult of the hero.[41] It appealed to Uriburu, the Prussianized soldier who felt that army discipline should be expanded to Argentine society.[42] It appealed to Uriburu, born of the landholding elite of Salta, who despised those politicians who catered to the immigrant masses. In 1929, Uriburu, guest of honor at a banquet given by his integral nationalist friends in the Munich Restaurant to celebrate the first anniversary of *La Nueva República*, raised his glass in a toast—to the continuing struggle against bad government (those politicians!) and the reorganization of Argentina.[43]

Thus on the eve of the 1928 presidential elections, conspiratorial factions within the army officer-corps were becoming part of an enlarged spectrum of political opposition to the Radicals. Modern Argentine militarism was not the creation of a monolithic army caste, but of politico-military factions led by officers and operating in a politically fluid situation. The Justo faction was the military ally of the liberal nationalist alliance of conservatives and Antipersonalists. Himself an Antipersonalist, General Justo became the leader of this conservative, restorationist alliance after the revolution of 1930. The Uriburu faction, on the other hand, represented the entrance of integral nationalism into the Argentine political arena, and was part of a radical-rightist movement against both Radicals and liberal nationalism or conservatism. However, both conspiracies were being hatched in a middle-class officer-corps that was still predominantly pro-Radical in sympathy, and the election of Hipólito Yrigoyen in 1928 gave the Radicals control of the centers of power within both the government and the army.

The army factions did not strike immediately against Yrigoyen after his election. The Radical ticket—Hipólito Yrigoyen–Francisco Beiró—had scored a resounding triumph over the Antipersonalists—Leopoldo Melo–Vicente Gallo—who had aligned with the Conservatives in a united front. The final tally was 838,583 to 414,026.[44] One

[41] Ibarguren, *La historia que he vivido*, p. 281. The author was a close friend and adviser of Lieutenant General Uriburu.

[42] Manuel Seoane, *Rumbo argentino*, pp. 145–146.

[43] Ibarguren, *La historia que he vivido*, p. 387.

[44] Etchepareborda, "Aspectos políticos de la crisis de 1930," p. 26.

characteristic of the new Argentine militarists was sensitivity to public opinion and so they were reluctant to move against a popular regime while it was operating with reasonable efficiency. When, in early 1929, officers of the Justo clique urged their leader to action, the general replied that Yrigoyen's election was too sweeping and it would be an error to stage a revolution at that time.[45] To Lieutenant General Uriburu, sensitive to the need for propaganda in the "conquest of the street,"[46] as he called it, the Argentine people must have seemed far from prepared to greet their savior.

Although in 1928 the shadow of the Great Depression was beginning to cast its gloom over Argentina, the popularity of the Radicals was soaring to new heights. Shorn of conservative Antipersonalist elements by the schism of 1924, the Radicals began to move leftward toward economic nationalism and social welfare. This new Radical party nationalism, combining the old dedication to political democracy with the new use of the state as an instrument of economic liberation and amelioration, held out the promise of a permanent middle-lower–class alliance within a broadly based political party. By 1927, the Radicals had made nationalization of petroleum a leading part of their economic program. In that year a coalition of Radicals and Socialists in the Chamber of Deputies was able to pass a bill calling for petroleum nationalization—in spite of opposition from Conservatives and Antipersonalists. Only continuing Conservative-Antipersonalist control of the Senate stood in the way of government expropriation of foreign oil concessions.[47]

Social welfare was a dominant theme in Yrigoyen's message inaugurating the congressional session of 1929. This brief address stressed the fact that existing "social legislation is inferior to the necessities of society," and called for more legislative protection for the laboring masses. He also emphasized the need to promote unionization in the

[45] Luna, *Hipólito Yrigoyen*, I, 461.

[46] Juan E. Carulla, *Genio de la Argentina*, pp. 24–25.

[47] Gabriel del Mazo, *El radicalismo: Notas sobre su historia y doctrina, 1922–1952*, p. 145. On the petroleum bill see Congreso Nacional, *Diario de sesiones de la Cámara de Diputados, año 1927*, IV, 447–478. During the years from 1928 to 1930, the Senate comprised nine Conservatives who generally voted with nine Antipersonalists, against seven Radicals and one Socialist.

interest of Argentine workers.[48] These themes were part of a new Radical nationalism. It was, however, destined to be short-lived. Radical nationalism was eclipsed in the years 1929–1930 owing to severe economic crisis and a complete collapse of popular presidentialism. By 1929, the effects of the worldwide depression were keenly felt in Argentina. The nation was subjected to a "state of affairs as novel as it was disturbing": a three-pronged condition of capital shortage, declining commodity prices, and shrinkage in international trade.[49] Europe could no longer provide the capital and the markets for Argentine meat and grains. The result was an adverse balance of trade that drained Argentine specie to other areas. At first, this development led to deflation and tight money, as paper currency was taken out of circulation in proportion to gold shipped abroad. After Argentina abandoned the gold standard on December 16, 1929, inflation was present in addition to general economic distress and unemployment.

In the face of this awesome crisis, all of the long-festering sores in the Argentine political system became acute. Popular presidentialism depended on the abilities of the chief executive, and Hipólito Yrigoyen was then seventy-six years of age and senile. Without presidential initiative, the legislature, divided between warring political organizations, proved barren of economic solutions. The Radical-controlled Chamber of Deputies and the Conservative-controlled Senate spent most of their time in debate on the credentials of newly elected rivals. Except for the manipulations of Yrigoyen's corrupt aides, government had come to a standstill.[50]

Although in fact Yrigoyen's ineptitude weakened loyal officers' resistance to conspiracy and revolt, his military policy was aimed at securing his hold on the army. Over the protests of his minister of war, General Luis J. Dellepiane, Yrigoyen continued his assault on professionalism by using political favoritism in making promotions.[51] In

[48] Mazo, *El radicalismo,* p. 145.

[49] Virgil Salera, *Exchange Control and the Argentine Market,* p. 46.

[50] Gálvez, *Vida de Hipólito Yrigoyen,* pp. 101–104; Roberto Etchepareborda, *Yrigoyen y el congreso,* pp. 38–39; Ramon Columba, *El congreso que yo he visto,* II, 94.

[51] See the text of Dellepiane's letter of resignation of September 3, 1940, in J. Beresford Crawkes, *533 días de historia argentina—septiembre de 1930–20 de febre-*

1929, in a move which was to become standard procedure to placate military discontent, he allotted twelve million pesos to raise the salaries of officers of the armed forces. It was the first such measure in nine years.[52] On the other hand, he suspended large-scale orders made during the Alvear administration for European military supplies. This move was deemed by many officers to be detrimental to the honor of the armed forces and the nation.[53] Such action, aimed at Justo's program of military modernization, tended to alienate further the already dissident faction of the army.

Against this backdrop of economic depression, collapse in popular presidentialism, and political manipulation of the military, the Justista and Uriburista factions of the army began in January, 1930, to plot together to overthrow the government. This alliance of liberal and integral nationalist factions was an uneasy one, ideological divisions having developed to reenforce the old professional rivalry between Justo and Uriburu.

As leader of the integral nationalists, Uriburu sought to make the revolution an exclusively military movement executed without the cooperation of the professional politicians. He felt that the revolution should be directed not only against the Radicals, but also against the institutions of republican-democracy. By managing without the aid of the Conservative-Antipersonalist political alliance, he would have no postrevolutionary commitments to the old order and would have free reign to alter the system of government. He envisaged himself as provisional president with virtually dictatorial powers for an unstipulated period. During this provisional government, although Uriburu did not make clear by what methods, basic legal reforms including the revision of the Sáenz Peña law would be enacted. Having ensured a qualified

---

ro de 1932, pp. 35–39. On the resumption of political manipulation of the military see Luna, *Hipólito Yrigoyen*, I, 452; Gálvez, *Vida de Hipólito Yrigoyen*, p. 411; "Subversiones de valores en el ejército," *La Prensa*, August 23, 1930, p. 13.

[52] Nicolás Repetto, *Los socialistas y el ejército*, pp. 209–222; G. Monseratt, *A través de los tiempos: Estudio historial sobre la equiparación de militares en retiro*, p. 197.

[53] Alfredo Colmo, "La situación," in *La Nación*, September 4, 1930, p. 8; Delfor del Valle, "La unión cívica radical y el ejército," *Hechos e Ideas* 1 (1935): 125.

suffrage, the provisional government would also make constitutional changes, the most important being to adopt corporate representation as in Italy.[54] Thus, Uriburu, representing the civilian and military integral nationalists, was planning a revolution of the right aimed at establishing a fascist-like state in Argentina.

To integral nationalists like Uriburu and his close friend, Juan E. Carulla, the liberal nationalist views of General Justo and his political allies represented a counterrevolution in the movement of 1930.[55] The liberal nationalists wanted a revolution to restore, under their supervision, republican-democratic institutions. They sought to overthrow the Radicals but not to alter Argentine laws and institutions. The liberal nationalists felt that the revolution should be a civilian-military movement, followed by a provisional government that would remain in power only until conditions necessary for holding national elections could be restored. Constitutional amendments, if deemed necessary by the representatives of the people elected under the Sáenz Peña Law, would be made only through procedures set forth in the constitution of 1853 (approval of two-thirds of each house and with a convention summoned for that purpose). To the Justistas the Sáenz Peña Law was an established and irreversible fact of Argentine political life.[56]

Leadership of this uneasy revolutionary alliance fell to Uriburu, who had seized the initiative in organizing the conspiracy. Justo, not wishing to endanger the movement by directly challenging its leadership, withdrew from the conspiracy and waited the proper time to exert his influence. The Uriburu conspiracy made little headway in the pro-Radical officer corps, and as late as August 12, 1930, successful execution of the revolution seemed only a remote possibility. The roll call of the revolution listed only 150 officers, most of them lieutenants. Not one of the crucial regiments of the capital nor the powerful Campo de Mayo garrison of the province of Buenos Aires could be counted upon to

---

[54] José María Sarobe, *Memorias sobre la revolución de 6 de septiembre de 1930,* pp. 24–37, 44–50; Diez periodistas porteños, *Al margen de la conspiración,* pp. 27–28.

[55] Carulla, *Genio de la Argentina,* p. 25.

[56] Sarobe, *Memorias,* pp. 19–22, 50–52; Diez periodistas porteños, *Al margen de la conspiración,* pp. 26–28.

join the revolution. Not even the Colegio Militar, the main force upon which Uriburu would ultimately rely for the execution of the revolution, was yet fully committed to the movement.[57]

Lingering pro-Radical sympathy in the officer corps does not by itself explain the paucity of revolutionaries at that date. For one thing many officers who were desirous of overthrowing Yrigoyen found Uriburu's integral nationalism too extreme. Also complete control of the revolution resided in Uriburu and the hard-core members of his faction: Lieutenant Colonels Juan Bautista Molina, Emilio Kinkelín, Alvaro Alsogaray, and Emilio Faccione. Recruitment was supervised by the integral nationalist zealot, Lieutenant Colonel Bautista Molina, and officers who did not assent, at least nominally, to Uriburu's fascism, were barred from the movement. Bautista Molina and Alsogaray also excluded high-ranking officers in order to maintain their own dominant roles in the movement.[58]

The weakness of Uriburu's conspiracy rendered it vulnerable to a prerevolutionary countermovement by a group of the liberal nationalist Justistas led by Lieutenant Colonels José María Sarobe and Bartolomé Descalzo. These officers strove to convert the revolution into a civilian-military movement with the avowed aims of safeguarding individual liberties, respect for the constitution and the laws of the nation, and a speedy return to normalcy so that elections could be held to replace the ousted Radicals. They felt that manifestoes spelling out the democratic, restorationist objectives of the movement would assure a favorable civilian reception for the revolutionary column as it marched into Buenos Aires. Representatives of a political alliance of Conservatives, Antipersonalists, and Independent Socialists (later to be known as the Concordancia),[59] were to be given a role in the execution of the revolution. Their participation would heighten the public image

---

[57] Juan D. Perón, "Lo que yo vi, de la preparación y la realización de la revolución del 6 de septiembre de 1930: Contribución personal a la historia de la revolución," in Sarobe, *Memorias*, pp. 293–294.

[58] *Ibid.*, p. 289.

[59] The Independent Socialists were a right-wing faction that split from the Socialist party in 1927. Led by Federico Pinedo and Antonio de Tomaso, the Independent Socialists joined the nascent Concordancia during the heated congressional sessions of 1929–1930.

of the revolution as a popular civilian-military movement against the Yrigoyen regime.[60]

With support from officers of the Escuela Superior de Guerra, the Justistas were able to impose their views on the Uriburistas. Revolutionary manifestoes were altered to suit the liberal nationalists, and the politicians were admitted as junior partners into the revolutionary planning so that they might serve as representatives of "the people" in calling upon key army regiments to rebel against the government. Although inclusion of this new Justo-Sarobe group raised the number of officers sworn to the revolution from 150 to 300[61] (out of an army officer-corps of about 1,600), the crucial regiments of the capital and the Campo de Mayo still remained doubtful. So it was planned that Uriburu would go to San Martín to put himself at the head of the cadets of the Colegio Militar and to rendezvous with 800 communications troops from El Palomar under Lieutenant Colonel Pedro Rocco. While the revolutionary column made its fifteen-mile march to Buenos Aires, planes from El Palomar and Paraná would drop Sarobe's manifestoes over the capital city, informing its residents that a liberal nationalist revolution had begun. The rest of the plan was compounded of audacity and confidence in the bandwagon impact of revolution in time of crisis.[62]

From the standpoint of military strength, the revolution was a gamble, with the Colegio Militar serving as Uriburu's ace-in-the-hole. The apathy and division of the government in the face of conspiracy were mainly responsible for the revolution's success. As early as 1928, Minister of War Dellepiane had carried out a military investigation that brought to light the existence of the Logia de San Martín.[63] However, a significant sign of Yrigoyen's mental decline was his failure to grasp the danger of conspiracy, and Dellepiane's warnings of disaffection in the army did not deter the president from resuming political

[60] Sarobe, *Memorias*, p. 65.

[61] Perón, "Lo que yo ví," in Sarobe, *Memorias*, p. 303. On the Justo–Sarobe counter-movement, see Sarobe, *Memorias*, pp. 102–137.

[62] Bartolomé Galíndez, *Apuntes de tres revoluciones, 1930–1943–1955*, p. 10.

[63] Cattáneo, *Entre rejas*, pp. 4–5.

manipulation of the military establishment. Nor did he pay heed to Dellepiane's pleas in 1930 that he take strong action against the Uriburu conspiracy.[64]

Yrigoyen's apathy was encouraged by conspirators within his own cabinet, who had come to believe that the Radical ship could be saved only by the president's resignation. Each attempt by Dellepiane to impress upon the president the gravity of the situation met with resistance from Minister of the Interior Elpidio González, Minister of Justice Juan B. de la Campa, and Chief of Police Juan J. Graneros. Having secret assurances that the revolution was aimed solely at forcing Yrigoyen's resignation and bringing Vice-President Enrique Martínez to power,[65] these cabinet conspirators sought to preserve their positions in two ways. First, by awaiting the proper time to solicit the resignation of Yrigoyen, and by planning that they would then clamp down on the conspiracy everyone knew existed. Also, in a gamble to preserve their own power should Yrigoyen be overthrown, they cooperated with the conspiracy by thwarting all attempts by Dellepiane and other loyal Radicals to convince the president of impending revolt.

With revolutionary pressures mounting, all hopes for effectively marshalling pro-Radical sympathy in the army officer-corps faded on September 3, 1930, when Minister of War Dellepiane, defeated by the cabinet conspirators, resigned.[66] His successor, Minister of the Interior Elpidio González, was a cabinet conspirator and this appointment meant that a military vacuum was created within the government. Two days later, the ailing President Yrigoyen, on the advice of his physician and the cabinet conspirators, transferred his powers to Vice-President Martínez.[67] By September 5, 1930, the cabinet conspirators had achieved their objectives, but their hold over a discredited government was to last for only one day.

---

[64] Sarobe, *Memorias*, pp. 83–85. See also Etchepareborda, "Aspectos políticos de la crisis de 1930," p. 37.

[65] Luna, *Hipólito Yrigoyen*, I, 464.

[66] Beresford Crawkes, *533 días*, pp. 35–39.

[67] Efforts by cabinet members to persuade Yrigoyen to resign are described in Diez periodistas porteños, *Al margen de la conspiración*, pp. 135–139.

On September 6, 1930, Lieutenant General José F. Uriburu, leading a small segment of the army comprised mainly of cadets of the Colegio Militar, the air force from El Palomar and Paraná, and eight hundred troops from the Escuela de Comunicaciones in El Palomar, conquered the Argentine government. Apart from a brief machine-gun flurry directed at the revolutionary column as it neared the Plaza del Congreso, no resistance was offered as the force made its triumphant eight-hour, fifteen-mile march south from San Martín to the Casa Rosada ("presidential palace"). Before a token force led by the ever-confident Uriburu, the Radical government fell as jubilant *porteños* roared their approval. Beginning with the Ministry of War, a complete collapse of command had occurred in the chain of army hierarchy, and not even one serious military encounter had marred Uriburu's seizure of power.[68] Modern Argentine militarism and political reaction had eclipsed Radical party nationalism.

The Argentine revolution of 1930 was not the work of a monolithic, self-perpetuating Prussian-type military caste seeking to impose its values and way of life upon civilian society.[69] Rather, it was the accomplishment of conspiratorial officer factions, led by rival generals, encouraged by civilian political groups, and using a basic shift in public opinion against the Radicals to execute a revolution of the right. Therefore, applying the general categories developed by the prominent military sociologist, Morris Janowitz, Argentine militarism can be described as emerging as "unanticipated" rather than "designed" militarism. "Designed militarism—the type identified with Prussian militarism—involves domination and penetration of civilian institutions by military leaders, acting directly and with premeditation through government and other institutions. Unanticipated militarism develops from a lack of effective traditions for controlling the military establishment,

---

[68] Excellent chronicles of the day of revolution are found in Roberto Etcheparreborda, "Cronología nacional," *Revista de Historia*, no. 3 (1958): 144–155; and Diez periodistas porteños, *Al margen de la conspiración*, pp. 171–183. On the collapse in the army chain of command, see Cattáneo, *Entre rejas*, pp. 19–22; and Luna, *Hipólito Yrigoyen*, I, 474–475.

[69] See Ismael Viñas, *Orden y progreso: La era del frondizismo*, pp. 31–33.

as well as from a failure of civilian leaders to act relevantly and consistently. Under such circumstances, a vacuum is created which not only encourages an extension of the power of military leadership, but actually compels such trends."[70]

[70] Morris Janowitz, *The Professional Soldier: A Social and Political Portrait*, p. 14.

PART II
MILITARISM AND NATIONALISM, 1930-1946

When, in 1930, integral and liberal nationalist factions of the Argentine army rushed in to fill the vacuum created by economic decline and governmental paralysis, political reaction had arrived *through* the military establishment and its leaders. The incoming factions by no means represented a majority of the army officer-corps. The majority of the corps, while aware of the necessity for political change, was still middle class, nationalistic, pro-Radical, though new divisions had arisen in the corps as in society at large. This fact underscores the necessity for the generalized approach to a consideration of Argentine militarism—that is, placing the army in the stream of larger political and social processes.

Due respect must be paid, however, to the autonomy of the army as a social institution. The generalized politico-military approach must be balanced by consideration of socio-institutional aspects since developments within the institution during a given period of time may be significant in conditioning the response of an important group of officers to events in the political arena at large. Army traditions, professional rivalries, changing modes of military thought, and foreign influences—none of these can be discounted in politico-military history.

Finally, in order to understand fully the development of Argentine militarism, both the politico-military and socio-institutional aspects must be related to other political and social forces in the decades following the revolution of 1930. That revolution revealed that Argentina, in the words of a visiting sociologist, "was and remains a fractured society."[1] So long as the centralizing force of presidentialism (supported by an army that was from 1880 to 1930, largely in accord with national policy[2]) was operating with reasonable efficiency behind democratic-republican forms, the deep divisions in Argentine politics and society did not rise violently to the surface. But just when popular presidentialism under the Radicals showed signs of evolving in 1928–1930 into a broadly based movement capable of permanently uniting the middle and lower classes behind political democracy, economic nationalism, and social welfare, it was overthrown by army factions representing a civilian elite divided along integral and liberal nationalist lines. During the next decade, army officers, formerly sympathetic to Radical nationalism, were faced with a choice between integral and liberal nationalism as these factions struggled for control of the army. Confronted with corruption and political sterility of liberal nationalist and Radical politicians, the broadly based, middle-class, pro-Radical sentiment in the officer corps was gradually transferred to integral nationalism. And so, by 1943, the army officer-corps emerged largely as a fascistoid middle sector supporting integral nationalism in a revolution against the professional politicians and foreign interests from above and the potential radicalism of the masses from below. By 1943, one significant part of the fracture of Argentine society was an army officer-corps largely at odds with the political system of the nation and therefore responsive to the aspirations of an integral nationalist elite.

While the Radicals managed to maintain the allegiance of most of the civilian middle class, the urban masses were by no means perma-

1 Irving L. Horowitz, "Modern Argentina: The Politics of Power," *Political Quarterly* 30 (1959): 401.
2 Jorge Abelardo Ramos, *Historia política del ejército argentino*, p. 56.

nently politicalized. Although Yrigoyen was prolabor, his hold over the Argentine masses was largely personalistic, and he failed to weld a permanent middle-lower-class alliance. The Socialist party, a leftist fragment of the Radical movement, that was later to undergo its own amoebalike divisions, never made much headway outside the city of Buenos Aires. Its moderate, evolutionary program alienated the firebrands, and its socialist anticlericalism and reformism were detestable to the conservative and religious. Too intellectual to rouse urban labor, the Socialists made virtually no inroads among the rural population or the new urban masses.[3] The Socialists also followed a policy of not interfering in the internal affairs of Argentina's labor movement. During the decade after 1930, they gave neither leadership nor inspiration to a labor movement that was characterized by apathy in the rank and file. In 1942, a revolt against the lethargic and bureaucratic Argentine trade union movement was led largely by the Communists. This revolt split the ranks of the Confederación General de Trabajadores (CGT) so that the quarter of a million organized Argentine workers were divided into rival organizations—the CGT No. 1 (the orthodox group, composed mainly of the railroad workers), and CGT No. 2 (the Communist and dissident-Socialist wing).[4]

As important in its effect on political events as the split in CGT was the changing social composition and mood of the urban masses. All of the political events that unfolded in the more than three decades after 1930 must be analyzed against the backdrop of a basic social transformation in Argentina. By 1943, a vast internal migration had brought rural labor streaming into the greater Buenos Aires area. Beginning in 1914, these internal migrants replaced immigrants from Italy and Spain in swelling the populace of the city. This growth was speeded by the expansion of industry during World War I, and the accelerated rate of industrial concentration in and around Buenos Aires after 1936. During the years from 1914 to 1943, the population of greater Buenos Aires doubled. The increase from 1,990,000 to 4,050,000 people raised political and socioeconomic problems of extraordinary magni-

[3] David H. Popper, "The Argentine Way," *Inter-American Monthly* 1, no. 1 (1942): 11, 45.
[4] Robert J. Alexander, *The Perón Era*, pp. 9–10.

tude.[5] By 1943, many urban workers were second-generation Argentines, sons of immigrants who regarded their fathers' allegiance to alien doctrines such as anarchism, socialism, and syndicalism as signs of foreignness. The new urban masses brought illiteracy and the oligarchy's concept of democracy from the countryside. Finding no permanent home in the traditional leftist parties, both sectors of the urban working class were, therefore, ready for identification with the nation-state through a native movement of social reform.[6]

From top to bottom, Argentina in 1943 was indeed "a fractured society." The army and labor were the two major pressure groups between the Argentine people and their government but neither the republican-democratic structure nor the fragmented political parties had responded to the nationalism and reformist aspirations of either of these groups. The liberal nationalist restoration during the years from 1932 to 1943, and its identification with electoral fraud, corruption, and the foreign interests, tended to discredit "democracy" in the eyes of nationalistic Argentines on all levels of society. The result was another political vacuum, filled first by the integral nationalists of the army in 1943 and then, during the years from 1943 to 1946, a military demagogue, Colonel Juan D. Perón, achieved power by combining the integral nationalism of the army with social welfare. Social welfare was an effective bridge to the newly politicized urban masses and there followed almost a decade of popular integral nationalism under Perón (1946–1955). The repercussions of this period are still keenly felt in Argentina.

---

[5] Gino Germani, *Estructura social de la Argentina: Análisis estadístico*, pp. 74–75.
[6] Alexander, *The Perón Era*, pp. 7–8.

2. The Army and the Politicians, 1930-1943

1717974

Just as the revolution of 1930 marked the eclipse of
the Radical party in the Argentine political arena, so it
stifled the pro-Radical sentiment in the predominantly middle-class
officer-corps of the army. Consequently, during most of the three
decades after 1930, Argentine militarism has borne the stamp of two
competing nationalisms of the right: integral nationalism, and liberal
nationalism or conservatism.

In the early 1930s the integral nationalists represented but a small
minority of the armed forces, since their program was then too extreme
for most officers. The majority of military men at that time were more
sympathetic to the liberal nationalism of Uriburu's rival General
Agustín P. Justo. Although Justo's faction had joined the integral
nationalists in overthrowing Yrigoyen, Justo, in league with a conservative alliance representing the old oligarchy and ambitious politicians of splinter parties, later sought to end Uriburu's military dictatorship, remove the armed forces from politics, and restore to the
nation the constitutional forms and personal liberties of western de-

mocracy. The conservative Justista program was deeply woven with Justo's own political ambitions and those of his followers, but as has been mentioned, it was rooted in the nineteenth-century liberal nationalism of Sarmiento and Mitre that emphasized civilian rule, democratic institutions borrowed from the western democracies, free trade, and the secular state.

From September 6, 1930, to February 20, 1932, Lieutenant General Uriburu served as the Provisional President of Argentina. To grasp fully the historical significance of Uriburu's regime, it must be examined from two related standpoints. The policies of his administration must be analyzed in order to understand its position as the first integral nationalist government in Argentine history, and his regime must be viewed as a historical interlude in which the prerevolutionary nationalist struggle for power was fought to a conclusion.

The major policies of the Uriburu regime were economic nationalism and brutal political authoritarianism with fascist pretensions. On the economic front, he reversed the policy of free trade that had been introduced and maintained by the liberal nationalist oligarchy, dependent on European markets for the sale of its beef, grains, and wool. According to official documents, the Uriburu regime considered it "the primordial duty of the Government to defend and protect the products of the nation."[1] In what was an important step toward protectionism in Argentina, Uriburu raised the general tariff rate by 10 per cent and placed additional special duties on some commodities. In order to diversify national production, the Junta de Abastecimientos and the Comisión Nacional de Fomento Industrial were formed to study methods for creating and stimulating new industries. Special commissions were also established to study foreign competition in grains, yerba mate, and wine-culture.[2]

Although Uriburu did not subscribe to the Radical party's desire to nationalize the petroleum industry, his regime was by no means responsive to foreign enterprise. To the dismay of the supporters of private petroleum interests, he refused to rescind earlier decrees re-

---

[1] Ministerio del Interior, *La obra de la revolución, reseña sintetica de la labor desarrollada*, pp. 61–62.

[2] Ismael Bucich Escobar, *Historia de los presidentes argentinos*, p. 571.

serving large areas for exploration by Yacimientos Petrolíferos Fiscales (YPF), the government oil agency established by Yrigoyen in 1921. Indeed, two months after taking office, Uriburu reserved the entire Tierra del Fuego for YPF. He also allocated ten million pesos to YPF for construction of plants and storage facilities.[3] The protection policy was extended to imports of refined petroleum products as well, and, even more important, Uriburu refused to yield to pressure from foreign and domestic oil interests on the price level of gasoline. A few weeks after the revolution, the foreign oil companies raised the price of gasoline, and tried to have the director of YPF do likewise. When YPF refused to do so, Uriburu upheld the autonomy of that agency, stating, "I am the instrument of no one."[4]

Except for protectionism, Uriburu's economic nationalism was in many respects similar to that of the middle-class Radicals. His philosophy, however, emanating from an integral nationalist belief in a military and civilian elite, was at once antiforeign and antidemocratic. There was, it should be noted, an industrial sector of the Argentine middle class which supported the Uriburu revolution. This sector was represented by economic nationalists like Alejandro E. Bunge, editor of the *Revista de Economía Argentina*, and Luis Colombo, president of the Unión Industrial Argentina. For nearly a decade and a half, this group had condemned the Radical politicians as demagogues attempting to raise living standards by raising wages instead of by stimulating industrialization through tariff protection. These economic nationalists welcomed the overthrow of the Yrigoyen regime and were quick to sense the common ground they shared with the integral nationalists of the army. They praised Uriburu's economic measures as evidence that the political revolution was to be followed by a financial and economic revolution. Uriburu's economic policies were all that the *Revista de Economía* had clamored for in the past and in Bunge's view the new trend pointed the way for future governments.[5]

---

[3] Yacimientos Petrolíferos Fiscales, *Desarrollo de la industria petrolífera fiscal, 1907–1932*, pp. 192–194, 213–220.

[4] Manuel Seoane, *Rumbo argentino*, p. 154.

[5] Alejandro E. Bunge, "La república argentina define su política economía nacional," *Revista de Economía Argentina* 28, no. 163 (1932): 3–4.

This civilian support of Uriburu's philosophy illustrates how a sector of the middle class in a transitional society may be willing to sacrifice political democracy for economic nationalism and industrial development. It will be profitable to remember this example in dealing with the large-scale conversion of the middle-class officer-corps to integral nationalism during the 1930s and 1940s. In 1930–31, however, Uriburu's integral nationalism was still unwelcome to the majority of both army officers and civilians.

In the political sphere, Uriburu threw to the winds prerevolutionary promises of respect for the constitution and the laws of the nation. These promises had been made under pressure from the liberal nationalist faction of the army and its political allies, and, once in power, Uriburu ignored them. Radicals were swept from even the most minor offices, and their leaders throughout the nation were dragged into police stations and beaten. There were accounts of the torture of Radical army officers and politicians in the federal penitentiary of Ushaía in Tierra del Fuego above Cape Horn. Uriburu also imposed an ironclad censorship on the press of the nation, suppressing the operation of many newspapers critical of his administration. *Crítica*, which had served as the headquarters of the liberal nationalist alliance and had done more to propagandize for revolution than any other newspaper, was one that was closed by government order. Its editor, Natalio Botana, given the choice of imprisonment or exile, left the country.[6]

As Ricardo Rojas, the famous literary leader of cultural nationalism in Argentina, described, the Uriburu dictatorship committed party persecution, torture, imprisonment without trial, suppression of free thought, search without warrant, censorship of the mails, police espionage, and arbitrary exile. Rojas himself joined the Radical party as the most effective way of fighting the Uriburu regime.[7] Nor was he unique in taking such action. Uriburu's authoritarianism was discrediting the whole revolution and driving democratic Argentines back into the Radical fold.

---

[6] Ysabel Fisk [Rennie], *The Argentine Republic*, p. 225; John W. White, *Argentina: The Life Story of a Nation*, p. 158.
[7] Ricardo Rojas, *El radicalismo de mañana*, pp. 95, 98.

Equally alarming to the liberal nationalists were Uriburu's manifestoes. A manifesto of October 1, 1930, informed frightened Argentines that Uriburu deemed the reorganization of public administration to be the prime need of the nation. Three major planks ran consistently through Uriburu's vaguely formulated, and often contradictory, public declarations about his program. First, the derogation of the Sáenz Peña Law by removing the secret ballot, thus divesting the "illiterate" masses of the vote and opening the way for electoral manipulation. Second, the adoption of corporate over geographic representation. And third, the formation of a nationalist party to replace the traditional political organizations and thus create a single-party state.[8]

To impose his program Uriburu utilized two sources of organized force: the professional army and paramilitary organizations of civilian supporters. Each Sunday of 1931 young integral nationalists of a paramilitary group, the Legión Cívica Argentina, were admitted to army barracks for military instruction and rifle practice. They were trained by a nucleus of officers under Lieutenant Colonel Juan Bautista Molina, hard-core member of the Uriburu faction during the revolution of 1930.[9] According to the preamble to the regulations of the Legión Cívica, legionnaires were to maintain themselves in constant preparation to defend the "public order when they are so required by the national authorities."[10] Uncertain of his hold on the army, Uriburu was organizing a personal force, and when criticized for such activity, he called the Legión Cívica the strongest national bulwark against the return of the Radicals.[11]

In the months after the revolution, Uriburu went to great lengths to try to bind the army to his administration. The contracts for armaments and war materials from Europe that had been suspended during Yrigoyen's two-year rule were resumed and paid for the the Uriburu regime.[12] Funds were made available to raise the quota of army con-

---

[8] For a useful summary-by-quotation of Uriburu's thought, see Carlos Ibarguren's introduction to José F. Uriburu, *La palabra del General Uriburu,* pp. 7–13.

[9] Oscar Troncoso, *Los nacionalistas argentinos,* p. 51.

[10] Atilio, E. Cattáneo, *Entre rejas: Memorias,* p. 44.

[11] J. Beresford Crawkes, *533 días de la historia argentina—6 de septiembre de 1930–20 de febrero de 1932,* p. 389.

[12] Ministerio del Interior, *La obra de la revolución,* p. 37.

scripts from 21,000 to 26,296, and enrollment in the Colegio Militar was increased from 350 to 700.[13] Uriburu's aide, Bautista Molina, was charged with classifying each officer on the basis of political inclination and with rewarding or punishing accordingly.[14] For those who cooperated with the Uriburu movement, life was to be one bed of roses. Promotions, expensive junkets to Europe and the United States, new cars, double salaries for filling civilian and military posts at the same time—all of these were offered in return for army support.[15] Finally, in a secret decree dated November 25, 1930, the Uriburu regime offered to pay all proven debts of Argentine army officers.[16]

The army was now knee-deep in politics and rent with bitter discord. One conspiracy organized against Uriburu soon after the revolution of 1930 was by a pro-Radical group called Legalists. This group had members in all five divisions of the army. While its leadership was centered in and around Buenos Aires, the site of political power, its greatest strength was in the regiments of the interior, to which many of the Legalists had been banished after the downfall of Yrigoyen. The leader of the conspiracy was Colonel Francisco Bosch, cavalry commander of the second army division with headquarters in the Campo de Mayo. In the city of Buenos Aires, headquarters of the first army division, the conspiracy was organized by Lieutenant Colonels Roberto Bosch, Sabino Adalid, Leopoldo Patalano, Luis S. Latorre, Aníbal Arce García, and Colonel Juan E. Palacios. In Paraná, headquarters of the third army division, the Legalist leader was Lieutenant Colonel Gregorio Pomar. The conspirators of the fourth army division, with headquarters in Córdoba, were led by Lieutenant Colonel Aníbal Montes. In the fifth army division with headquarters in Tucumán, the plot was headed by Lieutenant Colonel Atilio Cattáneo. So many pro-Radicals had been exiled to this outlying area that Cattáneo recruited 70 per cent of the officer corps.[17]

---

[13] Lisandro de la Torre, *Obras*, IV, 243–244.

[14] Silvio Santander, *Nazismo en Argentina*, p. 18.

[15] Luis L. Boffi, *Bajo la tiranía del sable*, p. 323.

[16] Text of this decree in Cattáneo, *Entre rejas*, pp. 55–56.

[17] Atilio E. Cattáneo, *Plan 1932: Las conspiraciones radicales contra el general Justo*, p. 62.

The execution of this Legalist conspiracy was, however, interrupted by a crucial deal with General Justo. Justo, in his struggle for power with President Uriburu, sought to bolster his military strength by aligning his liberal nationalist faction with the Legalists against the common enemy. Personal friendships within the officer corps were used to join the two factions in an uneasy alliance. Lieutenant Colonel Carlos D. Márquez, a thoroughgoing Justista, was a close friend of the brothers Roberto and Francisco Bosch, leaders of the Legalists. Conversations between Márquez and the Bosch brothers set the stage for discussions with Justo. During these discussions, the leadership of the Legalist conspiracy in the army was transferred, over the protests of many, to General Justo, with Colonel Francisco Bosch retained as chief of staff of the revolution. It was also decided that the rebellion would be delayed until after the presidential elections of November 8, 1931.[18]

Not all of the Legalists could reconcile themselves to dealing with a man who had cooperated in the overthrow of Yrigoyen in 1930. On July 20, 1931, Lieutenant Colonel Gregorio Pomar led the ninth infantry regiment of Corrientes in rebellion against the Uriburu regime. Since the movement was merely an uncoordinated provincial uprising, an isolated part of the conspiratorial network now largely under the control of Justo, it was doomed to failure. Pomar fled with a small group of rebels to Paraguay. On January 3, 1932, he returned to Argentina to lead a Radical rebellion mounted in the Uruguayan city of Salto and aimed at capturing the garrison of Concordia in the province of Entre Ríos. On the same day, Radical sympathizers led by the brothers Mario and Jorge Kennedy captured the town of La Paz in Entre Ríos. The government used air power against the provincial rebels and both revolts were easily suppressed.[19]

Although executed in defiance of Justo's leadership of the Legalist conspiracy, these uprisings did nothing to damage the general's presidential aspirations. Each military upheaval encouraged a growing conviction among the liberal nationalist politicians of the Concordancia that a military man was needed to lead the first administration after the

---

[18] *Ibid.*, p. 63.
[19] Cattáneo, *Entre rejas*, pp. 87–94; Gabriel del Mazo, *El radicalismo: Notas sobre su historia y doctrina, 1922–1952*, pp. 244–248.

dissolution of the provisional government. General Agustín P. Justo was such an officer. He could unite the Concordancia and now, owing to the alliance of Justista and Legalist factions, the army was largely under his control also.

Thus President Uriburu, lacking civilian support, also failed to gain control of the army. Furthermore, liberal nationalist fears of a Radical revival in reaction against Uriburu's policies were borne out by the results of the provincial elections in Buenos Aires on April 5, 1931. Since no one believed that the Radicals could make a comeback so soon after the revolution of 1930 had put them out of power, the Uriburu government kept hands off, and this election was a free and fair contest. In an excellent turnout, 463,000 citizens voted and the results struck a severe blow at Uriburu and all those associated with the revolution. Less than a year after the revolution had deposed Yrigoyen, the Radicals polled 218,700 votes, the Conservatives only 187,742.[20]

Recognizing from these results the end of their hopes of returning as popular leaders of the nation, the liberal nationalists realized that only electoral fraud could now restore them to power. Since supervision of the Buenos Aires elections was a responsibility of the minister of the interior, the liberal nationalist politico-military alliance— the Justistas and the Concordancia—accordingly pressured Uriburu to give them control of this position. Mortally ill now with cancer and having lost control of the army, Uriburu yielded to pressure. Integral nationalist Minister of the Interior Matías Sánchez Sorondo was replaced with former Minister of Public Works Octavio S. Pico. Pico was a supporter of Justo.[21] Now, Justo and the liberal nationalists controlled the two major levers of political power in Argentina—the army and the Ministry of the Interior.

The last stage in the liberal nationalist assumption of power was the presidential election of November 8, 1931, from which the Radicals were barred by executive decree. This left only an alliance of regional parties, the Progressive Democrats of Santa Fe and the Socialists, to oppose Justo and the Concordancia. The Progressive Democrat–Social-

---

[20] Bucich Escobar, *Historia de los presidentes argentinos*, p. 594.
[21] Torre, *Obras*, I, 230.

ist alliance had begun prior to the revolution of 1930 when, despite their opposition to Yrigoyen, these parties had shunned cooperation with army factions in the overthrow of constituted government. During the presidential campaign of 1931, the alliance backed the candidacy of Lisandro de la Torre, leader of the Progressive Democrats. They made militarism, as personified by Justo, the major issue of the election.[22] As Ysabel Fisk Rennie has ably pointed out: "The November elections were a return to the politics of the nineteenth century, with new refinements in fraud that were destined to circumvent the Sáenz Peña electoral mechanism. The police confiscated Libretas de Enrolamiento, the dead rose and voted, known Radicals were denied access to the polls, signatures were falsified, stamps and seals forged, ballot boxes broken open, fake ballots printed, and interventions made in provinces where necessary."[23] Needless to say, Justo won the election, and with his victory the revolutionary struggle for power came to an end.

On the afternoon of February 20, 1932, Argentines flocked into the streets of towns and cities throughout the nation to celebrate the end of the iron-fisted dictatorship of Lieutenant General Uriburu. On that day, a new president of Argentina, another general, Justo, was inaugurated. The liberal nationalists had triumphed over the integral nationalists. Still hopeful of becoming a popular president, Justo attempted to clear the air quickly of Uriburu's authoritarianism. Martial law and the state of siege were lifted, and Uriburu's fascist program was buried. The press regained freedom of expression. Political prisoners were released from jails, and the frontiers were opened to all but the most fanatic Radical exiles. "National conciliation" was declared the motto of the new government.[24]

Justo's desire to return the armed forces to their professional status was reflected by the officers chosen to represent the military establishment in the cabinet. Both the minister of war, Colonel Manuel A. Rodríguez, and the minister of the navy, Captain Pedro S. Casal, were officers who had been largely apart from conspiracies prior to and

[22] Bucich Escobar, *Historia de los presidentes argentinos*, pp. 601–602.
[23] Fisk, *The Argentine Republic*, pp. 227–228.
[24] Manuel Goldstraj, *Años y errores: Un cuarto de siglo de política*, p. 264.

after the revolution of 1930. During a long and distinguished military career, Colonel Rodríguez, an officer of great technical capacity, had earned the respect of most of the officer corps and the title, The Man of Duty. In the turbulent period following the revolution of 1930, when Uriburu and Justo had vied for control of the army, Uriburu had chosen Rodríguez to command the second army division with head-quarters in the powerful Campo de Mayo garrison. This despite the fact that Rodríguez had served in 1925 as Justo's aide in the Ministry of War. Rodríguez had also presided over the Círculo Militar in 1930, and, in that capacity, he had delivered a major address on July 10, 1931, to the banquet of comradery of the armed forces.[25] This speech, entitled "The Mission of the Army," was a major restatement of the liberal nationalist position on the role of the army in Argentine society, and was in the tradition of Mitre, Sarmiento, and Roca. The revolution of 1930 had changed nothing, Rodríguez argued. Those who believed that the revolution had transformed the army into a political instrument were deluding themselves. The "army is not a political force at the service of men or parties, but a child of the people who give it life, and it is at the service of the nation. It is guided by the old spirit of the Army of the Andes." Let parties and *caudillos* heed this message, and desist from attempting to infect the army with talk of conspiracy.[26]

Rodríguez's apparent zeal for military professionalism was not, how-ever, matched by prophetic powers. The fact was that the time had passed for national conciliation whether in the armed forces or in the political arena. By 1932, factions of the army had become part of an enlarged political spectrum, with the liberal nationalists as the con-servative right, challenged from the left by the Legalists, or Radicals, and from the extreme right by the Uriburistas or integral nationalists.

Soon after his 1932 election, President Justo, an old Antipersonalist himself, attempted to gain the support of the Radicals in order to broaden his base of civilian strength. But the Radicals, the nation's majority party, now strengthened by Alvear's return to the fold, de-

25 For a brief biography on Rodríguez, see *El hombre del deber: Una serie de semblanzas del Gral. Manuel A. Rodríguez*, pp. 17–22.
26 For text of Rodríguez's speech see *ibid.*, pp. 27–35.

clined such overtures. They chose instead to attempt the forceful overthrow of the government; that is, they returned to their pre-1916 policy of revolution and electoral abstention. Their choice of force thus perpetuated the schism of 1924, and forced Justo back to the liberal nationalist Concordancia for civilian support.[27]

The immediate threat to Justo's regime came from the army faction known as the Legalists. When the Radicals embarked upon a policy of revolution against the Concordancia, the Justista-Legalist alliance in the army broke down. Justo could easily cope with renewed Legalist conspiracy, for, having led the rebellion against Uriburu, he knew the group's inner workings and leading participants. He was aided also by the general ineptitude of the conspirators and by their persistent conflicts about the course to be followed. From 1932 to 1934, talk of conspiracy filled the coffee houses of Buenos Aires, and the waiters were almost as informed as the Justo regime on coming uprisings. This was, so to speak, rebellion over café italiano.[28]

A significant turning point in the conspiracy came on the night of June 28, 1932, when a retired major, Regino P. Lescano, was shot and killed by the police in the town of Curuzú Cuatía in the province of Corrientes. When the police searched Lescano's hotel room, they discovered documents and instructions he was carrying to Radical conspirators in the provinces of Corrientes, Entre Ríos, Santa Fe, and Chaco. Among the documents was a manifesto to be issued upon the outbreak of the coming Legalist revolution. This manifesto, an example of intense Radical nationalism, denounced the Justo regime on behalf of the "democracy and [of] the liberty of the Argentine people, of whom the Radicals represented an immense majority." It called for rebellion against the "heirs of the nefarious tyranny of General Uriburu, born of the coup of September 6, 1930, patronized by the imperialism of North American petroleum interests, which resuscitated government-by-caste in Argentina." It concluded with an appeal to the "dignified chiefs and officers, the noncommissioned officers, the cadets and the conscripts of the army and the navy" to "accompany us in the

[27] Goldstraj, *Años y errores*, p. 262.
[28] *Ibid.*, p. 275.

saintly rebel crusade for democracy and the political and economic independence of the Nation and its producing classes."[29]

Despite the Lescano disclosures, the Legalists, now led by Lieutenant Colonel Atilio Cattáneo, were determined to execute the rebellion scheduled for December 21, 1932. The plan called for explosions in key areas of the city of Buenos Aires, to be followed by uprisings in the provincial garrisons where most of the Legalist strength was located. But on December 15, 1932, conspirators in Buenos Aires accidentally discharged the explosives. In their hasty flight from the scene they left charred clothes, and also a list of persons to whom the explosives were to have been distributed.[30]

The Justo regime promptly brought the major Radical leaders, among them Marcelo T. de Alvear and the aged Hipólito Yrigoyen, into custody. They were released when Lieutenant Colonel Cattáneo testified that he alone had organized the revolt. Cattáneo was sentenced to nineteen months in prison. From December 16, 1932, to mid-1933, the national committee of the Radical party was not permitted to operate, and the Justo regime tightened its surveillance of political opponents and its control of the press.[31]

On June 5, 1933, after the Radical leaders had been released from prison, a new national committee was elected and preparations were made for a national convention to be held in the city of Santa Fe. From December 27 to 29, 1933, Radical politicians from throughout the nation assembled there to formulate the policy of their party. When the speeches and debates were ended, a majority of the delegates voted to continue the traditional policy of electoral abstention and revolution.[32] No sooner had the convention adjourned, than the gunfire of revolt was heard in the streets of Santa Fe. Armed civilians, reserve officers, and retired military men, led by two local Radical leaders, Alejandro Greca and Ovidio Molinas, were pouring into the streets of Santa Fe in an effort to capture the police stations, where arms were stored, and the telegraph office, which could sound the rebel cry

---

[29] Text of manifesto in *La Prensa*, July 6, 1932, p. 12.
[30] Cattáneo, *Plan 1932*, pp. 157–158.
[31] Mazo, *El radicalismo*, p. 234.
[32] Manuel Goldstraj, *El camino del exilio*, pp. 51–59.

throughout the nation. Simultaneous uprisings were launched by Radicals throughout the province of Santa Fe. On an island in the Río Uruguay, Legalist officers were apprehended by Brazilian army units as they prepared to join the movement. Only 150 armed men, under the leadership of Lieutenant Colonel Roberto Bosch, were able to flee the island and cross the river into the province of Corrientes. From there they marched to the town of Libres in an attempt to capture the eleventh army regiment. Two decades after the passage of the Sáenz Peña Law, the banner of the Radical rebels still read: "For popular sovereignty which is the liberty of the Fatherland."[33]

The uprisings of Santa Fe and Corrientes were quickly suppressed by loyal regiments of the army. Long before they had erupted Minister of the Interior Leopoldo Melo had been told of the plot, and had passed on the information to President Justo. Justo chose, however, to allow the uprisings to take place in order to link them to the convention of Santa Fe.[34] Army conscripts were ordered to arrest the Radical politicians gathered in Santa Fe. It was the largest political roundup of the Justo administration, and, despite their denial of complicity in the plot, more than a thousand embittered Radicals were shipped to the island of Martín García. "National conciliation" was ended, and the state of siege was reimposed by the Justo administration.[35]

Less publicized, but none the less important, was the military counterpart of the massive arrests of Radical leaders. This was the gradual purge of active Legalist officers from the Argentine army.[36] When divested of its military power, the Radical party—an ill-disciplined, unwieldy organization rent by factionalism—was hardly a dynamic political force in representing the majority of democratic and nationalistic Argentines. The death of Yrigoyen in 1933 left his old rival, Alvear, in seeming control of party leadership; but new divisions soon set in. From 1933 to 1935, the Radicals were divided into two warring camps, one favoring active participation in elections and the other electoral

---

[33] Mazo, *El radicalismo*, p. 245.
[34] Vicente de Pascal, "Argentina's Man of Destiny?" *Inter-American Monthly* 1, no. 7 (1942): 18.
[35] Goldstraj, *El camino del exilio*, p. 63; Mazo, *El radicalismo*, pp. 246–247.
[36] Cattáneo, *Plan 1932*, p. 67.

abstention and revolution. By 1935, when the Radicals abandoned abstention for participation, the party had reached its low point in leadership and internal unity. Even Radical historians affirm that this was a period of decadence in the history of their movement.[37]

The failure of Radicalism as an effective vehicle of popular, democratic middle-class nationalism in the transitional society of Argentina during the 1930s left only the rival integral and liberal nationalist factions to claim the allegiance of middle-class, nationalist army officers. The high-ranking members of President Justo's Logia de San Martín controlled the key posts in the army after his victory in the postrevolutionary struggle for power against the Uriburu faction.[38] By professional, political, or social ties, the Justista generals were identified with the ruling oligarchy and they were dependent for their military preeminence on the perpetuation of rule by the liberal nationalist oligarchy and the Concordancia. During the Infamous Decade of 1932–1943, the pseudodemocratic policies of the Concordancia enraged nationalistic Argentines in all social sectors outside the oligarchy and the commercial upper-middle class, and contributed significantly to the conversion of the army officer-corps to integral nationalism.

In the eyes of nationalistic Argentines, the Justo regime sacrificed the nation's economic independence for the interests of the landed oligarchy. The Roca-Runciman Treaty, signed in May, 1933, and renewed in 1935, served as the basis of Justo's program of economic recovery. This treaty provided assurances that the United Kingdom would not reduce its imports of Argentine beef below the quantity imported in 1932. In return, Argentina made many concessions. Apart from a limited sum to be deducted for servicing Argentina's debt to other nations, exchange earned from exports to Great Britain was to be reserved for remittances to Great Britain. In a supplementary accord, Argentina pledged to reduce tariffs on British goods to 1930 levels, while Great Britain agreed not to place new duties on Argentine products. A protocol was also drawn up to placate British stockholders who controlled Argentina's tramways, railroads, and public utilities. It promised to British investors in these sectors of the Argentine economy

[37] Mazo, *El radicalismo*, p. 237.
[38] Jorge Abelardo Ramos, *Historia política del ejército argentino*, p. 63.

"such benevolent treatment as may conduce to the further economic development of the country, and to the due and legitimate protection of the interests concerned in their operation."[39]

By offsetting preference within the United Kingdom, by reversing the protectionism of Uriburu, and, finally, by orienting the Argentine economy to that of the western democracies, the Roca-Runciman Treaty was clearly in the liberal nationalist tradition of the oligarchy. But historical events and the economic urgencies of a particular period defy all-inclusive categorization. To counteract the effects of economic depression, Justo and the liberal nationalists abandoned laissez faire for a directed economy, albeit along lines laid down by the landed oligarchy. Under Justo, the government fixed minimum prices for grain and assumed control of all foreign exchange operations. In effect a system of licensed importing was established. Foreign capital was induced to lend blocked funds to the government, and these were used to finance large-scale programs of public works. Unemployment was reduced by unprecedented road-building, and by constructing modern officers' quarters in garrisons throughout the nation.[40] In 1934, government control of the economy was enlarged further by the creation of a Central Bank, which, by virtue of its power to discount the paper of private Argentine banks, exerted significant influence over credit operations. By 1938 the Justo regime, aided by the expansion of European markets, had lifted Argentina to prosperity.[41]

However, increasing government intervention in the nation's economic life also meant increased opportunities for corruption. Along with charges of *vendepatria*, or "selling out the Fatherland to foreign interests," the Justo regime was accused of rampant corruption. Most of the muckraking in this period was carried out by the Socialist–Progressive Democrat alliance, but their findings enraged army officers and nationalists in all quarters against the professional politicians. In the political realm, the Justo regime represented what one army officer

---

[39] George Pendle, *Argentina*, pp. 78–79.
[40] On Justo's program of military modernization, see Poder Ejecutivo Nacional, 1932–1938. *Ejército: Ferrocarriles del estado*, section on "Construcción militares realizados en el periodo 1932–1937," VI, no pagination.
[41] Pendle, *Argentina*, pp. 80–81.

has called the "enthronement of electoral fraud."[42] The problem of needing to use force to influence elections while maintaining the appearance of a nonpolitical army was solved by ordering army troops confined to their barracks on election days, and leaving the work of electoral intimidation to armed police. Political opponents who insisted on casting their votes were mistreated, and even shot. Enrollment books were seized, poll-watchers expelled, ballots adulterated, and ballot-boxes stuffed.[43]

A leading beneficiary of electoral fraud was Roberto Ortiz, who was elected in 1938 as successor to President Justo. Ortiz, a member of the Antipersonalist faction, had been hand-picked by Justo for the presidential ticket, along with Miguel Angel Cárcano, a Conservative with liberal leanings. Cárcano had not won the vice-presidential nomination however, and this attempt by Justo to perpetuate his control resulted in fragmentation of the Concordancia since the Buenos Aires Conservatives, in rebellion against his domination, had nominated their own vice-presidential candidate, Robustiano Patrón Costas. In the end, a compromise candidate, Rámon Castillo, was nominated and this was a severe blow to Justo's prestige.[44] In addition seeds of future dissension were sown between Castillo, who would assume the powers of the presidency in 1940, and Justo, influential in Argentine politics until his death in 1943.

Soon after his election by unabashed fraud, President Ortiz repudiated corruption and pledged himself to the restoration of democracy in Argentina. During a dynamic first year in office, he redeemed this pledge. Honest elections were guaranteed in the provinces of Tucumán, Entre Ríos, La Rioja and Mendoza. Federal intervention annulled fraudulent elections in the provinces of San Juan, Buenos Aires and Catamarca. Each of these interventions served as a dramatic example of the president's determination to democratize the Argentine political system. In San Juan, Ortiz dismissed a personal friend, who, while serving as federal interventor, had disobeyed orders to guarantee the hon-

[42] Ramón Molina, *Defendamos nuestro país*, pp. 249–250.
[43] *Ibid.*
[44] *Noticias Gráficas*, "Un negro cuarto de siglo (IV)," December 1, 1955, p. 11.

esty of provincial elections. In the province of Buenos Aires, Ortiz struck at the very core of Conservative strength by intervening to unseat Manuel Fresco whose machine had corrupted the gubernatorial elections of 1939.[45] And disagreement over elections in Catamarca drove a permanent wedge between the president and Vice-President Castillo. Although instructed by Ortiz to see that the elections were held without fraud, Castillo, being true to his Conservative cohorts, permitted the use of corruption. Upon his return to Buenos Aires, Castillo was chased out of the president's office with heated denunciations ringing in his ears. Nor did he return until 1940 when illness forced Ortiz to transfer the government to him as vice-president.

Viewed from the standpoint of Argentine militarism, Ortiz's government represented the last civilian administration that was popular enough to resist political forces with access to power through the army. The revival of democracy won broad popular support for the Ortiz administration since it enabled the Radicals to gain control of the Chamber of Deputies through honest elections. On the other hand, powerful enemies were made on the right. By refusing to be Justo's tool, Ortiz had alienated the ex-president, who still wielded great influence in the army and in political circles. Hated by the Conservative faction of the Concordancia, Ortiz was anathema to the elitist civilian and military integral nationalists. Having broken the dikes of electoral fraud, he had forced the lines to be sharply drawn on the issue of full-fledged democracy. On the left, his regime drew its support from members of both factions of the Radicals as well as from the Socialist–Progressive Democrat alliance. Within the army, he maintained the allegiance of Minister of War Carlos Márquez, a former thorough-going Justista who had broken with the general and now gave full support to the president's program.[46] But on the right, three competing forces—Justo and his faction of the army, Vice-President Castillo and the Conservatives, and the integral nationalists, both civilian and military—now shared one objective: undermine the Ortiz regime and, if possible, also discredit Márquez.

[45] *Ibid.*, "Un negro cuarto de siglo (III)," November 30, 1955, p. 10.
[46] On Ortiz-Justo, and Márquez-Justo splits, see White, *Argentina*, p. 165.

Their objective was accomplished, in part, when Ortiz, suffering from diabetes, was brought to the point of blindness in 1940. By July 3, 1940, Ortiz had to transfer his presidential powers to Vice-President Castillo. But his cabinet was retained and the president continued to wield influence in the government through bedside conferences with its members. One month after the presidential reins were transferred to Castillo, the Palomar Land Scandal provided an important showdown in the struggle over Argentine democracy.

The Palomar Land Scandal involved the sale of a tract near the Campo de Mayo to the Ministry of War at the price of 2,450,303 pesos. This tract had been purchased by the government from Luis M. Casas, who had bought it on option from its owners at 65 centavos a square meter and then, the very same day, had sold it to the Ministry of War for 1 peso 10 centavos a square meter. The price paid to Casas was about one million pesos more than its estimated value,[47] and it was alleged that the profits were divided with influential persons in the government. As in all such transactions, the decree for the purchase of the tract had been signed by Minister of War Márquez.

A special senate committee, comprised of Alfredo Palacios, Héctor González Iramain, and Gilberto Suárez Lago, was appointed to investigate the transaction. During its investigation, the senate committee summoned some of Argentina's most important politicians, army chiefs, and congressmen. The evidence implicated a number of officers and politicians. However, the committee report assigned ultimate responsibility for the land purchase to Minister of War Márquez, although the charge was one of negligence rather than dishonesty.[48]

The Palomar Land Scandal could have been written off as one more episode in an era when governmental corruption was not unusual. But competing politico-military forces were at work to make the issue a focal point for larger conflict. While the senate committee was in session, the issue brought integral nationalists of the army into direct conflict with the prodemocratic minister of war. The integral nationalist leader, General Juan Bautista Molina, land expert of the Ministry of

[47] *New York Times*, August 20, 1940.
[48] The major documents on the Palomar scandal are brought together in Benjamín Villafañe, *La tragedia argentina*, pp. 116–133.

War, who was also involved in the transaction, sent a letter to the senate committee charging Márquez with assigning responsibility for the deal to Bautista Molina and other officers in order to shield his own guilt. Minister of War Márquez countered quickly by placing Bautista Molina under sixty-day arrest and by ordering precautionary measures for all six army divisions against a possible integral nationalist uprising.[49]

President Ortiz, although willing to concede that fraud and corruption had been present in the Palomar transaction, contended that forces of the right were exaggerating the issue to discredit his administration. For Justo and for the Castillo supporters, the scandal presented a perfect opportunity to weaken Ortiz's lingering power. For the integral nationalists, it was a symptom of decadent democracy in action. On August 23, 1940, Ortiz resigned his office in a gesture that was really a direct appeal for support from the Argentine people. His letter of resignation focused on what he considered the larger issues in the episode: "In my government the nation has returned to its traditional democratic life. . . . The Palomar land scandal has been used to confront our democratic system as if it were a necessary consequence of the same—a relationship established in an effort to shake confidence in the system. The desire for dishonest profit is a result of human imperfection and not a consequence of any constitutional condition."[50]

Ortiz's challenge to the antidemocratic forces proved successful. The maneuver aroused such a wave of popular protest that a joint session of Congress voted 170 to 1 to reject the president's resignation. The lone vote cast for acceptance was that of Senator Matías Sánchez Sorondo, integral nationalist and minister of the interior under Uriburu. The surge of public support for Ortiz convinced most integral nationalists of the army that their day had not arrived. As one foreign correspondent stated, "democracy had won an historic victory."[51]

But this defense of his administration sapped the dwindling strength of the blind president. Soon after his legislative victory, Ortiz agreed to permit Vice-President Castillo to organize a cabinet to replace the

[49] *New York Times*, August 22, 1940, p. 6.
[50] Villafañe, *La tragedia argentina*, pp. 134–136.
[51] *New York Times*, August 26, 1940, p. 4.

one that had resigned during the Palomar investigation. With Castillo's assumption of such powers, the popular base of the administration was dissolved immediately, and Argentina was returned to government controlled by minority politico-military forces representing the landed oligarchy. Between September 2 and 7, 1940, Vice-President Castillo organized a cabinet of "conciliation" to reunite the Concordancia. No friend of Justo, Castillo was, nevertheless, forced to recognize the general's enduring influence by appointing Justistas to the all-important Ministries of War and the Interior. General Juan M. Tonazzi was named minister of war and Miguel Culaciatti, an Antipersonalist, was appointed minister of the interior. Only one appointee, Guillermo Rothe as minister of justice and public instruction, represented Castillo's own Conservative clique, while Daniel Amadeo Videla, named minister of agriculture, represented the Conservatives of Avellaneda. Although integral nationalists of the army had no representative in the cabinet, the small group of integral nationalist naval officers were represented when Rear Admiral Mario Fincatti was appointed minister of the navy.[52]

Without either popular support or influence in the army, Castillo was forced to concede key cabinet posts to Justo in order to fill the power vacuum surrounding his administration. It should be noted that by 1940–1942 the Justista, or liberal nationalist faction, despite the numerous contradictions and historical ironies involved in its position, had come to represent the constitutionalist, neocivilianist, and proally clique of the army. Still ambitious for the presidency in 1943, and still willing to use fraud to attain his goal, Justo had nevertheless foresworn military revolt.[53]

The reunited Concordancia was, in the end, shattered on two major issues: the international situation and the presidential succession in 1943. While appearing to be subordinate to Justo, Castillo paid little heed to Justista cabinet members.[54] The inevitable break between the

[52] *La Vanguardia*, "Documentos para la historia," July 17, 1945, p. 3.
[53] *Ibid.*
[54] David H. Popper, "The Argentine Way," *Inter-American Monthly* 1, no. 1 (1942): 11.

two leaders came through disagreement over the issue of Argentine neutrality in World War II. Castillo was striving against mounting international pressure to maintain this neutrality. Justo, with his traditional liberal nationalist orientation to the western democracies, publicized, in typically dramatic fashion, his desire to align Argentina with the allies in World War II. When Brazil declared war on the axis on August 22, 1942, Justo flew to Rio de Janeiro as an "honorary general" to offer his services to President Getulio Vargas. This gesture embarrassed the Castillo regime, and when asked his opinion of Justo's journey, the vice-president sharply replied: "I am not interested in the travels of foreign generals."[55]

Castillo's determination to maintain a policy of strict neutrality was partly shaped by the rise of profascist integral nationalism in the army, a threat that had grown in magnitude and audacity since 1934. After Uriburu's death in 1933, the integral nationalists had returned to their barracks determined that they would one day strike again against the republican-democracy of the professional politicians. The uprising of 1930 had provided revolutionary training for integral nationalist captains and lieutenant colonels, who would return as colonels and generals to lead the movement of 1943. Beginning in 1934, integral nationalist generals Juan Bautista Molina and Benjamín Menéndez, supported by junior officers—Juan Filomeno Velasco, Humberto Sosa Molina, Franklin Lucero, Pedro P. Ramírez, and Emilio González— conspired anew against their arch rivals in the Justista faction.[56] Throughout the period 1932–1943, this profascist faction increased its strength under the inspiration of foreign authoritarian movements. By 1941, two separate networks of integral nationalist conspirators, headed by Bautista Molina and Menéndez, were plotting to overthrow the government.

Bautista Molina scheduled his uprising for February 14, 1941. The night before the revolt, however, General Adolfo Espíndola, commander of the first army division and a Justista, happened to inspect

[55] Pascal, "Argentina's Man of Destiny?" 1, no. 7 (1942): 18.
[56] Juan E. Carulla, *Al filo del medio siglo*, pp. 221, 226–227, 244.

one of the rebel regiments. Much to his surprise, the troops were sleeping in combat uniforms and boots. Espíndola made no mention of this occurrence prior to his departure from the barracks. Fearful that, despite his silence, he suspected a conspiracy, many of the key officers bowed out at the last moment. When Minister of War Tonazzi learned of Espíndola's findings, he ordered an immediate investigation. The conspirators claimed that their troops were ordered to sleep fully equipped as part of training for a period of A.O.P. (Alteration of the Public Order).[57] Since none of the conspirators was relieved of duty or subjected to disciplinary action, this explanation may have been accepted; on the other hand, it is likely that the weak Castillo regime now felt obliged to appease the integral nationalists.

With each passing day, the integral nationalists of the army grew bolder. In early September 1941, General Benjamín Menéndez, leader of his own conspiracy, wrote an article for the profascist newspaper *Pampero* calling for the "elimination of politicians."[58] He was ordered confined to his home under surveillance for two months. Two weeks later, the Castillo government averted an integral nationalist uprising in the army aviation school in Córdoba and at the air base in Paraná. The commander of the aviation school, Lieutenant Colonel Sustaita, cohort of Bautista Molina, was arrested along with Major Bernardo Menéndez, officer in charge of the Paraná base.[59]

By 1942 integral nationalism had spread to the key army posts in the city of Buenos Aires and to the Campo de Mayo garrison. But a final integral nationalist bid for power was constantly being delayed by conflict over leadership and tactics. In addition to such as the Bautista Molina–Menéndez split, the integral nationalists were divided on whether cooperation with President Castillo in a "legal" revolution was preferable to an outright seizure of power by the army. On one objective the conspirators did agree: the displacement of liberal nationalist or Justista influence from the Ministry of War, with subsequent downward pressure to unite the officer-corps behind integral nationalism.[60]

---

[57] Gontran de Guemes, *Así se gestó la dictadura: "El GOU,"* pp. 9–12.
[58] Quoted in the *New York Times*, September 10, 1941, p. 6.
[59] Ibid., September 25, 1941, p. 1.
[60] Guemes, *Así se gestó la dictadura*, pp. 14–16, 19–21.

Agreement on this objective led to the formation of the secret military lodge, Grupo Directivo de Unión Espiritual Unificador (GDUEU). A forerunner of Grupo de Oficiales Unidos (GOU), GDUEU organized, in the army officer-corps, a network of secret cells dedicated to the spread of the integral nationalist conspiracy. Its major objective was the displacement of the Justistas from the Ministry of War and the top posts in the army. The leading GDUEU spokesman was General Domingo Martínez, chief of the Buenos Aires police, and it was he who presented integral nationalist demands to Vice-President Castillo.[61]

In 1942 Castillo was in no position to ignore the demands of GDUEU, because his ties with the liberal nationalist faction of the army were strained by disagreement on the international question and on the 1943 presidential succession. Lacking civilian support as well as effective control of the army, Castillo was now willing to align his regime with the integral nationalists, hoping thereby to preserve his power and to control the coming election. On November 17, 1942, in what turned out to be the first act of the Argentine revolution of 1943, General Juan Tonazzi was forced to resign as minister of war. With his resignation, Justista power in the army was destroyed. His successor was the integral nationalist cavalry chief, General Pedro P. Ramírez, who quickly installed his cohorts in the key posts of the army.[62]

There was no Justista counter-movement. On January 11, 1943, General Tonazzi served as pallbearer in the funeral of ex-President Justo, ringing down the curtain on another era of Argentine politico-military history.[63] The integral nationalist victory in the struggle to control the army was not merely the product of organization and tactics. Mainly it reflected the rising force in the Argentine army, one that was to play a dominant role in politics for two decades to come. The alliance of a Justo-controlled army with the liberal nationalist oligarchy was finished. By 1943 the army officer-corps largely represented a fascistoid middle sector bent on transforming Argentina into a regimented industrial society geared to glory and war.

[61] *La Vanguardia*, "Documentos para la historia," July 17, 1945, p. 3.
[62] *Ibid.*
[63] *La Prensa*, January 11, 1943, p. 6.

3. Social and Institutional Aspects of Argentine Militarism: A Hypothesis

In tracing the rise of integral nationalism to dominance within the officer corps and to ultimate domination of the state, it is not sufficient to focus solely on the relationship of the army officer-corps, or dominant factions thereof, to institutional, social, and political developments in Argentina. Due consideration must also be given to the autonomy of the army as an institution—that is, to the values engendered by the military way of life that have conditioned political action. Not only is it important to identify the socio-institutional factors that contributed to the rise of integral nationalism in the officer corps during the late 1930s and early 1940s, but also it is necessary to develop certain variables that facilitate an analysis of the changing political positions of the military in Argentina since the organization of The New Army.

The tortuous course of Argentine militarism is, in part, explained by a basic dichotomy of values in the army. As has been stated, *the Argentine army is both a traditional and a modern institution, and it is torn by these conflicting values.* The traditional-modern conflict is written into the profile of the Argentine army officer. He is at once largely middle class, conservative, "Catholic," and nationalistic. Contrary to popular impressions, he is not recruited from the social elites of the provinces. A recent study of the social and geographic origins of Argentine generals indicates that they are drawn with surprising constancy from the urban areas of the littoral, especially from the city and province of Buenos Aires. The Argentine army officer-corps has not been a self-perpetuating military caste, but has been open to sons of both creole and immigrant families.[1] It has long been recognized by scholars that the corps serves as a vehicle for socially ambitious members of the middle class. As James Bruce, United States ambassador during the Perón era, observed: "Very few of Argentina's smartly uniformed, sword-wearing Army officers come from the wealthiest class. There is a sprinkling of old *estancia* family names in Army rosters, but it has never been a rich man's career. Most leaders are from the ambitious middle-class families—Spanish, Italian, German, Irish."[2]

Social origins and class bias have, however, rarely been the key factors in determining the political positions of the army. Instead, the political positions of army factions reflect corporate or institutional values. Sociologically speaking the Argentine army is an authoritarian institution that inculcates hierarchical and conservative values in those who undergo its training. Those who do not display these archetype values sink in the hierarchical scale and are consigned to professional anonymity.[3]

In past analyses of the rise of integral nationalism in the army, emphasis has been placed on the predispositions of officer-candidates and on their authoritarian and Germanic training. The very selection of an army career is often indicative of personal predispositions to order and discipline over freedom of the will.[4] Before the revolution of 1943,

[1] José Luis de Imaz, "Los que mandan: Las fuerzas armadas en Argentina," *América Latina* 7 (1964): 43–45.

[2] James Bruce, *Those Perplexing Argentines*, pp. 303–304. On the social origins of the army officer-corps, see also Benjamín Rattenbach, *Sociología militar: Una contribución a su estudio*, pp. 143–147.

[3] Imaz, "Los que mandan," pp. 42–43.

[4] Luis Rodolfo González, "Ideas Contrary to the Spirit of May and Their Re-

officer candidacy was open to all youths, between the ages of sixteen and twenty-one, who could raise the necessary 3,000 to 5,000 pesos for fees.[5] By 1946, the number of scholarships was raised to equal the enrollment of 750, making the Colegio Militar a fee-free institution.[6] The army was thus an open institution for those with personal predispositions towards its values and training. Many who entered the army came from immigrant homes wherein democratic conditioning was often quite lacking.[7]

During the malleable years of military training, from sixteen to twenty-one, predispositions that had often determined the choice of an army career were reenforced in the Colegio Militar. Entrance into the Colegio Militar was by annual competitive examinations, covering a wide range of academic subjects: arithmetic, algebra, biological sciences, world geography, ancient, medieval, and modern history, Spanish and French.[8] How rigorous these examinations were cannot be determined. But having entered the Colegio Militar, the cadet who was not willing to subordinate all else to his profession did not last long. From cadet to high-ranking officer, Argentine military men pursued their careers with an intensity that shaped a unilateral personality, since professional considerations overrode all others. Immersed in military affairs, officers came to pride themselves on their separateness from the civilian population.[9]

An intensification of authoritarian attitudes was necessary to survive the rigors of training in the Colegio Militar. This spit-and-polish army, trained on the Prussian model, demanded of the cadet blind obedience to command, strict hierarchical relationship between officer and conscript, and application of a rigorous code of honor to every facet of

---

percussion in Argentine Political Life: A Military Opinion at the Service of Definitive Pacification," trans. K. H. Silvert, in *Letters and Reports Written for the American Universities Field Staff, 1955–1958*, pp. 6–9.

[5] Ray Josephs, *Argentine Diary*, p. 62.

[6] *Memoria del ministerio de guerra presentada al honorable congreso de la nación, 4 de junio 1946–4 de junio 1947*, p. xi.

[7] González, "Ideas Contrary to the Spirit of May," pp. 6–9.

[8] Armando Duval, *A Argentina, potencia militar*, II, 386.

[9] Benjamín Rattenbach, *Estudios y reflexiones*, pp. 85–87; Bruce, *Those Perplexing Argentines*, pp. 304–305.

military life. Rebels who refused even the slightest renunciation of their personal will were labeled Republicans and quickly dismissed from the corps. Since the permanent officer corps, not congressmen, controlled appointments to the Colegio Militar, a perpetuation of type was assured.[10]

Officers destined for key posts in the general staff and high echelons of the army were given advanced training in the Escuela Superior de Guerra. The Escuela de Guerra was the hub whence German influence spread through the Argentine army. Organized in 1901 on the Prussian model, it was staffed largely by a German training mission under its first director, Colonel Alfred Arendt. From 1901 to 1914, high-ranking German officers instructed the future military leaders of Argentina, and not one serious conflict marred this period of service collaboration. Beginning in 1905, Argentine army officers were sent to Germany for military training, and from 1909 to 1914, six students of the war academy attended German maneuvers annually. When in 1914 the German mission was recalled to serve in World War I, its influence was perpetuated by Argentine officers who had served as assistants.[11]

Soon after the war, the Argentine government engaged a six-man German mission headed by General W. J. Kretchmer. It was destined to remain in Argentina until 1940. Post–World War I efforts by France (Germany's traditional rival for military influence in Latin America) to make inroads into the Argentine army were effectively blocked by Inspector General José F. Uriburu. Uriburu had spent six months in training with the Uhlan Guards of Berlin in 1908 and was an ardent Germanophile. When appointed inspector general in 1923, he named as his adviser a Prussian general, Wilhelm von Faupel, a skillful military organizer who exercised considerable influence in the army down to 1927.[12]

The United States did not enter the rivalry for influence in Latin American armies until 1938, when the sending of military missions

[10] González, "Ideas Contrary to the Spirit of May," p. 10; Bruce, *Those Perplexing Argentines*, pp. 304–305.

[11] Duval, *A Argentina*, II, 368–369.

[12] Fritz T. Epstein, "European Military Influences in Latin America," pp. 144–146.

became part of United States planning for hemispheric defense against Nazi expansion. By that time, the six-man German mission in Argentina was headed by General Günther Niedernführ and comprised two colonels, one lieutenant colonel, a major and a captain. Whereas eighteen Argentine officers were receiving instruction in Germany, only five were studying in France. Most of the directors of the Colegio Militar had been trained under German instructors and tended to impart their bias to the cadets. The textbooks, regulations, organization, drilling techniques, and uniforms of the Argentine army were patterned after those of Germany. A survey made in 1938 of the 169 works by foreign military experts translated for the Biblioteca del Oficial, the important series published by the Círculo Militar, indicated that ninety-six were German, fifty-seven were French, nine were English, seven were Italian, one Swedish, and one Japanese.[13]

Most investigators agree that Germanization contributed significantly to the development of integral nationalism in the Argentine army.[14] Four decades of German military training (1901–1940) carried with it a spiritual conditioning that inclined many Argentine officers toward authoritarianism as opposed to the democratic principles of their own nation. General Luis Rodolfo González, speaking in the Círculo Militar in 1956, and looking back at the "far-reaching consequences" of Germanization, stressed the fact that German military instruction could not be divorced "from the spiritual from the ideological."[15] Many of the authoritarian-minded, German-trained, Argentine officers developed a mentality that placed little faith in the general citizenry, the professional politicians, or the slow workings of the democratic processes. These attitudes were intensified by electoral fraud and governmental

---

[13] T. R. Ybarra, *America Faces South*, pp. 186–187; Silvano Santander, *Nazismo en Argentina: La conquista del ejército*, p. 24; Ruth and Leonard Greenup, *Revolution before Breakfast*, p. 8; Fritz T. Epstein, "Argentinien und das Deutsche Heer," in *Geschichtliche Kräfte und Entscheidungen*, p. 293; Carlos von der Becke, "La République Argentine et l'armee argentine," *Revue Militaire Générale* 4, ser. 2 (1948): 462.

[14] George I. Blanksten (*Perón's Argentina*, pp. 307–308) cites German military training as one of the three major factors in determining the role of the Argentine army in politics.

[15] González, "Ideas Contrary to the Spirit of May," pp. 12–13, 18.

corruption in all quarters during the Infamous Decade (1932–1943).
There is no doubt that authoritarian and Germanic military training
contributed to the rise of integral nationalism in the Argentine army
officer-corps. However, the cool, long-range view of the historian
indicates that the thwarting of historic army drives by the regular
vehicles of political power was also an important influence. These historic army drives are the permanent factors in what we have called the
traditional-modern dichotomy of values.

On the traditional side, army indoctrination imbued the officer with
a simple, but fiery, patriotism. This patriotism with a capital *P* was the
legacy of the institution's historic nationalizing role in the winning of
independence, the consolidation of the nation, and as the fount of patriotic values for youth in an immigrant society. The army officer, often of immigrant parentage, came to view himself as the supreme
patriot, the man of simple honor in an institution that was the repository of national tradition. The mission of the officer, as one lieutenant
has written, was to teach "the fatherland, before all and above all, the
fatherland which is the native earth, which is the home, which is the
school, which is honest and productive work, which is the family, the
institutions, the honor, which is the respect for our sovereignty syn-
thesized in the sun of our flag."[16]

Along with the simple, traditional patriotism, most army officers
shared an "elemental conservatism."[17] This was not the conservatism of
a particular political party. Rather, it was the conservatism of the
military bureaucrat drawn to accepted procedures and, more important,
of the patriotic defenders of the state drawn to traditionalism.

Catholicism—but not the confessional variety—appealed to the army
officer as the moral cement of an ordered society.[18] Hierarchically conditioned by his profession, he valued social order above all other values.
Beneath the movements of the masses, which he deeply distrusted, he

---

[16] Germán R. Teisseire, "Influencia del ejército en el desarrollo de los valores
materiales y morales del pueblo argentino," *Revista Militar* 99 (January–February,
1953): 37.

[17] Carlos Cossio, *La política como conciencia, Meditación sobre la Argentina de
1955*, pp. 147, 158.

[18] Juan José Hernández Arregui, *La formación de la conciencia nacional (1930–
1960)*, pp. 495, 497.

tended always to smell the influence of alien doctrines, such as communism. This tendency had been aroused during the riotous strikes of the Tragic Week of 1919, when the army was called in to cope with the large-scale labor disorders.[19]

Side by side with these traditional army values was a modern nationalism that called for autarchy, industrialization, and technical modernization.[20] This nationalism, related to interest in a national war machine, included a drive to free the economy from foreign influences and dependence on foreign markets. This strong technocratic drive also bolstered antagonisms in the German-trained army against the western democracies—England and the United States. Army nationalists suspected these nations of influencing Argentine politics through alliances with the oligarchy, and through large-scale investments in important sectors of the nation's economy. They believed that the alliance between the oligarchy and the foreign interests was aimed at keeping the nation agricultural.

Such military preoccupation with the political and economic processes of the nation was intensified, in the late 1930s and early 1940s, when officers accepted the "integral" concept of national preparedness. Acceptance of this concept represented the adaptation of a contemporary vogue of military thought to the justification of a perpetually peacetime army bent on continued expansion of its influence. In the 1930s it formed part of the army officer's defense against pacifism, disarmament, and, most important, against the perennial complaints of leftist politicians about excessive military expenditures. The "integral" concept was stated most succinctly by Minister of War Juan D. Perón in the conclusion to his speech of June 10, 1944, at the University

[19] Alfredo A. Baisi, *La revolución faltante*, p. 30.

[20] For the most detailed lamentation by an integral nationalist concerning the plight of an economically dependent nation, and resulting political implications, see Mariano Abarca, "La industria y la dependencia nacional," *Revista de Economía Argentina* 43 (May, 1944): 66–67. Even a thoroughgoing liberal nationalist Justista like General José María Sarobe (*Política económica argentina*, pp. 13, 18, 101–102) approved of the drive for autarchy and industry in the interest of the national war machine. See also Julio Sanguinetti, *Nuestro potencial económico industrial y la defensa nacional*, p. 304. On p. 12 of Eduardo A. Grimaldi's *Industria siderúrgica argentina, antecedentes y comentarios*, bold print declares: "IT IS TO THE MINISTRY OF WAR THAT THE NATION OWES ITS STEEL INDUSTRY."

of La Plata: 1) war is a socially inevitable phenomenon; 2) even peace-loving nations must, therefore, be in continuous preparation for war; 3) the "National Defense of the Fatherland" is an integral problem which requires governmental coordination of all the nation's resources; it cannot be improvised when war knocks at the nation's door. Militarily, then, the army officer wanted strategy lifted to the place of diplomacy and statecraft in the formulation of national policy.[21]

A summation of the army officer's values points up the inherent dichotomy in his position. Most Argentine army officers favored a powerful military, as the major index of national prestige in a modern industrial society ordered by traditional values. Hence, the army wanted modernization, but was unwilling to pay the price—the erosion of traditional values and the rise of new social forces (that is, an industrial proletariat). For example, industrialization, so strongly desired by the army officer, undermines simple traditional values, brings new political and social forces into being, and threatens the patrilineal family. How to promote nationalistic modernization while coping with its impact on traditional society, was the fundamental dilemma of the army officer.

The quest by the army for a vehicle for these conflicting drives serves as an integrating hypothesis in explaining the tortuous course of militarism in Argentina. In the five decades after the definitive organization of the nation in 1880, strong presidential governments, whether oligarchical or Radical, retained the allegiance of the army. From 1880 to 1916, officers of Argentina's New Army were identified with the liberal nationalism of the landed-commercial oligarchy, the modernizing elite at that time. This was the era of dominant Roquista influence in the army, when, like other middle-sector government officers, the top brass served the oligarchy. The oligarchy, in turn, served the officer

---

21 Juan D. Perón, *Significado de la defensa nacional desde el punto de vista militar.* Perón's speech, along with many essays by military men reflecting the integral concept, is reprinted in Universidad Nacional de La Plata, *Curso de cultura superior universitaria: cátedra de defensa nacional*, pp. 50–79. See also, Juan Lucio Cernadas, *Estrategia nacional y política de estado*, p. 21; Ernesto Fantini Pertiné, *Inquietudes militares de la época*, pp. 133–134; and V. Andrada, "El consejo de la defensa nacional," *La Prensa*, June 24, 1943, p. 5.

corps by modernizing, professionalizing, and Germanizing the army. Social order and military modernization thus went hand-in-hand.

From 1916 to 1930, most army officers identified with middle-class Radicalism. Professionalization had led to the displacement of the older Roquista generals by junior officers drawn from Argentina's enlarged middle class. These new senior officers came to see in Radicalism the great national movement of the day. While Radicalism promised the middle class control of the government, it then posed no threat to the social order. Furthermore, officers of the New Army were attracted to the first Yrigoyen regime (1916–1922) by its independent, neutral foreign policy in World War I. In the late 1920s they were hopeful that the new Radical nationalism would bring social order and modernization to Argentina. Their hopes died in the years from 1928 to 1930 when the ship of state foundered under the senile Yrigoyen.

During the late 1920s there began to be serious disaffection in the ranks of the army officer-corps. One faction, led by General Justo, had profited greatly from an alliance with the Antipersonalists of Alvear in the years from 1922 to 1928. In contrast to Yrigoyen's curious financial austerity toward the military, the Alvear administration provided Minister of War Justo with the funds to modernize the army. General Justo and his faction responded by becoming the political instrument of an alliance between Antipersonalists and Conservatives. Like their Antipersonalist political cohorts, the members of the Justista faction aligned themselves with the liberal nationalist oligarchy. Hence, the Justo faction veered towards traditionalism and conservatism.

Another dissident faction that emerged in the 1920s was that of Lieutenant General Uriburu, who represented the appearance of integral nationalism in the army. The Uriburistas were hostile to the free-trading liberal nationalist oligarchy for having used democratic institutions to deliver the nation to foreign interests. They were also opposed to the demagogic politicians of the Radical middle class, who, while avowedly nationalistic, manipulated the masses for the sake of power. Only the army, the Uriburistas believed, could redeem Argentina through social order and nationalism. The Uriburu faction sought to combine military rule, political authoritarianism, and economic nationalism. Traditional values of elite rule and social order were to be reconciled with modern drives for industrialization, protectionism, and economic nationalism under the rule of a military strongman. Only in the light of conflicting army values can the Uriburu position be understood. That Uriburu espoused fascist ideology, only underscores the drive to have economic modernization while coping by force with its social repercussions.

The overthrow of Yrigoyen in 1930, achieved by the temporary union of liberal and integral nationalist factions of the army, represented political reaction executed through the army. Temporarily disillusioned by the collapse of popular presidentialism, army officers with Radical sympathies, although a majority, were unable to marshal their forces against the minority rebel factions. After the revolution, while Uriburu served as provisional president (1930–1931), his rival, General Justo, gained control of the army by forging an uneasy alliance between his own liberal nationalist faction and a group of Radical officers known as the Legalists. Uriburu had gone to great lengths in attempting to win control of the army; but in 1931 integral nationalism was still too radical for army officers. When Uriburu, confronted by rising military opposition, was forced to hold presidential elections in 1931, Justo, through fraud and electoral manipulations, emerged as the victor.

The Justista-Legalist alliance broke down soon after Justo took office in 1932. Dependent largely on the old, free trading, liberal nationalist oligarchy for civilian support, the Justo regime soon alienated the pro-Radical Legalists. As has been stated, the Justo regime launched the Infamous Decade, and during this period (1932–1943), nationalistic army officers became disillusioned with all professional politicians. On the one hand, they were angered by the sell-out of the nation to foreign interests in league with the oligarchy. The depth of their disdain for the oligarchy was revealed by a joke which was widely circulated in the army in 1943: "Upon organizing the nation, the Argentine patrician class received a house on Calle Florida and an *estancia* in the province; it mortgaged the *estancia*, sold the house, and just when it was about to sell the Fatherland, we intervened with the revolution of June 4, 1943."[22] On the other hand, army officers found no outlet in the Radical party for their nationalism. Divided in tactics, rent by feuds

---

[22] Roque Lanús, *Al servicio del ejército*, p. 36.

over leadership, excluded from power by corruption, Radicalism again proved inept as a civilian vehicle for army nationalism. Neither the traditional oligarchy nor middle-class Radicalism satisfied army drives for social order and nationalistic modernization. Furthermore, many of the active Legalists had been purged from the army as a result of unsuccessful uprisings from 1931 to 1934, and thus Radical influence in the military was further decreased. Confronted by the choice between the Justista faction with its alliance with the hated oligarchy, and the Uriburista brand of super-nationalistic militarism, most army officers opted for the latter. Lacking a legitimate political outlet for their values, they again seized the state in 1943 in an integral nationalist revolution aimed at social order and modernization through authoritarian military rule.

The extent of the army officer-corps' conversion to integral nationalism is indicated by the fact that in 1943 the secret lodge, GOU, that had executed the revolution, had recruited about 60 per cent of the 3,600 officers of the Argentine army.[23] From 1930 to 1943, the integral nationalist faction had grown from a distinct minority of the officer corps to a force of the first magnitude. The figure also indicates that a large-scale political conversion of frustrated ex-Radical officers had taken place.

That ex-Radical officers might some day join forces with integral nationalist supporters of military dictatorship, had been foreseen by ex-President Marcelo T. de Alvear. In 1937, Alvear, an expert on military affairs, stated: "The gravest error of General Uriburu was leading the army against Radicalism. The army reflects the people, and our people is 70% Radical. And it may follow, that some day this 70% of Radicals in the army will rebel; then they will be isolated; disavowed by the majority of the people which chastises it unjustly, repudiated by the rest, they will deem themselves obligated by the circumstances to implant a dictatorship of the middle class, without support from within and outside the nation, incompetent and disoriented, despotic and anarchical."[24]

---

[23] Josephs, *Argentine Diary*, p. 140.
[24] *La Vanguardia*, "Documentos para la historia," July 17, 1945, p. 3.

The emergence of the army as a fascistoid middle sector in 1943 was, then, not primarily the result of authoritarian training and Germanic influences, although these were indeed contributing factors. It was rather the result of conflicting army drives that had found no other outlet in the political arena. Still it should not be denied that the early military victories of Nazi Germany in World War II awakened historic pro-German sympathy in the Argentine army and helped convince many officers that dictatorship, organized along authoritarian lines for internal stability and external glory, represented the wave of the future.[25] Other foreign stimuli also had an influence. Many Argentine officers were deeply impressed by the alliance of sword and cross in the Franco dictatorship of Spain. It was in agreement with their value system to see the Spanish *caudillo* as the bulwark of Catholicism against hated communism. Others admired the fascist regime of Mussolini in Italy, and were impressed by the Italian conquest of Ethiopia.

In view of the forty years of service collaboration between the two armies, it is not surprising that it was the German model that most deeply influenced Argentine officers. Nazi German expansion awakened the racist, imperialist urges of integral nationalists in the Argentine army and served as inspiration for their aspirations for hegemony in a South American bloc freed from Yankee influence. In their view, such hegemony would also establish the military superiority of the "master Latin race" of "white" Argentines over the mixed races of Brazil, Argentina's historic rival for Latin American leadership.[26]

Although the integral nationalists declared their independence of the corrupt influences of political parties of all persuasions, they were prepared to accept the assistance of civilians with their own political beliefs. Civilian integral nationalists had been drawn largely from the ranks of discontented intellectuals, the provincial elite, and, to a certain extent, the clergy. As the army moved towards integral nationalism in the late 1930s, a fundamental change was occurring in the civilian

---

[25] González, "Ideas Contrary to the Spirit of May," pp. 16–17. Also Juan E. Carulla (*Latinomérica en picada*, pp. 142–144) records an unusually frank conversation between the author and an Argentine general, who gives his reasons for admiring Germany.

[26] Josephs, *Argentine Diary*, p. 139.

movement. Civilian integral nationalism became deeply permeated by Catholic, corporative, Hispanophile, and pro-Franco thought.[27] Gaucho folklore and *rosismo* were, to a large extent, eclipsed by a Catholic nationalism that stressed the church-sword alliance in the political regeneration of Argentina. Henceforth, civilian integral nationalists will be referred to in this analysis as Catholic nationalists.

Despite their dedication to Catholicism as a force for social order, not all integral nationalists of the army were willing to make the dictates of an authoritarian nation-state subject to the approval of the church. However, most army officers agreed with the views of the Catholic nationalists on most issues. Both groups shared a belief in authoritarian government using strict control to inculcate military values and church ethics. Both hated the professional politicians and the "illiterate" masses, and were in favor of rule by the military elite. Both supported a xenophobic nationalism that stressed hatred for the western democracies, suspicion of foreign economic interests, and an urge, often repressed, towards expansionism. Both groups were advocates of economic nationalism, protectionism, and industrial modernization, but were unwilling to face the effects of these on traditional society.

Further complicating the study of the socio-institutional aspects of Argentine militarism is the tendency of the military establishment to divide politically along both vertical and horizontal lines. The navy has often been in opposition to army cliques, and, in both branches, political tensions between commissioned and noncommissioned officers in what is known as the question of military castes have caused deep rifts.

Owing to the army's numerical superiority, its distribution in garrisons throughout the nation, and the fact that military revolt can not succeed without extensive territorial occupation by ground forces, that branch has been by far the most politically powerful. But no study of Argentine militarism can ignore the navy. Since 1943, it has played an increasingly significant political role, first as an unwavering opponent of integral nationalism and later as a staunch foe of Peronism.

---

[27] Oscar Troncoso, *Los nacionalistas argentinos*, pp. 52–57; Juan E. Carulla, *Al filo del medio siglo*, p. 227.

Naval opposition to integral nationalism and the proletarian-oriented Perón dictatorship has often been attributed to the social origins of that branch's officer corps. It is common to assume that the naval officer-corps—drawn from the elites of the coastal provinces, and linked to the agrarian and commercial interests of Buenos Aires—reflects the liberal nationalist, civilianist tradition of the oligarchy and upper middle class. In a recent study of the resurgence of militarism in Latin America, Edwin Lieuwen has explained naval opposition to Peronism by asserting that the officer corps "tends to originate in the upper middle class, a class traditionally opposed to any socio-political advance of the labor-left."[28]

Such assumptions of social superiority were labeled as myths by naval officers whom the author interviewed in Argentina. They remain unproven owing to the navy's reluctance to make information on social origins available to scholarly research. It should also be noted that other observers, handicapped by the same dearth of data, have written that the social origins of the naval officer-corps do not differ significantly from those of their middle-class counterparts in other branches of the military or in the liberal professions.[29]

More important than the still unresolved question of social origins is the distinction, made by political scientist James W. Rowe, between "acquired political tastes" and "inherited class interest."[30] The naval officer may come from the same social stratum as his counterpart in the army, but institutional values of upper-class behavior[31] cause him to identify with elites from his civilian habitat. Whether middle class or no, the fact is that in the eyes of Argentine civilians entrance into the naval officer-corps does confer a status higher than does entrance into the army officer-corps.

In view of his geographic origins and institutional norms of behavior, the naval officer in the Buenos Aires area must certainly have

[28] Edwin Lieuwen, *Generals vs. Presidents: Neomilitarism in Latin America*, pp. 15, 23.
[29] Carlos A. Florit, *Las fuerzas armadas y la guerra psicológica*, p. 42; E. F. Sánchez Zinny, *El culto de la infamia: Historia documentada de la segunda tiranía argentina*, p. 460.
[30] James W. Rowe, *Argentina's Restless Military*, p. 7.
[31] Florit, *Las fuerzas armadas*, p. 42.

experienced a pull towards identification with elites. To a larger extent than even the army officer-corps, naval officers have been drawn from the province and city of Buenos Aires.[32] Prior to 1930, 49 per cent of Argentine naval officers were drawn from the capital city of Buenos Aires and still another 21 percent from the province.[33] Of the eighty-six men admitted to officer candidacy in 1936, forty-one were drawn from the capital and twenty-four from the province.[34] Hence, if naval officers sought to confirm their adopted social status by identification with civilian elites, they were likely to do so in terms of the liberal nationalist tradition of the oligarchy and upper middle class in and around status-conscious Buenos Aires.

Naval political views are also shaped by the cosmopolitan nature of the profession. The naval career presents an opportunity for travel beyond the national soil. Conditioned by the international environment of life at sea, the naval officer's perspective is rarely a strictly national-istic one.[35] The naval officer is thus drawn not to the xenophobic and narrow integral nationalism, but to the more cosmopolitan liberal na-tionalist tradition.

At home, the naval officer does not share the army officer's martial self-consciousness and pride in his separateness from the civilian popu-lation. Many naval officers avoid wearing their uniforms in public. In an army-sponsored book containing the memoirs of a conscript, a broadside is leveled at the navy for this practice. While on leave, the army conscript meets a naval officer and strikes up a friendship. Their introduction is marred, however, by the conscript's failure to recognize the naval officer's rank.

"Excuse me," the conscript states, "I am unfamiliar with naval rank."
"Are you from the interior?" asks the naval officer.
Army conscript: "No, I am from the capital."
Naval officer: "Then how is such ignorance possible?"
Army conscript: "I don't know, sir. But I must use my reason, since I

[32] Imaz, "Los que mandan," p. 44.
[33] "La escuadra y la escuela naval; breve reseña histórica" in *Los viajes de la "Sarmiento,"* p. 27.
[34] *Memoria del ministerio de marina correspondiente al ejercicio 1936*, pp. 25–26.
[35] Florit, *Las fuerzas armadas*, p. 43.

have never seen a naval officer in uniform on the streets of Buenos Aires; I don't know why this is so, but that's the way it is. On the other hand, I have seen many foreign naval officers in uniform, as if they were proud of wearing it."[36]

Like civilian liberal nationalists, naval officers tend to admire the political forms and personal liberties of the western democracies. This admiration has been bolstered by many decades of service collaboration with western democracies. As has been stated, the technical side of service collaboration can never be divorced from the spiritual and political. Whereas the Argentine army was the recipient of four decades of German military training, the navy was guided first by Great Britain and later by the United States. From the 1890s to the mid-1930s, British ships, equipment, and instruction prevailed in the Argentine navy.[37] Beginning in 1935, a three-man United States training mission was assigned to assist in instruction at the Naval War College.[38] This inaugurated a period of United States–Argentine service collaboration that has lasted down to this day.

The Argentine navy's democratic traditions are, however, in the words of Edwin Lieuwen, of the "classical Greek, privileged-class type . . . . "[39] In this respect, they approximate the outlook of the Argentine liberal nationalist civilian elites. Life aboard ship, with all its cooperative activities, precludes the strict hierarchical relationship typical in the army between officers and men. In the army, conscripts still respond to orders with the humble, "Yes, my general," or whatever their superior's rank is at the time. In the navy, "Yes, sir" will suffice.

It should be stated, however, that naval officers have not been unanimous in defense of the liberal nationalist tradition. In 1934 an integral nationalist officer clique, headed by Admiral Abel Renard, was organized in the navy, and later came to be associated with the army factions of Bautista Molina and Menéndez.[40] Prior to the revolution of 1943, a

[36] Santiago M. Peralta, *Memorias de un conscripto*, p. 89.
[37] Teodoro Caillet-Bois, *Historia naval argentina*, pp. 513, 517.
[38] United States, Department of State, *Papers Relating to the Foreign Relations of the United States, 1934*, IV, 541.
[39] Lieuwen, *Generals vs. Presidents*, p. 15.
[40] *La Vanguardia*, "Documentos para la historia," July 17, 1945, p. 3.

group of ambitious integral nationalist junior naval officers, headed by Captain Alberto Teisaire, was linked to the GOU conspiracy.[41] And during the Perón regime, some naval officers, in order to advance professionally, cooperated with the dictator.

In both army and navy the question of military castes sometimes became a divisive factor. Despite the closer relationship between officers and men, in the navy, a social gulf persisted, and during the Perón dictatorship it came dramatically to the fore. The noncommissioned officers of the navy, drawn from the Peronist lower class, were pitted during this period against the commissioned officers, who were staunch foes of the dictator. On at least two separate occasions, during Perón's election in 1946 and during a naval plot against the dictator in 1951, noncoms planned counterconspiracies against their superiors.[42] In the army most of the noncoms were drawn from the lower class, and they harbored serious grievances against the commissioned officers who were mainly middle class.[43] Like his relatives in civilian society, the noncom sought higher pay, improved social standing, and the opportunity to enter the officer corps. During the 1930s, the Radical Legalists, conspiring to overthrow the oligarchy,[44] exploited these issues. Just as Perón stole the allegiance of the lower class by social welfare, he won the support of army noncoms by catering to their demands for greater recognition.

[41] Guillermo D. Plater, *Una gran lección*, pp. 33–35.

[42] Aníbal O. Olivieri, *Dos veces rebelde: Memorias*, p. 15.

[43] On the social origins of the noncoms, see Rattenbach, *Sociología militar*, pp. 143–147.

[44] J. Beresford Crawkes, *533 días de la historia argentina—6 de septiembre de 1930–20 de febrero de 1932*, pp. 312–313; *El hombre de deber: Una serie de semblanzas del Gral. Manuel A. Rodríguez*, p. 48.

4. The Revolution of 1943 and the Rise of Colonel Juan D. Perón

The Argentine revolution of 1943 began within the Castillo government in 1942, when control of the army and the Ministry of War was transferred from the liberal nationalist Justistas to the integral nationalists of the GDUEU. The revolution of 1943 was to represent the withdrawal of military support from the discredited Castillo regime as well as the assumption of direct control of the government by the integral nationalists. This seizure of the state by the integral nationalists was facilitated by a political vacuum in the Argentine government. While the GDUEU had forged some kind of integral nationalist unity within the army, civilian and democratic forces in the political arena were torn by divisions and demoralization.

An examination of the civilian forces on the eve of the military revolution of 1943 underscores this point. In this rich agrarian state, impelled by wartime industrialization towards the status of a transitional society, a sector of the landed oligarchy still ruled. As political leaders, however, Castillo and his Conservative cohorts were a far cry from the proud liberal nationalist oligarchy of the nineteenth century. Under Castillo, tutelary democracy had come to mean electoral fraud and corruption. Lacking popular support, confronted by strife within his own political organization, and having lost the allegiance of the Justista faction of the army, Castillo had turned to the pro-German integral nationalists for the force necessary to perpetuate his personal brand of elitism. This faction of the army, although it cooperated with him for a time, was in reality the enemy of the liberal nationalist oligarchy.

Soon after Justo's death, Castillo faced open revolt within the Concordancia, as political leaders looked ahead to the presidential succession. On January 24, 1943, Minister of Justice Guillermo Rothe, Conservative leader of Córdoba, declared his candidacy. His bid was met by separate declarations issued by Rodolfo Moreno, Conservative governor of Buenos Aires, and the powerful Robustiano Patrón Costas, Conservative from Salta. Finally the Antipersonalist wing of the Concordancia countered by offering its own presidential candidate, Juan Cepeda, of Rosario.[1]

Castillo's strategy to perpetuate his political power was to reunite the Concordancia and to make a public display of the loyalty of the integral-nationalist–controlled army to his regime. His formula for reuniting the Concordancia was to support the Robustiano Patrón Costas–Manuel de Iriondo ticket, Iriondo being a Antipersonalist leader of Santa Fe. Well-publicized Saturday dinners with high-ranking officers were meant to dramatize Castillo's alignment with the army.[2] In reality, Castillo was the slave, not the master, of the army.

While the Concordancia was splitting, the middle-class democratic parties were attempting to form a popular front to stave off militarism. The principal obstacle to this movement was the majority party of the nation, the Radicals, who claimed to be the rightful heirs to political power in Argentina. Since the revolution of 1930, a deep sense of resentment and betrayal had permeated the Radical camp, and made its members willing to use any tactics to regain their former legal power.

---

[1] Bernardo Rabinovitz, *Lo que no se dijo. Sucedió en la Argentina* 1943–1956, pp. 12–13.
[2] "Documentos para la historia," *La Vanguardia*, September 18, 1945, p. 5.

It will be remembered that the Radical movement bore the personalistic, authoritarian stamp of Hipólito Yrigoyen, and that he had sought to use the professional army as the servant of popular presidentialism instead of excluding it from politics. During the decade after Yrigoyen's death in 1933, the Radical party underwent division, deterioration, and loss of popularity. In 1943, Radical nationalism, still the major vehicle of the middle-class struggle against the oligarchy, forsook civilianist democracy by declining to enter into a popular front with the Socialists and Progressive Democrats. Instead, the Radicals, desirous of power at all costs, chose to deal with the integral nationalist Minister of War Ramírez, and offered him their party's nomination for the presidency.[3]

With the movement for democratic union shattered, the integral nationalists of the army, catered to by the Concordancia and the Radicals alike, were in a commanding position. Disdainful of democracy, the integral nationalists were nevertheless willing to use its institutional façade to accomplish their objectives and bring the army to power. An aroused civilian populace might have obstructed the integral nationalist assumption of power, for army officers have always been sensitive to public opinion. But tainted by a decade of graft and electoral fraud, neither the Concordancia nor the Radicals was capable of arousing a pessimistic and apathetic public. In 1943 "the average man-in-the-street," wrote Ysabel Fisk [Rennie], "was embittered and disillusioned by the spectacle of the fraud and corruption of the Conservative governments. The government bureaucracy, which is filled on the spoils system, was swept clean of the opposition and filled with incompetents who were friends of Conservative politicians. The touchstone to success was pull. With it, the most incompetent and dishonest man was made. Without it, no one, no matter what his education, no matter what his intelligence, could get so much as a clerical position. The young people who came of age in the decade 1930–1940 were a frustrated generation. Politically and economically they were ciphers. Graduate engineers, graduate chemists, graduate teachers found every avenue closed to them. Cynicism became the fashion, and this generation was so

---

[3] *Ibid.*, October 9, 1945, p. 3; Ysabel Fisk [Rennie], "Argentina: The Thirteen-Year Crisis," *Foreign Affairs* 22, no. 2 (January, 1944): 265.

thoroughly, so effectively submerged that it has almost no representatives in Argentine politics today."[4]

A strong labor movement, capable of paralyzing the economy by general strike, also might have deterred the integral nationalist takeover. But, the CGT having split into rival organizations in 1942, organized labor was both weak and divided. Furthermore, neither organized labor nor the middle-class democratic parties had reached the new urban masses who, beginning in the 1930s, came pouring into Buenos Aires from the countryside. These denizens of the misery shacks which rimmed the city were to find their champion in the integral nationalist Colonel Juan D. Perón.

This, then, was the vacuum into which the army moved in 1943: a divided oligarchy, a fragmented middle-class popular front, an apathetic public, a weak and disunited labor movement, and a lower class yearning for political and social integration in a strongly nationalist state. While these fissures were coming to the surface in the fractured society, the GDUEU, later GOU, forged the unity and leadership necessary for military revolution.

After the revolution of 1943, the GDUEU became the GOU. Henceforth, the term GOU will be used continually in this interpretation, since both organizations were part of a single historical movement. Although it is not possible to determine with certainty when the GOU was actually formed, it is likely that the secret lodge came into being in July or August, 1942.[5] It was patterned after the Japanese Bushido, a military lodge identified with extreme nationalism in that country.[6] It was dedicated to uniting the army politically and defending it against all enemies. GOU agents were organized in secret cells in army garrisons throughout Argentina, and they held regular meetings to share a common pool of political information.[7]

---

[4] Fisk, "Argentina," p. 263.

[5] "Documentos para la historia," *La Vanguardia*, July 17, 1945, p. 3.

[6] Luis Rodolfo González, "Ideas Contrary to the Spirit of May and Their Repercussion in Argentine Political Life: A Military Opinion at the Service of Definitive Pacification," trans. K. H. Silvert, in *Letters and Reports Written for the American Universities Field Staff, 1955–1958*, p. 9.

[7] Extracts of GDUEU statutes in "Documentos para la historia," *La Vanguardia*, July 17, 1945, p. 3.

Although the GOU regulations described the lodge as an organization with no formal chief, it was actually directed by a group of sixteen officers of varying rank.[8] Most of these officers were colonels who, having served together in the Mendoza garrison in 1940, organized an integral nationalist faction known as Cruzada de Renovación. After leaving Mendoza, the officers of the Crusade, foremost among them Colonel Juan D. Perón, spread their doctrine throughout the nation. Their slogan was Gobierno, Orden, Unión (Government, Order, Union), and the letters GOU also came to stand for Grupo de Oficiales Unidos (Group of United Officers).[9]

That colonels played a major role in organizing the GOU is a point of no little significance. Professional and political ambitions have always been intense at the colonel's level in the Argentine army. For socially upward-striving officers, the rank of general meant entrance into the nation's elite. This explains why an examination of the rosters of the Uriburu conspiracy, the Legalist schemes of the 1930s, and the movement of 1943 indicates that a large number of participants were lieutenant colonels and colonels. As the highest ranking officers able to claim the personal allegiance of the conscripts, the colonels were both ambitious and powerful enough to throw professional restraints to the winds.[10] Furthermore, many of the colonels who organized the GOU had received revolutionary training as captains and majors in the conspiracy of 1930. Their leadership in organizing the revolution of 1943 and their success in imposing their political views on the officer corps, showed that ranking integral nationalist generals, Bautista Molina and Menéndez, had lost control of the movement.

After the revolution of 1943, the colonels would emerge like mushrooms in the political sunshine. Prior to the revolution, the GOU did need ranking generals as window-dressing and as instruments of authority to unite the officer corps. They received such support from a group known as the Five of the Jousten (named after a hotel in central Buenos Aires where the high-ranking conspirators met). The Five of the Jousten were Generals Pedro Ramírez, Arturo Rawson, and

---

[8] Bonifacio del Carril, *Crónica interna de la revolución libertadora*, pp. 24–25.
[9] Ray Josephs, *Argentine Diary*, pp. 138–139.
[10] *Ibid.*, p. 64.

Diego Masón, and Rear Admirals Sabá Sueyro and Benito Sueyro.[11] Both Ramírez and Rawson were especially prized by GOU as frontmen for the revolution. Ramírez, former chief of staff of the Menéndez conspiracy, was the ranking general of the army and provided the necessary military authority. Although Rawson was proally and reputedly had prodemocratic leanings, his position as senior officer of the Campo de Mayo garrison made him a valuable addition to the conspiracy.

As has been stated, the first GOU objective was control of the Ministry of War. This was arranged with President Castillo through GOU representative General Domingo Martínez, chief of police of Buenos Aires. After the Ministry of War was transferred to General Ramírez in November, 1942, the GOU embarked upon its second objective—absorption of the democratic forces, an end to the popular front, and its own assumption of power through the democratic processes.[12]

The willingness of Radical politicians to name Minister of War Ramírez as the candidate for the presidency spelled the end of democratic union. With the promise of Radical support, Ramírez next tried to force "his president," Castillo, to select him as presidential candidate on the Concordancia ticket. To complete the plot to foist integral nationalism on the nation through legal revolution, Castillo was asked also to appoint Ramírez minister of the interior, the position giving best control of the elections of 1943. The minister of war appointment was to be transferred to General Diego Masón, Ramírez's colleague among the Five of the Jousten. If the Radicals balked on delivering their support to Ramírez, militarism and integral nationalism would come to power using the old Concordancia techniques of electoral fraud.[13] Either way, or both ways, the GOU stood to gain.

President Castillo, however, refused to submit to such pressures and ordered Ramírez to resign. This created a complete vacuum around his government, since the GOU, the only powerful and united force in the nation, withdrew its support from his regime. When, on June 4, 1943, Castillo committed the final act of his political suicide by naming

11 "Documentos para la historia," *La Vanguardia*, October 9, 1945, p. 3.
12 *Ibid.*, October 2, 1945, p. 3.
13 *Ibid.*, October 9, 1945, p. 3.

proally, Conservative, Robustiano Patrón Costas as his successor, the pro-German GOU ordered ten thousand troops from the Campo de Mayo to overthrow the government.

The actual revolutionary operation on that day was led not by Minister of War Ramírez, but by General Arturo Rawson, senior officer at the Campo de Mayo. Much to the dismay of the GOU, the bold Rawson declared himself president, violating a prerevolutionary oath to share power in a triumvirate with Rear Admiral Sabá Sueyro and General Ramírez.[14] Even more alarming to the pro-German integral nationalists was the fact that upon seizing the presidency, Rawson dispatched aides to the United States embassy with assurances that Argentina would forsake neutrality for inter-American solidarity in World War II. These moves so enraged the colonels of the GOU that they threatened to throw the president out of the window of the Casa Rosada unless he resigned immediately.[15] On June 6, 1943, Rawson resigned. He was replaced by Minister of War Ramírez.

The revolution of 1943, a purely military coup, was at once antioligarchical, antiliberal, antidemocratic, anticommunist, and sought no support from the Argentine masses. Disdaining both the professional politicians and the masses, the integral nationalists represented a fascistoid middle sector. Emerging as they did from the army, they could see only the military elite as the rulers of a regenerated Argentina.

The historical tradition of the revolution was revealed in a decree of September 2, 1943, honoring the memory of Lieutenant General José F. Uriburu "who led the liberating movement" of 1930.[16] A decade after his death, Uriburu, once the leader of only a small integral nationalist minority in the army, had become the hero of the officer corps. This fact indicates the basic political changes that had occurred in the army since 1930.

Government under the integral nationalists of the army became a decree-issuing mill, with an average of eighty-seven decrees being is-

---

[14] *La Prensa*, December 5, 1943, p. 8.

[15] Juan D. Perón to Professor Robert Alexander, in personal interview, Madrid, September 1, 1960. Used by permission of Professor Alexander.

[16] Text of decree is in Bartolomé Galíndez, *Apuntes de tres revoluciones, 1930–1943–1955*, p. 35.

sued daily to govern everything from morals to heavy industry.[17] These decrees dramatized the traditional-modern dichotomy within the army. As revolutionaries of the radical right, the integral nationalists endeavored to inculcate traditional values of God, Fatherland, and Family. As modern nationalists, they also endeavored to transform Argentina overnight into a self-sufficient, industrial war machine.

The resolve to establish social order by authoritarian means was made dramatically clear with the announcement of three important decrees on December 31, 1943.[18] The first dissolved the political parties, placing their activities outside the law. By early 1944 a journalist in Buenos Aires was able to report that "practically every pro-democratic organization here has been barred, banned or beaten out of existence."[19] The second decree regulated the press, depriving newspapers of virtually all freedom of expression. Censorship was also imposed on radio stations and movies. "Alien," or "communist," Jewish newspapers were closed down.[20] The ministry of the interior ordered the arrest of anyone suspected of having communist contacts. The third decree reversed the secular, liberal nationalist tradition in education by making religious, that is, Roman Catholic, teaching obligatory in the public schools. God, family, and morality, the simple traditional values, became dominant themes of the military decrees. Societies of Free Masons were ordered closed. Divorce advertisements inserted by lawyers in Buenos Aires newspapers were stricken from the press as threats to "the Christian principles on which family life is founded, [as] attacks [on] family unity" and "against Argentina's traditional principles." Women in business or public life were to be objects of scorn, threats to the traditional patrilineal family. The military regime quietly removed women from key positions in the government.[21]

Military decree, by dictating everything from the length of women's dresses to the ideals of a child's education, was to cleanse society. Taxidance cabarets, where a drink bought female companionship, were re-

[17] Josephs, *Argentine Diary*, p. 170.
[18] Galíndez, *Apuntes de tres revoluciones*, p. 68.
[19] Josephs, *Argentine Diary*, p. 265.
[20] *Ibid.*, pp. 116, 190.
[21] *Ibid.*, pp. 47, 67, 90.

stricted to specified neighborhoods. The "new" Argentines were to be reared on the virtues of supernationalism and militarism. A decree of September 27, 1943, ordered primary schoolteachers to "take advantage of every opportunity to exalt the sentiment of the Fatherland . . . [and] to give military glory and deeds of arms the preferred place which they deserve."[22] Physical education in the schools was taken over by the army. Preconscription military training was ordered for children from twelve years of age.[23]

Along with this dose of Spartan traditionalism, modern industrialism was to come to Argentina. In line with the integral concept of war, the Council of National Defense was created, "with the end of assuring in time of peace the strictest cooperation of the distinct organisms of State in activities related to defense."[24] In part, the industrial drive, with its emphasis on production of war material, was spurred by the rivalry with Brazil, which was receiving heavy Lend-Lease aid from the United States. In addition, however, industrial modernization was a deeply rooted historical aspiration in the army.

In their drive to industrialize Argentina, the integral nationalists adopted measures characteristic of a war economy. All factories were to devote themselves to defense-related industries. Lacking in iron, Argentina imported scrap from Spain and Paraguay. Law number 12,709 created the Dirección General de Fabricaciones Militares, which combined capital from the state and from private firms and began the development of eighty factories.[25] Expanded government intervention in the economy characterized a policy of autarchy and forced industrialization designed to defend the economy from fluctuations originating outside the nation. Expenditures, especially those of the military, were multiplied, taxes increased, and new sources of revenue were tapped. From 1941 to 1946, total national expenditures increased by 123.7 per cent. Military expenditures accounted for 62.9 per cent of this in-

22 George I. Blanksten, *Perón's Argentina*, p. 188.
23 Ruth and Leonard Greenup, *Revolution before Breakfast*, p. 18.
24 República Argentina, Presidente, 1944 (Farrell), *Mensaje y Memoria, 1943–4 de junio, 1944*, pp. 104–105.
25 "Dirección General de Fabricaciones Militares, Ley No. 12.709" in General Manuel N. Savio, *Ley de Fabricaciones Militares: Conceptos que fundamentaron su proyecto*, pp. 19–25.

crease, having jumped from 21.2 per cent of national expenditures in 1941, to 44.3 per cent by 1946.[26]

True to the Uriburista, integral nationalist tradition of protectionism, the military regime reversed the liberal nationalist policy, sponsored by the beef and wheat interests of the oligarchy, of free trade with Europe. On June 6, 1944, a decree was issued authorizing the executive to raise import duties by as much as 50 per cent in order to stimulate and protect native industry.[27] The measure was meant as another step in the creation of an industrial base for the national war machine.

More attention was, of course, devoted to the production of armaments than to any other industry. Arms made in Argentina by Argentines was the theme that linked militarism to industrialization to nationalism. A native 35-ton tank, the Tiger, constructed of parts from no less than eighty-five separate plants in Argentina, became a much publicized feature of the armaments program. In line with the new emphasis on air power, the government constructed an all-Argentine fighter plane, an imitation of the PT-19 Fairchild trainer, called the DL-22. For the first time, heavy artillery, machine guns, depth charges and aerial bombs became regular items of production in Argentina. The driving force behind the Argentine armaments program was reputed to be Austrian munitions magnate, Fritz Mandl.[28]

Hurriedly contrived and lacking essential raw materials (coal, iron and steel), the industrial war machine squeaked of "scrap and spit." However, the new integral nationalist Tiger roared stridently of expansion. Inspired by German conquest, the integral nationalists issued sensational secret circulars that told of the coming of Argentine hegemony in a South American bloc freed from Yankee influence. One of the secret circulars of the military government read as follows:

> Argentina is surrounded by hostile governments, which are inspired by ideals different from ours. We must not give in to this Bloc of United Nations, but on the contrary oppose them with all our force.

[26] Robert A. Rennie, "Argentine Fiscal Policy," *Inter-American Economic Affairs* 1, no. 1 (June, 1947): pp. 52–53.

[27] *Ibid.*, p. 69.

[28] "Show of Strength," *Business Week*, July 1, 1944, pp. 114–116.

The United States is our enemy.

Russia is our enemy.

The anti-Argentine circle will be broken by defeating the present Spanish-speaking governments surrounding us, replacing them by governments supporting our own purposes.

All of these governments will be united in a regional league of La Plata, which will demand the adhesion of all Hispanic-America, beginning with Peru. Brazil will be induced to join the Eastern Bloc. If she does not agree she will be reduced to neutrality by placing 120,000 men at her back. The Eastern Bloc will be connected with Spain, and through Spain with the Axis. It is now possible, with the use of maximum efforts, to separate England and the United States.[29]

Sharing as they did the same goals as the integral nationalists of the army, the Catholic nationalists of Argentina had a field day after the army seized the state. Their administrative experience was sorely needed and their influence was especially important in the area of public education and information,[30] where the integral nationalists were determined to inculcate militarism, supernationalism, and church doctrine. They also occupied key positions in other areas of the government: David Uriburu was named interventor in Corrientes; Alberto Baldrich interventor in Tucumán; and, Admiral L. Scasso interventor in Córdoba. Mario Amadeo, destined to become an important figure in Catholic nationalist circles, was appointed director of political affairs in the Ministry of Foreign Relations.[31]

As the Catholic nationalists secured a foothold in the government, they became more audacious in their pronouncements on Argentina's destiny. Gustavo Martínez Zuviría, anti-Semitic minister of justice and public instruction, proclaimed the church-sword alliance in the revolution. The *niños bien*, fascistoid sons of provincial oligarchs, gathered in the Club del Plata to praise the revolution as being in the tradition of Dictator Juan Manuel de Rosas. Friar Castellani, influential rector of the University of La Plata, raised the banner of Hispanidad, which de-

---

[29] Text of circular is in Carlton Beals et al., *What the South Americans Think of Us*, pp. 316–317.

[30] William B. Bristol, "Hispanidad in Argentina, 1936–1945," pp. 124–125.

[31] Oscar Troncoso, *Los nacionalistas argentinos*, pp. 67–68.

nounced Argentina for having abandoned Spain in 1810 and supported the use of Catholicism as Argentina's road back to the mother country.[32]

Few Catholic nationalists could envision themselves ever being eclipsed as the major civilian suport of the revolution by the leaders of labor. In their drive to industrialize Argentina, the integral nationalists of the army brooked no disobedience from the working class. A decree of July 20, 1943, placed severe restraints on labor union activities, especially those "alien to their true character."[33] During the first months of the military regime, an offensive was launched against organized labor. Unions were intervened, leaders jailed, labor organs suppressed.[34] Then on October 27, 1943, a historic but unpublicized event took place: Colonel Juan D. Perón was appointed as head of the Department of Labor and Social Security. It was seemingly an unimportant post, the department being merely a branch of the Ministry of the Interior. Perón would, however, use this post to change the course of the revolution, to give it a broad social base, and to facilitate his climb to power as the new champion of Argentina's underdogs. His superior in the all-important Ministry of War, General Edelmiro Farrell, was in reality a front-man for Perón.

Perón's initial power stemmed from his position within the GOU and the army. Months before he launched his program to win the masses over the revolution, he had been a leading contender for power in military circles. After the revolution of 1943, control of the GOU passed from the powerful sixteen officers to what was called the Big Four: Colonel Juan D. Perón, chief of the secretariat of the Ministry of War; Colonel Enrique González, secretary to President Ramírez; Colonel Emilio Ramírez, chief of police of Buenos Aires (replacing Martínez); and Colonel Eduardo Avalos, chief of the powerful Campo de Mayo garrison.[35] In the Ministry of War, Perón served as

---

[32] Silvio Santander, *Nazismo en Argentina: La conquista del ejército*, pp. 30–31.

[33] Text of decree in *La Prensa*, July 21, 1943, p. 7.

[34] Jorge Abelardo Ramos, *América latina: Un país*, p. 168.

[35] Carril, *Crónica interna de la revolución libertadora*, p. 29. Contra-almirante Guillermo D. Plater (*Una gran lección*, pp. 41–42) not only names the Big Four as the directorate of GOU, but also states that Perón was head of the group.

recruiter for the GOU and was reputed to be the rising force within the lodge. In November, 1943, Perón boasted to Chilean correspondent Abel Valdés that the GOU controlled 3,300 of the 3,600 officers of the Argentine army. GOU members were required to give proof of their allegiance by depositing signed letters of resignation on Colonel Perón's desk.[36]

But, while increasing his military power, Perón also undertook to change the orientation of the revolution by giving it a broad social base among the Argentine masses. That a military man would seek to lead the working class, came at first as a shock to Catholic nationalists.[37] In general, army officers tended to look upon labor activity as a species of crime, if not of treason. But Colonel Perón, at forty-nine, was no ordinary army officer. He had the ability to store and to utilize life experience. In his own words, he had long been interested in social problems. During his years as an officer, Perón had conversed with conscripts who came from impoverished families, lacked decent clothes and entered the army barefoot. He had traveled widely in Argentina in the service of the army, and was keenly aware of the miserable conditions under which people lived and worked in many provinces. During the years from 1938 to 1940 while on a study mission in Europe, he witnessed the social transformations in progress in Italy, France, Germany, and Spain.[38] He had participated in the Uriburu revolution of 1930 as a captain, and had no doubt drawn many lessons on revolution from that experience. Hence, Perón combined insight into social problems with practical revolutionary experience.

The story of Perón's program for the masses has already been told in great detail in other works. As early as September, 1943, Perón, General Farrell, and Colonel Juan Filomeno Velasco, seeking civilian support for the revolution, had been in communication with the Socialist labor leaders, Angel Borlenghi and José M. Argana. They first attempted to win the allegiance of labor by offering government posts to union leaders. The labor leaders, however, refused to join a de facto

---

[36] Interview quoted in *La Prensa*, November 12, 1943, p. 6.

[37] See Mario Amadeo, *Ayer, hoy, mañana*, p. 19.

[38] Perón to Alexander, in personal interview, Madrid, September 1, 1960. Used by permission of Professor Alexander.

government as long as it was de facto, and, more important, they sought concrete proof of the government's concern for the working class.[39] Within less than one year, Perón furnished the evidence by passing 29 new labor laws and taking part in 311 labor disputes and 174 settlements, thereby making his name a household word to 2,852,000 Argentine workers. Wage rates were fixed at from eleven to eighteen per cent above their previous levels, giving labor a definite stake in the perpetuation of Perón's influence.[40]

By winning the allegiance of the working class, Perón avoided Uriburu's error of attempting to build a revolutionary regime on such fragile fulcrums as the Church and the 300,000 to 500,000 Catholic nationalists.[41] For those in the lower class who refused to see the light, Perón could always brandish the iron fist hidden by the soft glove of paternalism. As early as October 28, 1943, forty-eight leaders of established labor unions were arrested.

Although he had added an "army" of workers to his already impressive military power, Perón still faced two major challenges: control within the GOU and within the political arena at large. Each of the three other members of the Big Four in the GOU was a powerful rival. Colonel Enrique González had by-passed the office of undersecretary of war in favor of the presidential secretariat, a position whence he could keep tabs on President Ramírez and that he converted into a center through which all cabinet decisions had to pass.[42] Firmly ensconced in this position of power, González was the leading opponent of Perón's program for the popularization of integral nationalism. As chief of police of Buenos Aires, Colonel Emilio Ramírez enhanced his influence as one of the regime's strong-men by sponsoring the creation of a national police force. The last of the Big Four was Colonel Eduardo Avalos, commander of the powerful Campo de Mayo garrison, which is pointed at the city of Buenos Aires like a dagger. Avalos

---

[39] José M. Argana to Robert Alexander, in personal interview, Buenos Aires, October 30, 1946. Used by permission of Professor Alexander.

[40] Germán Arciniegas, *The State of Latin America,* trans. Harriet de Onís, p. 57.

[41] Estimate of number of Catholic nationalists is from Saxtone Bradford, *The Battle for Buenos Aires,* p. 140; pages 137–138 contain a complete list of the many Catholic nationalist organizations in 1943.

[42] Josephs, *Argentine Diary,* p. 141.

would lead the coup of October 9, 1945, the last major military threat to Perón's assumption of power.

In his struggle for power within GOU, Perón was aided considerably by the international situation. When on January 26, 1944, President Ramírez bowed to United States' pressure and severed Argentine relations with the axis, it set in motion a series of significant developments within the military power structure. On February 24, 1944, President Ramírez, only shortly before referred to as the spirit, brain, and arm of the revolution, was forced by a group of officers led by Perón to resign the presidency. He was replaced by General Farrell, an officer of little political ambition and a front-man for Perón. With the retirement of President Ramírez, Colonel Enrique González lost his power in the presidential secretariat and Colonel Emilio Ramírez was relieved as chief of police, thus removing two of Perón's rivals in the Big Four. Colonel Ramírez was replaced by Colonel Juan Filomeno Velasco, who would convert the police into a tool of Perón. On February 27, 1944, Colonel Perón, defeating a bid by General Juan C. Sanguinetti for the post, was named minister of war by the GOU. In early July, 1944, Perón defeated a drive for the vice-presidency led by General Luis Perlinger, minister of the interior. On July 6, 1944, Perlinger was removed from the Ministry of the Interior, and two days later, Perón was appointed vice-president.[43]

Perón was now the most powerful man in Argentina, holding three offices simultaneously (Department of Labor, Ministry of War, and the vice-presidency). Although the backing of labor was necessary for his long-range possession of power, Perón's first need was to consolidate his military support in the dangerous game of army politics. To strengthen his hold over the armed forces, he accelerated military expenditures. They soared from 291 million pesos in 1941, to 1,428 million in 1945, representing about 50 per cent of the government's annual expenditures. He also intensified the production of army equipment in Argentine factories and reorganized the army in a way that pleased commanders under him.[44]

---

[43] Carril, *Crónica interna de la revolución libertadora*, pp. 30–32, 35–36; Greenup, *Revolution before Breakfast*, p. 170; Santander, *Nazismo en Argentina*, pp. 29–30.
[44] Greenup, *Revolution before Breakfast*, pp. 169–170.

At the same time, Perón moved to stifle and to weaken his opposition within the military establishment. In March, 1944, a large group of high-ranking officers called for the return of the army to its nonpolitical functions and for the restoration of normalcy. Perón countered with the first large-scale purge, relieving many generals of their posts, delaying the promotion of other officers, and later forcing them into retirement. To gain the support of other officers, he issued on October 5, 1944, General Order No. 18, urging military men to submit their opinions on important problems to him as part of their duty as patriots.[45] Furthermore, Perón tied army commanders to his regime by assigning them police and political functions. These officers were ordered to submit bimonthly reports on civilian political activities in their regions.

To completely consolidate his control over the army, Perón strove to undermine the power of Colonel Eduardo Avalos, his lone remaining rival in the Big Four. The number of troops under the command of Avalos in the Campo de Mayo was decreased, while the number of secret service and police was expanded under Perón's cohort, Colonel Filomeno Velasco. The number of police in Buenos Aires soared to thirty thousand, a force some considered sufficient to check any sudden move from the Campo de Mayo.[46]

The major challenge to Perón's army-labor-police combination came in the famous October Days of 1945. It came from an uneasy coalition of the navy, the Campo de Mayo garrison headed by Colonel Avalos, and an alliance of the democratic parties, student organizations and some labor and professional associations. On October 9, 1945, the Campo de Mayo garrison, applying pressure on the Farrell regime, forced Perón to resign the three posts he held in the government. There followed the appointment of Admiral Héctor Vernengo Lima to the Ministry of the Navy and Colonel Avalos to the Ministry of War. These officers exemplified the basic division that existed in the military forces of the anti-Perón coalition.

---

[45] Roque Lanús, *Al servicio del ejército*, pp. 32–33, 49–50, 55.

[46] Joseph Newman, "Perón Copies Axis Strategy," *New York Herald Tribune*, December 26, 1945, p. 24.

Admiral Vernengo Lima, a liberal nationalist, was the ranking officer of the navy. He had replaced Captain Alberto Teisaire, leader of the naval integral nationalists, in the Ministry of the Navy. Except for the small integral nationalist faction, the liberal nationalist naval officer-corps was hostile to the rise of Perón.[47] Moreover, the navy, long engaged in a bitter service rivalry with the army, had been hostile to the ascendancy of the GOU in the early stages of the revolution. Naval opposition to Perón reached its height during the October Days of 1945 when Admiral Vernengo Lima joined forces with Colonel Avalos in deposing him. The navy sought to turn the government over to the Supreme Court, an institution identified with the Justista era and the liberal nationalism of the oligarchy.

Although most of the allied civilian forces supported this objective, Colonel Avalos and his army integral nationalists disagreed. Their aim was to have the government transferred to Amadeo Sabattini, the Radical leader of Córdoba. Confronted by Perón's popular integral nationalism, the Avalos group supported a return to the Radical nationalism of the Yrigoyen period.[48] Here was a historical echo of the days when the middle-class army officer-corps supported Radical nationalism.

While this divided coalition squabbled over the way to fill the void created by Perón's dismissal, opposition forces were in motion. With Perón arrested and held in custody on the island of Martín García, the CGT, encouraged by Colonel Domingo Mercante and Eva Duarte, called a general strike for October 17, 1945. The police, prepared for the event by the Peronist Colonel Filomeno Velasco, would make no effort to oppose demonstrations by labor.[49] When on October 17 200,000 workers poured into the center of Buenos Aires, shouting "our lives for Perón," the future dictator had accomplished his next objective. Now, "the government needed Perón to tranquilize the peo-

---

[47] Aníbal O. Olivieri, *Dos veces rebelde. Memorias*, p. 15; Blanksten, *Perón's Argentina*, pp. 314–316.

[48] Gabriel del Mazo, *El radicalismo: Notas sobre su historia y doctrina, 1922–1952*, p. 57; Ramos, *América latina*, p. 175.

[49] Luis Gay, Secretary General of CGT, to Robert Alexander, in personal interview, Buenos Aires, November 22, 1946. Used by permission of Professor Alexander.

ple, and Perón needed the government to tranquilize [the divided] army."[50]

After his triumph of October 17, Perón placed his supporters in key government posts, but he refused to take office. Devoting his energies to preparations for elections in February, 1946, he formed a new party, the Partido Laborista, to nominate him for the presidency. The Partido Laborista was pledged to the nationalization of public utilities, to provision of hospitals and homes for the workers, the aged, and the sick, and to the defense of gains made by the lower class during Perón's tenure as secretary of labor. By claiming that his popular integral nationalism was the successor to the Radical nationalism of Yrigoyen, Perón won the support of a dissident group of Radicals. The Church, its position bolstered in the past by the integral nationalists, supported Perón. By warning that his defeat would mean the restoration of the liberal nationalist oligarchy, Perón struck fear into the lower-class sector of the electorate. He also engaged in a bitter duel with the leftist Unión Democrática—the Radicals, the Socialists, and the Communists—who, lacking a constructive program, concentrated on branding Perón as a fascist.

Perón expanded his support by placing his program under an umbrella of traditional Argentine nationalism and fear of intervention by the Colossus of the North. Using the slogan "Braden or Perón," he cleverly converted his government's duel with Spruille Braden, former ambassador to Argentina and now undersecretary of state at Washington, into an issue of national pride. Two weeks before the election, Washington answered by publishing the *Blue Book*, or *Consultation among the American Republics with Respect to the Argentine Situation*. Summarizing the proaxis activities of the integral nationalist regime during the war, the *Blue Book* boomeranged as a diplomatic maneuver. It served only to reenforce Perón's claim that he was defending Argentine independence against the United States.

The elections on February 24, 1946, supervised by the army, were the first honest contest since the election of Yrigoyen in 1916. Both the Partido Laborista and the Unión Democrática had free access to the

50 Plater, *Una gran lección*, p. 61.

radio and to all parts of the nation, and there were more newspapers opposed to Perón than in favor of him. The only advantage enjoyed by Perón was the transmission of some of his speeches on all radio stations.[51] The popular vote was close; it gave Perón about 1.5 million votes to 1.2 million received by José P. Tamborini, the Unión Democrática candidate. In the electoral college, however, Perón polled 304 votes to the 72 for his opponent. Peronists also won two-thirds of the seats in the Chamber of Deputies, and all but two seats in the Senate.[52] Popular integral nationalism had arrived in Argentina.

[51] Mariano Reinaldo Martínez, *Notas imparciales para la historia del peronismo*, p. 9.

[52] George Pendle, *Argentina*, p. 103.

PART III
PERONISM AND THE ARMY,
1946-1955

$\mathbf{B}$efore discussing Peronism and the army, it is necessary to describe the nature of that political phenomenon in terms of both its historical uniqueness and its similarity to other forms of modern dictatorship. The sociologist Irving L. Horowitz has suggested that since Argentina "was and remains a fractured society," it is perhaps best to view Peronism "in parts before attempting general observations." He states:

In economics, Peronism represented a variety of Italian corporate syndicalism; in politics, Bonapartist rule was wedded to a typical Latin American innovation—the strong man regime employing various parties and power factions to keep dissidence and discontent from translating itself into effective action; in intellectual affairs, Peronism veered sharply from the French rationalism and positivism that played such a large part in the educative reforms of the great Domingo Sarmiento, towards the mystique of the nation. Clericalism and anti-scientific trends in philosophic thought became *au courant*. The legend of Martín Fierro, the gaucho Paul Bunyan, and the myth of Evita Perón's saintliness, did much to render inept what was once the finest educational system in the Americas.[1]

As for the social base of Peronism, Horowitz writes:

This was achieved through the first large-scale development of trade union-ism as the primary means of workers' organization, the first concentrated effort at the emancipation of the peasant from virtual serfdom, the eleva-tion of women of all social strata to a position of legal equality, the socialisation of health and welfare, and, finally, the continued strengthen-ing of nationalistic tendencies first etched a hundred years ago in *la era Criolla*. That this was undertaken to establish a basis for Argentina becom-ing the "Colossus of the South"—a strong state of expansionist designs and a self-sustaining economy—does not vitiate the fact that Peronism was a social revolution.[2]

Stressing the fact that Peronism was indeed a social revolution, Gino Germani, Argentina's foremost sociologist, has compared it with classic forms of fascism. He found that the Argentine form differed from the others in that it fostered the social and political integration of the urban and rural working class, while the European fascisms were built funda-mentally on the lower middle class. Rapid industrialization and massive urbanization in Argentina after 1930 tore the masses from their tradi-tional setting, leaving them uprooted, without a place in the established parties, and largely void of union experience. The Argentine middle class, on the other hand, also of recent formation through nineteenth-century immigration, had found a home in the democratic parties, es-pecially the Radical party. Hence, in Argentina widespread middle-class fears of sinking into the proletariat did not exist. In Argentina the problem was to integrate the uprooted masses, to give them a political home by substituting Social Justice for the fascist motto, Order, Disci-pline, Hierarchy. Furthermore, whereas other forms of fascism stressed forced social collaboration under an all-powerful state, Peronism fea-tured mass antagonism toward the oligarchy.[3]

---

[1] Irving L. Horowitz, "Modern Argentina: The Politics of Power," *Political Quarterly* 30 (1959): 401–402.

[2] *Ibid.*, p. 402.

[3] Gino Germani, *Integración política de las masas y totalitarismo*, pp. 10–15.

Peronism did, nevertheless, emulate European fascism in both its supernationalism and its appeal to an ambitious sector of the industrial middle class. In some of its features, it also resembled the popular-nationalist authoritarianism of underdeveloped areas. However, by the time Perón came to power Argentina was moving out of the underdeveloped category and had become a transitional society.[4]

By using the term popular integral nationalism this interpretation seeks to stress the fact that Peronism was deeply rooted in the history of Argentina. Peronism is viewed as the adaptation of the integral nationalism of the army to mid–twentieth-century conditions in that country. Upon assuming office in 1946, Perón resumed military rank, and it was as a professional soldier that he ruled Argentina during the next nine years. This is not to say that Perón was not a thoroughgoing opportunist; indeed, his personality was like a "tube" through which all Argentine history passed and was channeled for selfish, demagogic purposes. However, he also brought to demagoguery the habits of the army officer, and, at the outset, his regime was geared to the fulfillment of three integral nationalist aspirations.

First, popular integral nationalism provided the substantial civilian support that was a prerequisite for enduring military rule. It must be recognized that Argentina, though deeply divided, was no inchoate, emerging nation. In 1946, it was a country of ample political sophistication—with a democratic tradition, with organized political parties, with many power factors, with professional organizations and a labor movement. In such a society, the army could not rule alone for long periods of time; the continuance of military rule depended on substantial organized civilian support. The laboring masses and a sector of the middle class provided this and enabled Perón to cloak his dictatorship in the traditional democratic-republican forms of the nation.

Second, popular integral nationalism, featuring an alliance of the army and captive labor, enabled the officer to have nationalistic modernization while promising him social peace through a proletariat tied to the authoritarian state. Hence, the second function of Peronism was to bridge the traditional-modern dichotomy of values in the army. To

[4] Arthur P. Whitaker, *Argentina*, p. 105.

many army officers it seemed as if a formula had been found at last for both social order and modernization.

Third, though wary of advances by the *descamisados*, many integral nationalist army officers proved willing to gamble on Perón, for he promised to deliver their long-cherished hope—a strong army, as the major index of national prestige, in a powerful, united, industrialized state. For this they were willing, albeit reluctantly, to trade their monopoly of the state for an alliance with labor. In any case, the massive labor demonstrations of October, 1945, having raised the threat of social revolution, convinced army officers that the demands of order dictated a partnership with labor under Perón.

At first sight the army-labor alliance seems like a historical anomaly, and, to a large extent, it was. Historically, the two forces were antagonistic. On the other hand, both were motivated by similar sociopsychological drives. Nationalism, militant and determined, served as a common denominator for both. Both the army officer and the *descamisado* sought identification in a strongly nationalist state. For the army officer, often of immigrant parentage, identification with the nationalist state was further proof of the purity of his patriotism. For the worker, recently removed from the taint of alien parental doctrines of anarchism and socialism, or drawn from the backlands to the city where he was mocked as a *cabecita negra* ("little blackhead"), identification with a nativist nationalist labor movement promised new dignity. Therefore, while the army-labor alliance was uneasy, it was also welded by strong nationalist drives on the part of both forces.

Although the army-labor alliance under Perón was uneasy, it should not be concluded that all army officers were hostile toward the masses. In fact, Perón's prolabor measures should not be viewed as the work of a military apostate. Many army officers, like Perón, had served in the provinces and were aware of the poverty of the lower class. Many had written reports and articles on the deprivation of the peon masses of the interior. Some officers developed a paternalistic attitude toward the poor, which led them to support Perón's efforts to improve the condition of the lower classes.[5]

[5] Robert A. Potash, *The Army and Politics in Argentina, 1928–1945*, p. 286.

The relationship of the army to the Peronist dictatorship may be divided into two major periods. During the first period of his dictatorship, 1946 to 1951, Perón manipulated, divided, balanced, and catered to the demands of the army. The army, the most important power factor in the Peronist structure, was to have its demands satisfied—but, at the same time, its influence was to be continually undermined. Despite his complex political maneuverings, Perón respected the traditional status of the army during this period. The second period of Perón's dictatorship, 1952 to 1955, unfolded against the backdrop of the economic decline that ended the dream of the speedy conversion of Argentina into a powerful, united, industrial state. In the face of rising military opposition, Perón sought to convert the army from a traditional institution of state into a more creative and integral part of the dictatorial apparatus. In this period he set out to *remold* the army, to alter its traditional allegiances to institution and historic Fatherland. His effort to bend the army's loyalties towards the Peronist state was part of his general totalitarian campaign during this period. The effort to make the army "his" army was carried out both by indoctrination and by an intensification of traditional methods of bribery.

5. The Army in the Peronist Structure, 1946-1951

Perón was never the complete master of the Argentine army. From the very outset of his regime, the officer corps of the army was divided into three groups: those who had supported his candidacy; those who had opposed him to the point of seeking his resignation and retirement from the army; and those, probably the majority, who had remained neutral in the struggle.[1] Soon after taking up the reins of government, Perón moved against his avowed enemies, and fifty army officers, among them four generals, were purged, along with many naval chiefs and aviators.[2]

Against lingering opposition within the military, Perón was quick to raise the threat of social revolution by the *descamisados*. He continually warned that in the event of his overthrow, Argentina would be the

[1] Arturo J. Zabala, *La revolución del 16 de septiembre*, p. 23.
[2] Congreso Nacional, *Diario de sesiones de la Cámara de Diputados, año 1950*, IV, 3528.

scene of a blood bath similar to the Spanish Civil War. Balancing labor against the army was a major device by which he hoped to retain power and to still the guns of the military. In the first hours of his rule, he made a significant statement to his close associates. "In order to sustain myself in power," he said, "I need 'insurance' of one million workers to obey me blindly and with whom I will be able to defend myself from whatever action by the military; and 'reassurance' of one hundred thousand bayonets to impede excessive advances by the popular masses."[3]

To Perón the carrot was always as important as the stick. And so he sought by word and deed to win the military to his regime. To the military men, he depicted his "New Argentina" as an "organized community" in which the armed forces serve as the "vertebral column," sustaining the whole organism, "forming part of the national unity, not as an inert part, but like a live organ integrated with all and integrated by the rest."[4]

As an active agent in the formation of the "New Argentina," one function of the military was to furnish leadership. Perón's cabinets consistently included officers of the armed forces in civilian posts. Army officers were installed as the provincial governors of Buenos Aires, Córdoba, Corrientes, Tucumán, Entre Ríos, and Mendoza. Important posts in the government, in the Railroad Administration and the National Energy Administration, for example, went to Peronist army officers. The chief of the federal police came consistently from the army officer-corps.[5]

The armed forces also played an important role in Perón's economic programs for Argentina. Integral nationalist officers of the army backed his efforts to convert the nation into a powerful, united, self-sufficient war machine, free of foreign control and the influence of the colonial oligarchy. As ardent supporters of heavy industry in Argentina, the

[3] Arnaldo Orfila Reynal, "Breve historia y examen del peronismo," *Cuadernos Americanos* 84 (November–December, 1955): 15.

[4] Speech by Perón at the dinner of comradery of the armed forces, July 5, 1950, quoted in *La Prensa,* July 6, 1950, pp. 5–6.

[5] Robert Alexander, *The Perón Era,* pp. 114–115. See also, George I. Blanksten, *Perón's Argentina,* p. 310.

army welcomed its role in the supervision of much of the first Five-Year Plan. Control of the production of war materials and the vast area of related activities was vested in the Dirección General de Fabricaciones Militares under General Manuel N. Savio. This agency of the army was also given the power to explore and exploit the mines which delivered the raw materials for munitions and other heavy industries.[6] To assure the success of a large-scale plan to modernize the material, buildings, and plants of the army, the Five-Year Plan placed a vast permanent fund at the disposal of the Ministry of War.[7] The army, in the words of reporter Ray Josephs, was "given authority to spend and act without public accounting in a manner never before legally permitted in the New World."[8]

To supplement lags in the domestic production of arms, heavy purchases of foreign equipment were made through IAPI (Argentine Institute for the Promotion of Trade). Immense quantities of war equipment, especially planes, jeeps, and tanks, were imported and purchases of United States war surplus alone soared to $500 million. During the first eighteen months of the regime, ship after ship brought war surplus equipment to Argentine shores. Planes from the United States, England, Canada, and other countries were imported in particularly large quantities, for air power was now considered the key to national power.[9]

Along with power, new weaponry, and lavish quarters, Perón made the Argentine armed forces the highest paid in the world. In 1948, he signed a bill granting a 30 per cent increase in base pay to officers of the army, navy, and air force. Except for the rank of second lieutenant, the Argentine military man received more money than his opposite number in the United States armed forces. Based on the rate of exchange of 480 pesos for 100 United States dollars, comparative pay for the two armies was as follows:

[6] Manuel N. Savio, *Ley de Fabricaciones Militares: Conceptos que fundamentaron su proyecto,* pp. 8–9.

[7] Presidencia de la Nación, Secretaria Técnica, *Plan de Gobierno, 1947–1951,* I, 241.

[8] Ray Josephs, *Latin America: Continent in Crisis,* p. 350.

[9] *Ibid.,* p. 352; Alejandro Magnet, *Nuestros vecinos justicialistas,* pp. 104–105.

	Argentine	United States
Lieutenant General	$11,250	$8,800
Major General	10,000	8,800
Brigadier General	8,750	6,600
Colonel	7,000	4,000
Lieutenant Colonel	5,000	3,850
Major	4,250	3,300
Captain	3,250	2,760
First Lieutenant	2,500	2,400
Second Lieutenant	2,125	2,160

The rates of pay were the same for comparable grades in the respective navies.[10]

However, while satisfying the material demands of the army, Perón strove to undercut its power. Like other power factors, it was to be checked and divided as well as bought. To avoid having the branches unite against him, Perón encouraged service rivalries. "So long as their surplus energies are used up in fighting one another, they won't have the strength to bother me much," he is reported to have said.[11] In the years from 1945 to 1949, the size of the army was reduced by one-third, to 70,000 men.[12] Meanwhile Perón slowly and quietly built up the strength of the police forces under the civilian Ministry of the Interior. Bribe-divide-balance was deemed the key to the maintenance of power.

Under the Perón regime, the gradual undermining of hierarchical discipline in the army, begun prior to the revolution of 1930, was continued and intensified. Whereas Uriburu had catered to the generals, and Castillo to the colonels, Perón courted the junior officers. Sudden promotion to the higher ranks was held out as the reward for the loyalty of junior officers. New cars and homes kept them satisfied in lulls between frequent purges.[13]

This downward politicalization of the army reached to the cadets of

[10] Mac R. Johnson, "Argentina gives 30% Base Raise to Officers" in *New York Herald Tribune*, July 3, 1948, p. 3.
[11] Edwin Lieuwen, *Arms and Politics in Latin America*, pp. 69–71.
[12] *Ibid.*
[13] Mary Main [María Flores], *The Woman with the Whip: Eva Perón*, pp. 156–157.

the Colegio Militar. A new policy of appointments to the military academy seriously curtailed the professional army's influence. Whereas previously, appointments to the Colegio Militar were made by a committee drawn from the army officer-corps, under the Perón system, appointments were to be made by congressional committees from the Peronist-controlled legislative branch. Moreover, the costs of military education were to be borne by the government. By March, 1949, shortly after these changes were made, the Colegio Militar, saturated by Peronist political philosophy, was inculcating loyalty to the party and government over loyalty to the army as an institution.[14] Here was a sign of things to come.

The final level at which Perón cultivated the personal allegiance of military men was that of the noncommissioned officers and he was highly successful in exploiting the question of military castes. First, he made a special effort to appeal to the sergeants' keen sense of dignity. They were provided with new uniforms that closely resembled the uniforms of commissioned officers. Furthermore, as early as 1946 Perón declared that he supported giving the vote to the noncommissioned officers.[15] When on September 20, 1948, a general order was issued granting them the franchise, General Humberto Sosa Molina, minister of war, was so worried that he addressed the noncoms, warning them that the right to vote meant only that; it did not imply the right to free expression of political opinions—that could lead to the dissolution of the armed forces and even civil war.[16]

The noncoms did eventually play a significant political role, supporting Perón and serving as his chief spies within the armed forces.[17] In 1954, Perón, in a move of profound importance, rewarded the noncoms by granting them access to commissions in the army officer-corps.[18] This move, further evidence of the thoroughgoing politicali-

[14] *Hispanic World Report* (later changed to *Hispanic American Report*) 2, no. 1 (April, 1949): 19.

[15] "Mensaje presidencial" in Congreso Nacional, *Diario de . . . Cámara de Diputados, año 1946*, I, 123–124.

[16] Virginia Lee Warren, "Argentine Warns Minor Army Aides," *New York Times*, September 22, 1948, p. 7.

[17] Reynaldo Pastor, *Frente al totalitarismo peronista*, p. 161.

[18] Congreso Nacional, *Diario de . . . Cámara de Diputados, año 1954*, I, 178–179.

zation of the army, won for the dictator the enduring allegiance of many noncoms.

Although constantly checked and undermined, the army continued to exert strong influence within the Peronist structure. The Perón dictatorship drew its strength from five principal sources. Most important were the twin pillars of real and potential force: the army, which had brought Perón to power, and the captive labor unions of CGT, which had legalized his regime by its massive vote. Two other sources of power were the political forces that, along with the army officer-corps, formed the elite of the regime—the Catholic church and the Catholic nationalists. The fifth source of Peronist strength was the new and powerful group of industrial magnates who had risen to power as members of the Perón government or as friends of the ruling clique.[19] They represented the industrial sector of the Argentine middle class that, since 1930, had proved willing to sacrifice democracy for industrialization.

While these five groups within the Peronist structure all helped maintain his dictatorship, they also threatened it through continuous conflicts with each other. Meanwhile, outside the Peronist structure, the traditional political parties were in constant conspiracy with the liberal nationalist navy and with prodemocratic officers, discontented military men purged by Perón, and military opportunists seeking to replace him.

In a sense, Peronism, having brought together traditional and modern forces, each with competitive stakes in the regime, represented political opportunism enthroned. The dictator did, however, attempt to develop a doctrine to cover his dynamic and conflicting power structure. Perón called this synthetic doctrine Justicialism, a third position between communism and capitalism. Significantly, the major characteristic of Justicialism was fluidity in balancing the four forces that motivated men and society—materialism and idealism, individualism and collectivism. To balance these conflicting, though essential forces, the state must move to the center or to the right or left according to specific circumstances.[20]

Justicialism was, in reality, an ideological coating for Peronist prag-

[19] A. W. Bunkley, "Peronist Crisis," *Yale Review* 39 (Spring, 1950): 404–405.
[20] The best analysis of Justicialism is in Blanksten, *Perón's Argentina*, chap. 12.

matism. The fact is that Perón was never able to evolve an ideology capable of overriding the specific stakes that each supporting source of power had in his regime. Of the army's stake, much has already been said. Under Perón, the state also sustained the Catholic religion in many ways. He supported mandatory Catholic teaching in the public schools, declaring their prime function to be that of implanting "God in the consciences [of students], exalting the spiritual over the material."[21] Prelates were given subventions. Scholarships were provided for seminaries. Contributions were made to churches and religious colleges. Economic aid was given to other needy religious institutions. Religious congresses and publications were subsidized. Catholic movements against pornography were supported by the state.[22]

Perón's support of the Catholic church also pleased the Catholic nationalists. "This small but violent minority had supported Nazism and Fascism, hated the United States, and saw in Peronism a chance to put into operation its nationalist-expansionist-totalitarian ideology."[23] They were gratified by Perón's campaigns against the liberal nationalist oligarchy, and they also supported Perón's friendliness towards Franco Spain and his resistance after 1946 to conciliatory overtures from the United States. As an extension of the third position in domestic policy, Perón posed as the world leader of a middle way between the East and West in foreign affairs.

The workers of CGT, as important as the army in supporting the Perón regime, sought higher wages, bonuses, a shorter work-week, and a sense of identity in the nationalist state. Their commitment to popular integral nationalism was joined to worship of Perón's wife, Eva, who, after her husband's inauguration, became the power in the Secretariat of Labor, CGT, and the women's branch of the Peronista party. From these positions, Eva Perón successfully supported the demands of the *descamisados*, and they continued to benefit from the regime despite the onset of inflation after 1949. Eva also supervised a newly created

[21] "Mensaje presidencial" in Congreso Nacional, *Diario de sesiones de la Cámara de Senadores, año 1949*, I, 34.

[22] Hernán Benítez, "La iglesia y el justicialismo," *Revista de la Universidad de Buenos Aires*, no. 24 (1952): 357–358.

[23] Bunkley, "Peronist Crisis," pp. 404–405.

Ministry of Health, charged with the construction of hospitals and carrying out campaigns against disease. Along with these official duties, Evita ("little Eva") endeared herself to the masses through the Social Aid Foundation, a vast philanthropic organization financed by trade union and other contributions. Through the foundation, clothes, food, medicine, and money were distributed to the poor. Hence, in almost patristic-matristic fashion, the Peróns personified the twin pillars of power. With fiery harangues, Eva specialized in demagoguery for the masses, enabling Juan to concentrate on the army "and, in doing so, to maintain his status as officer and gentleman."[24]

Eva Perón was linked by personal and business ties to Miguel Miranda, who personified the fifth force supporting the regime. Representing the new economic oligarchy that supervised the industrialization program, Miranda was Eva's tutor in finance and her partner in a company that monopolized the importation of drugs.[25] Both were also leading objects of military disdain during the early years of the Perón regime. For the traditionalist army officers, Miranda and Eva personified the most hated results of modernization. They viewed Miranda as the selfish, grasping modern industrialist and Eva as the lady demagogue who roused the masses to political action.

As head of the Argentine Institute for the Promotion of Trade (IAPI), created by decree in May, 1946, Miranda exercised vast powers over the economy. His was the disastrous yet lucrative task of financing a program to retain the support of the army, of the *descamisados*, and of the industrial oligarchy. This program, called the Miranda Plan, provided for heavy government spending in the investment side of the economy in order to purchase war material, build an arms program, and support vast industrialization projects. It also involved pumping money into the consumer section of the economy through higher wages, bonuses, and pay for an expanded bureaucracy. Hence, both investment capital and consumer capital were to be increased simultaneously. But at whose expense? The answer: that of the liberal nationalist landed oligarchy. IAPI was given a monopoly over export-import trade, along

---

[24] Arthur P. Whitaker, *Argentina*, pp. 113–114.
[25] Main, *Woman with the Whip*, p. 144.

with the power to buy up all of Argentina's agricultural produce and to sell it whenever the highest price was offered. Designed to benefit from a hungry postwar Europe, this program was in the long run to undermine the rich agricultural and pastoral exchange-earning capacity of Argentina.

Until 1949, the program brought into the government the money necessary for arms, industrialization, and the purchase of foreign-owned utilities and railroads. The Perón regime undertook industrialization through the first Five-Year Plan (1947–1951), which concentrated on the expansion and development of oil, gas and hydroelectric resources, and on the importation of capital equipment. Another important accomplishment of the regime was the repatriation of foreign investment as typified by the purchase during 1947 and 1948 of the deteriorating British-owned railroads. For all varieties of nationalists, including those of the military, Argentina seemed on the road to becoming Economically Free, Socially Just, and Politically Sovereign, as the Peronist motto read.

But by 1949 Argentina's economic situation had begun to deteriorate. Miranda had forecasted vast sales of agricultural commodities to the European Recovery Program at high prices, or at best, that a World War III would mean the purchase of such goods at any price. But neither situation materialized. Furthermore, agricultural production, discouraged by the policies of IAPI, began to stagnate. This was followed in the early 1950s by a combination of declining agricultural prices and severe droughts in Argentina. With agricultural production declining, the peso sank in value and by 1949 the Argentine gold reserve had declined to one-third its prewar level. The gross national product declined from 62.3 billion pesos in 1948 to 49.3 in 1952.[26] Inflation began to haunt the nation.

Economic decline spelled disaster for Perón's efforts to quickly transform the nation into a powerful, united, industrial state. This followed on the heels of the failure of Perón's expansionist designs in Latin America. In inter-American politics, Perón had attempted to fulfill in-

26 Whitaker, *Argentina*, pp. 136–137.

tegral nationalist aspirations for expansion. During the initial years of his regime, his efforts to extend Argentine influence in Latin America were made through his contacts in the armies of other nations. Relations had been established between the GOU and similar lodges in the Bolivian, Chilean, Paraguayan, and probably the Peruvian and Venezuelan, armies. Many of the officers of these lodges had formerly belonged to the secret continental lodge known as the Condors, which linked German-trained military men from throughout Latin America.[27] Totalitarian-minded and believing the army to be the only reliable institution in Latin American politics, these officers had all been admirers of Nazi Germany. With the encouragement of Argentina, these secret military lodges had executed revolutions in Bolivia in December, 1943, in Peru in October, 1948, and in Venezuela one month later. Similar conspiratorial elements were thwarted in their efforts to establish an army regime in Chile.[28] On December 16, 1948, Chilean President Gabriel González Videla, commenting on Peronist penetration of his nation's army, declared "that there is a continental conspiracy in existence."[29]

Although Argentine influence played a role in encouraging the revolts, Perón was less successful in maintaining his influence over foreign military men once they were in office. The Villarroel regime in Bolivia, until it was overthrown in July, 1946, maintained closer ties with the United States than with Argentina. The military dictatorship in Venezuela also became more preoccupied with consolidating its friendship with the United States than with serving as a subordinate to Perón. In Lima, the Odría dictatorship, although at first advised by Peronist representatives, turned against the Argentine dictator in the early 1950s.[30] Never able to compete with the United States on the level of financial strength, Perón's efforts to make Argentina an expansionist power must have been seriously weakened by the deterioration

---

[27] Raúl Damonte Taborda, *Ayer fue San Perón*, p. 12.
[28] Robert J. Alexander, "Peronism and Argentina's Quest for Leadership in Latin America," *Journal of International Affairs* 9 (1955): 48.
[29] Damonte Taborda, *Ayer fue San Perón*, pp. 25–26.
[30] Alexander, "Peronism and Argentina's Quest," p. 49.

of the economy. As a result, the first stage in the attempt to create a
Greater Argentina proved a keen disappointment to integral nationalists of the army.

In the wake of economic decline and international failure, the first
serious reverberations within the Peronist structure occurred. These
were sparked by a series of illegal wildcat strikes in February, 1949.
With the economy weakening and threatened by strikes, the army began
to express long-standing grievances. Eva Perón was an object of military hatred down to her death in July, 1952. She offended the traditionalism of the army in many ways. She was despised as a woman and ex-
showgirl in politics. For the army, bred in traditional respect for the
patrilineal family, the woman's place was in the home. Yet Perón, an
army officer, had basically altered the role of women in Argentine society. He had organized the women's branch of the Peronist party, and
placed Eva at its head. In 1947, women were given the vote for the
first time in Argentine history. Aside from disapproving of the rise of
feminine influence in general, the military hated Eva as the personification of the power of CGT and, above all, as one who promoted class
strife over social order.

The integral nationalists of the army also hated Miranda and the industrial oligarchy. The military disdained them for their corruption and
for their challenge to the army's influence in the industrialization program. Whereas Miranda and his cohorts favored light industry to fit
the resources of Argentina, the army supported the development of
heavy industry as the base for its war machine.[31]

Under the leadership of Minister of War Sosa Molina, the army used
the crisis of 1949 to present three major demands to Perón. First, Miguel Miranda and the industrial oligarchy, having led the nation to economic crisis and having looted the sick economy, must be purged. Second, Eva Perón must go; she must move quietly out of politics and the
leadership of CGT. Third, Perón must choose, once and for all time,
between the army and labor forces in his regime.

Pressured from both the left and right forces within the structure of
his regime, Perón made his choice by the end of February, 1949. He

[31] Enrique Rivera, *Peronismo y frondizismo*, p. 225.

turned to the right. Miranda had been forced to resign in January, 1949, and in compliance with army demands, his staff was also purged. Perón also brought his old GOU rivals, Colonels Emilio Ramírez and Enrique González, back into the government as military watchdogs.[32]

Perón would not, however, capitulate on the issue of Eva's role in politics. Nor would he make concessions to the army and then permit its leader, General Sosa Molina, to retain power. When, in late 1949, Eva was refused entrance into the Campo de Mayo, Perón used the incident for a showdown with Sosa Molina. By forcing Sosa Molina to have the responsible officer courtmartialed and demoted, Perón undercut the army officers' confidence in their minister of war. Sosa Molina was then quietly "promoted" to minister of defense, a new and politically innocuous post in which he would have little direct contact with the armed forces.[33]

The second major army challenge to Perón's power came in 1951. By this time economic recession and inflation were firmly rooted in Argentina and military men had many reasons for their discontent. By 1950, the construction of military factories, barracks, and other installations had come to a virtual halt. Perón's cabinet had been progressively converted into a civilian body, and civilians were beginning to take over important posts in the government also.[34] Once again it was Eva, and all she personified, that ignited military resistance to Perón. In August, 1951, a vast, labor-sponsored rally was held to support Eva's candidacy for the vice-presidency. Appalled at the prospect of a woman as commander in chief in the event of Perón's death, the army applied intense pressures for the withdrawal of her candidacy. That Eva was forced to withdraw was only one sign of the deep discontent that now seethed within the army.

In 1951, the army officer-corps was once again divided roughly into three groups. About 40 per cent of the corps was staunchly Peronist, bound to the regime by personal and professional gains. About 20 per cent of the corps was skeptical of the regime if not opposed to it, and this group was growing. The failure of Perón to deliver a powerful,

[32] Bunkley, "Peronist Crisis," pp. 409–411.
[33] *Ibid.*, pp. 410–411; Main, *Woman with the Whip*, pp. 157–158.
[34] Lieuwen, *Arms and Politics in Latin America*, p. 69.

united industrial state had obviously taken its toll. The remaining 40 per cent was passive, cautious, and neutral, seeking to avoid a civil war at all costs. The air force was deemed to be weakening also in its loyalty to the Perón regime, and the liberal nationalist navy had never really been in the camp at all.[35]

There were at least three conspiracies in the making within the armed forces in 1951.[36] The most powerful of them was led by General Eduardo Lonardi, who was closely linked to the Catholic nationalists. Lonardi was supported by many army officers and virtually all of the navy and air force.[37] Convinced that inflation had undermined Perón's labor pillar of power, these conspirators were ready to strike as soon as possible.[38]

But on September 28, 1951, a premature revolt was led by General Benjamín Menéndez, long-time integral nationalist leader. With some air support from the bases of Palomar, Morón, and Punta del Indio, Menéndez sought to initiate a sudden march on Buenos Aires from the Campo de Mayo. Thwarted by Peronist noncoms in his effort to move on Buenos Aires with thirty Sherman tanks, Menéndez started off with only two tanks, three armored cars, and two squadrons of cavalry. Manifestoes were scattered on Buenos Aires by twenty planes in a force led by Captain Vicente M. Baroja from the naval air base at Punta del Indio. But Peronist artillery stopped Menéndez's column at El Palomar and thus quickly squelched the abortive upheaval.[39]

Recognizing that the Menéndez revolt was a sign of large-scale disaffection in the armed forces, Perón moved quickly to meet this serious threat to his regime. He assumed complete control of the armed forces for 180 days, declaring the nation to be in a "state of internal war," and a special tribunal, the Superior Council of the Armed Forces,

---

[35] Russell H. Fitzgibbon, "Argentina after Eva Perón," *Yale Review* 43 (Autumn, 1952): 35–36.

[36] William Horsey of United Press International to Marvin Goldwert in personal interview, Buenos Aires, February 17, 1961.

[37] Mario Amadeo, *La encrujicada argentina*, pp. 30–31.

[38] George Pendle, "Perón and Vargas," *Fortnightly Review* 176 (November, 1951): 723–725.

[39] *Hispanic American Report* 4, no. 10 (September, 1951): 28–29.

was appointed to make the necessary large-scale purges.[40] Thirty admirals were forced into retirement, along with Minister of the Navy Teodoro E. Hartung.[41] The special tribunal later purged nine generals, including General Angel Solari, commander in chief of the army, and General Felipe Urdapilleta, commander of the first army division in and around Buenos Aires. From two to three hundred army officers, including General Menéndez, were imprisoned, and not a few were tortured.[42] Although none of the conspirators was executed, Perón, in a move unprecedented in Argentine politico-military history, denied pensions to the families of those imprisoned. No wonder that the faction of 1951 became the rabid anti-Peronists after the dictator was overthrown in 1955.

The disaffection of 1951 also reenforced Perón's determination to build up military power where he could control it. Soon after the Menéndez revolt, he removed the Argentine coast guard from navy supervision and placed it under the Ministry of the Interior.[43] The national gendarmerie, its numbers and weaponry increased, was taken from the army and also placed under the Ministry of the Interior.[44] By the end of 1952, the police forces at the disposal of the government had increased to about 150,000 men, more than double that of the army (70,000). The police forces included the gendarmerie, the coast guard, the Buenos Aires and provincial police, the federal police and its dependencies, the federal coordination, the special section, the control of state, and the security guard.[45] It appeared that the police forces were being enlarged to serve as a counterweight to the army in case of civil strife.

But Perón had still another threat in store for his rebellious military colleagues—the nightmare of an unleashed, armed, *descamisado* horde. As early as July, 1951, at a banquet of comradery of the armed forces, Perón had made military men anxious by declaring that since the func-

[40] Congreso Nacional, *Diario de . . . Cámara de Diputados, año 1951*, III, 2201.
[41] Aníbal O. Olivieri, *Dos veces rebelde: Memorias*, pp. 39–40.
[42] Magnet, *Nuestros vecinos justicialistas*, p. 101.
[43] Text of decree in *La Nación*, February 14, 1952, p. 1.
[44] Magnet, *Nuestros vecinos justicialistas*, p. 101.
[45] Damonte Taborda, *Ayer fue San Perón*, p. 42.

tion of the armed forces was external defense, it was "insidious" to suggest that the "creation of an organically popular force" at home would lead to conflict between workers and soldiers.[46]

Despite deep-seated disaffection in the armed forces, successful military revolt depended largely on a basic change in public opinion. Peronist purges had taken their toll of rebellious activists by imprisoning them or forcing them into retirement. Only a fundamental change in public opinion could sap the will of loyalists to resist and stir the doubtful into rebellious action. And the elections of 1951 proved that Perón's popularity endured. Less free and fair than the electoral contests of 1946, the campaign of 1951 involved persistent harassment of Perón's Radical opponents. Nevertheless, Perón's victory was impressive and proved that his attraction to the masses remained. He polled 4.6 million votes in comparison to 2.3 million for the Radicals. The Peronist party won all of the seats in the Senate and reduced the number held by the Radical minority in the Chamber of Deputies from forty-five to fourteen.[47]

[46] Text of speech in *La Nación*, July 7, 1951, p. 4.
[47] George Pendle, *Argentina*, p. 119.

6. The Move toward Totalitarianism: The Army and the Decline of Peronism, 1952-1955

The Perón regime was a materialistic dictatorship. Although it featured a sometimes fanatical worship of the nationalist state, its continuance depended on the ability of the dictator to meet the competitive demands of its two main sources of power—the army and labor. Beginning in 1952, the economic situation made this increasingly impossible. Between 1948 and 1952, the gross national product dropped from 62.3 billion pesos to 49.3 billion pesos. This meant there was a marked decline in per capita income, for in the same period the population increased from about 15.4 to 18 million. Even the favored industrial sector declined at the same time that the value of agricultural products was decreasing. Droughts from 1949 to 1951 cut the production of grain, and, along with plummeting exports, Argentina witnessed a reversal in the terms of trade after 1947. Prices paid for imported capital goods rose while prices received for Argentina's agricultural produce declined. Except for a brief revival in 1950 and 1951 during the Korean War, economic recession and inflation took hold in the land.[1]

The economic crisis hastened basic changes in the Perón regime— changes that alienated the various power groups that constituted his support. From 1952 to 1955, since Perón was unable to buy the support of his sources of strength, he attempted to dominate them by turning leftward towards political authoritarianism. While continuing his threats to form labor militias, he launched, in 1953, a vast program in the armed forces of Justicialist indoctrination. In other words, he tried to change the traditional status of the armed forces, making them "his" military establishment. A series of attacks against the Catholic church, begun in November, 1954, and intensified down to mid-June, 1955, alienated members of the clergy and the Catholic nationalists. To the dismayed civilian and military integral nationalists, Perón's assault on the church was striking proof that he was out to wreck traditionalism through a drive for totalitarian control.

In domestic economics and foreign policy, Perón remained the supreme pragmatist. During the years from 1952 to 1955, he moved to the right in these spheres. To bolster Argentina's faltering economy, he began to favor employer over worker and profit-making over social justice. This policy, which also included the encouragement of foreign investment in Argentina, undoubtedly alienated Peronist labor on the left, and hastened the polarization of the regime. In 1953, he abandoned his expansionist, anti-Yankee policy for rapprochement with the United States, a trend that was climaxed two years later by a contract with Standard Oil for the development of Patagonian petroleum reserves. This whole series of moves alienated archnationalists in the right and the left ranks of Peronism, hastened the polarization of the army-labor alliance, and encouraged conspiracy within the armed forces.

One such conspiratorial network was uncovered in the armed forces in 1952, almost as Perón began his second term. True to army tradition, the conspiracy was the work of a secret military lodge, the Logia Sol de Mayo. The chief of the lodge was Colonel Francisco Suárez, a

[1] Arthur P. Whitaker, *Argentina*, pp. 136–137.

retired army chief of staff. The lodge included more than one hundred military conspirators, mostly retired, that is, purged, from the armed forces. Its membership ranged from ex-integral nationalist members of the GOU, like General Elbio Anaya, to former Radical officers, such as General Toranzo Montero.[2] The plot was uncovered when a civilian conspirator was arrested and tortured. He divulged both the names of military men involved and the details of the conspiracy. The coup, planned for execution on February 2, 1952, involved not an armed rebellion by army units, but an attempt to assassinate the President and Señora Perón. Among the one hundred conspirators arrested in a lightninglike roundup on the day of the assassination attempt were a number of army officers and some members of the Radical party. Later arrests led to the imprisonment of twelve naval officers along with a few members of the air force.[3] Those imprisoned were tortured by Peronist interrogators.

Perón now, more than ever, distrusted the professional army. On April 18, 1952, he issued a general order that stated that all important army posts in the area of Buenos Aires were to be filled only by officers of "proven adhesion to the Justicialist Government."[4] Wary of sudden thrusts from nearby garrisons or another assassination attempt, Perón built up a cordon of security around Buenos Aires. Another general order, of the same date, revealed his fear of assassination. It declared that in case of an attempt on the president's life, the government would answer with thousands of avengers from the CGT and the Peronist party, who would wipe out domestic and foreign agents connected with such plots.

The Peróns also moved to strengthen the labor sector and to revive the army's haunting fear of bloody civil war. In 1952, Eva, smarting from the Menéndez and Suárez conspiracies, purchased arms for the workers of CGT through the Social Aid Foundation. The Argentine firm of Ballester Molina delivered five thousand pistols and two thou-

---

[2] Rogelio García Lupo, *La rebelión de los generales*, p. 61.

[3] E. F. Sánchez Zinny, *El culto de la infamia: Historia documentada de la segunda tiranía argentina*, p. 465; *New York Times*, February 6, 1952, pp. 1, 11.

[4] Reynaldo Pastor, *Frente al totalitarismo peronista*, p. 159; *Libro negro de la segunda tiranía*, p. 247.

sand carbines, by order of Eva, to militant CGT members.[5] The arming of the *descamisados* was made public by the sensational revelations of the Radical publication, *El Ciudadano*. It described Perón's decision and gave details of the plans to form labor militias from the ranks of CGT. Five thousand *descamisados* of "absolute confidence" had already been enrolled, and they were divided into "shock troop detachments," "special mission" units, and "reserves." Their function was not to engage the "enemy" in hand-to-hand combat, but to serve as a mobile striking force against weak rebel points.[6] This seemed like a direct challenge to potential rebels in the military, and perhaps an omen of things to come.

But after the death of Eva on July 26, 1952, the situation was soon changed. Then the newly strengthened CGT, headed by José Espejo, made a bid for more power. Soon after Eva's burial, Espejo declared himself to be the "custodian" of her remains, "today, tomorrow, and forever."[7] This, of course, carried the planned implication that anyone, including Perón himself, seeking to curb CGT was attacking the guardians of Eva's tradition. Perón made short shrift of this bid by labor for independence and dominance within his regime. In response to army pressure, he himself assumed leadership of the Social Aid Foundation, and ousted José Espejo, leader of the CGT "army" of six million workers, selecting a Peronist puppet to succeed him. This action placed CGT directly under Perón again. Although Perón continued to arm the workers periodically with machine and antitank guns, the idea of labor militias was temporarily dropped and the general strike remained the CGT's chief weapon. Perón was not about to become dependent upon an army of labor, for balance was still his key to power.[8]

Beginning in 1952, there was also a new emphasis upon making the army a more creative contributor to a regime reeling under economic setbacks. Economic necessity forced the regime to sponsor a program of *autobastecimiento* ("economic self-sufficiency") for the expensive army. On May 21, 1952, Perón declared his willingness to expand the

---

[5] Alejandro Magnet, *Nuestros vecinos argentinos*, p. 222.

[6] *El Ciudadano* quoted in "Perón's Private Army," *Time*, March 24, 1952, p. 41.

[7] Milton Bracker, " 'Alone'—New Chapter in the Perón Drama," *New York Times Magazine*, August 24, 1952, pp. 10, 28, 30.

[8] Arthur P. Whitaker, *The United States and Argentina*, pp. 170–171.

army's economic role by granting to the Ministry of War full power and resources to achieve self-sufficiency for the institution.[9] Military centers of production soon found themselves equipped to provide essential material for officers, noncoms, and civilian personnel of army posts throughout the nation.[10] This held out the promise that the army, turned into a virtual business enterprise, would be able to maintain its standard of living on a permanent basis, regardless of changes in civilian administrations.

For *autobastecimiento* the army was expected to pay a dear price. The political facet of the attempt to make the army a more creative contributor to the regime came like a totalitarian bolt of lightning. In 1953, the new mission of the army, according to the Perón regime, became that of "safeguarding the greatest interests of the nation" in the light of "National Doctrine."[11] This new mission included a vast plan to indoctrinate and educate all military personnel along Justicialist lines.

Under the new program, army unit chiefs became the "creative agents" of Peronism. Fully indoctrinated themselves, these officers were to teach Justicialism to conscripts as the foremost criterion of army loyalty. They were thus to become the "creative commands," teaching loyalty, above all else, to the Peronist state. In launching the Course of Orientation of Unit Chiefs, Perón himself declared that the teaching of his doctrine as the prime focus of military loyalty would "culminate in the realization of a permanent custom of correct conduct on the part of the men."[12] In other words, politicalization was now to reach downward to the conscripts, as the Perón regime used National Doctrine to eclipse traditional loyalties and even perhaps loyalty to military superiors. Furthermore, all military men, from general to conscript, were to be indoctrinated. Here was an overt effort by Perón to convert the army from a traditional institution into a Peronist institution. Where, officers might ask, would Perón stop?

[9] Congreso Nacional, *Diario de sesiones de la Cámara de Diputados, año 1952,* I, 160.

[10] Franklin Lucero, *El precio de la lealtad,* pp. 63–64.

[11] "Ministerio de Ejército" in Congreso Nacional, *Diario de sesiones de la Cámara de Diputados, año 1954,* I, 176–181.

[12] "Curso de orientación para jefes de unidad," *Revista Militar,* no. 622 (November–December, 1953): 7–26.

The Catholic church was soon to ask the same question. During the early years of his regime, Perón actively sought and gained church support through a number of measures which have already been described. By 1950, however, a rift had begun to appear between Perón and the church. Many of the diehard Peronist labor leaders viewed Catholicism as anachronistic in the modern, industrialized, syndicalist state they hoped to create. They began to demand social changes that were unacceptable to the Catholic church, such as the legalization of divorce and of prostitution. Furthermore, the women's branch of the Peronist party and female enfranchisement had weakened the church's influence on the female population of the urban centers of Argentina. Finally, in the public schools there occurred, with the passage of time, a decided shift in emphasis from the teaching of Catholicism to the inculcation of Justicialism. This caused grave concern in clerical quarters.[13]

In a sense, Peronism represented the projection of the traditional-modern dichotomy of values to the national scene. This was evident in the church-state conflict that was to follow. Peronist industrialization and modernization were aimed at the creation of a nation largely free from traditional values, especially in the *descamisado* sector. Yet, Peronism drew much of its support from army officers, churchmen, and Catholic nationalists, all of whom were deeply concerned with the preservation of traditional and religious values. As Peronism grew more totalitarian, the conflict between the demands of modern dictatorship and those of traditionalism was certain to sharpen.

There was, however, a difference between conflict, always a characteristic of the Peronist structure, and a head-on collision. In 1954, Perón, the shrewdest dictator of the twentieth century, provoked a head-on collision with the Catholic church and the traditionalist forces. Why he did this still remains a mystery. H. L. Matthews, *New York Times* reporter in Argentina in 1955, queried many Argentines on the question and found that "no two explanations are the same."[14] Current historical interpretation on the problem remains at the same quizzical level.

[13] "Church and State in Argentina," *World Today* 12 (February, 1956): 62.
[14] H. L. Matthews, "Juan Perón's War with the Catholic Church," *Reporter*, June 16, 1955, pp. 19–20.

Perhaps the most feasible explanation of Perón's attack on the church is that suggested by Bonifacio del Carril. According to Carril, the attack was the climax of the state's battle with the church for the minds of youth. In 1954, Minister of Education Armando Méndez San Martín, a new power in the Perón cabinet, proposed the formation of the Union of Secondary Students to organize and indoctrinate Peronist youth. The Catholic church openly opposed this move as well as all demonstrations by the new organization. Persistent church opposition, constant and efficient, had wounded Perón's pride. Encouraged by left-wing laborites, he now prepared to wage open war against the Catholic church in a move prompted more by emotion than by his usual cold and calculating shrewdness.[15]

Still another interpretation holds "that the first motive for this attack upon the church was resentment of any attempt to bring Catholic influence to bear within CGT or on its members.[16] Perón was reportedly bitter about the plans of certain clergy to form a Christian Democratic party since it might cut into his *descamisado* following. He also suspected direct Catholic infiltration into the ranks of labor.

According to another interpretation, the attack on the church was a diverting action meant to attract attention from economic recession, the failure of expansion, and the hated contract with Standard Oil.[17] If attention was what Perón wanted, he could not have picked a more controversial issue.

To these interpretations may be added a point of view that the church, being the only undivided power factor in Argentina, was too much of a challenge to the regime. Perón wanted the church fragmented like the other power factors. "Like all absolute rulers, he [Perón] has a touch of megalomania."[18]

Although most cabinet members pleaded with Perón not to undertake the politically suicidal assault on the church, Minister of the Interior Angel Borlenghi and Minister of Education San Martín supported

---

[15] Bonifacio del Carril, *Crónica interna de la revolución libertadora*, pp. 38–39.
[16] John Murray, S.J., "Perón and the Church," *Studies* 44 (Autumn, 1955): 260.
[17] Antonio Benedetti, *Perón y Eva: Trayectoria y fin de un régimen*, p. 188.
[18] Matthews, "Perón's War with the Catholic Church," p. 22.

the move.[19] Hence, the support for the attack came from the left-wing labor elements in the cabinet, that is, from those intent on having modernization take its toll on the traditional values of the nation. After a series of day-long meetings with cabinet members, governors, legislators, and CGT leaders in October, 1954, Perón decided to launch his assault on the church in the next month.

The conflict between Perón and the church erupted with sudden bitterness in November of 1954 and intensified until mid-June, 1955. During that time, Perón legalized divorce and prostitution, proposed an end to Catholic influence in education, and advocated the taxation of church property. The Peronist police arrested a large number of priests and lay churchmen. On May 1, 1955, Perón's supporters called for the complete separation of church and state. Violent demonstrations and counterdemonstrations followed, including a Peronist attack on the archiepiscopal palace in Buenos Aires. When church officials disobeyed an order forbidding the annual Corpus Christi procession, Perón, on June 14, expelled two Catholic prelates from Argentina. On June 16, Perón was excommunicated by the Catholic church.

Beneath the violent surface events of the church-state conflict surged profound changes in the whole Peronist structure. The satellite integral nationalist forces (members of the clergy and Catholic nationalists) were alienated, of course, by the conflict. The traditionalist, Catholic army officers were also antagonized by Perón's assault on religious values.[20] Through their chaplains and intensely religious wives, army officers were reminded of their duties to the church. To dramatize their disappointment with the army's reluctance to move more quickly against the government, religious women would relinquish their seats on buses to officers.

The fact that resistance to Perón had increased on the right, led to answering pressures from government cliques and labor groups on the left.[21] Perón was, however, in no position to respond to the labor left,

---

[19] Olivieri, *Dos veces rebelde: Memorias*, p. 100.

[20] Magnet, *Nuestros vecinos argentinos*, p. 222.

[21] José Luis Romero in *Ciclo de Mesas Redondas: Tres revoluciones (los ultimos veintiocho años)*, pp. 120–121.

for by 1952 the Argentine economy had sunk into deep depression. Gone were the large exchange reserves built up during and after the war by the high prices paid for Argentine foodstuffs. The rationing of beef and the importation of wheat were grave signs of the decline of Argentine agriculture. A two-year series of droughts had impoverished the *campo* ("provinces"). As long as the rationing of fuel slowed down both industry and transportation, Argentina also found it difficult to secure ample replacements of arms and factory machines. Inflation struck at the wages of all, including the favored *descamisados*, some of whom could get only part-time work.

In 1953, Perón decided to reorient his economic policies to cope with depression. Demands by the *descamisado* for a general wage increase were resisted; the cycle of inflation, wage hikes, and then more inflation had to be halted. Labor was also told to produce more in order to shore up the nation's faltering economy. For the *descamisados*, this was a strikingly new kind of government talk.

To save the foundering economy, Perón also reversed himself on the cherished idea of economic independence. In 1953 he decided that the cooperation of the "capitalist-imperialists" was necessary if the economy was to recover. On August 26 of that year, the Perón government passed a law designed to attract foreign investment in the industrial and mining sectors of the economy. Although many restrictions were placed on these investments, the law marked an important step in Perón's turn to the right.[22]

In quest of foreign capital, Perón moved in 1953 toward a rapprochement with the United States. The move was significant not only as a basic reversal of foreign policy, but also because it dramatized the failure of Perón's bid for hegemony in Latin America against the influence of the Colossus of the North. In his unsuccessful attempts to expand Argentine influence in Latin America, Perón had used a number of devices. Along with influencing foreign military revolts he also began, soon after his inauguration in 1946, to propagandize for the economic union of South American countries. As part of this effort to promote Argentine-sponsored Spanish Americanism over

---

[22] Whitaker, *The United States and Argentina*, pp. 175–176, 203–204, 208.

United States-sponsored Pan Americanism, specially trained labor attachés were placed in neighboring countries to spread Peronist propaganda and to infiltrate their labor movements. An international labor federation was established under Peronist leadership, and given the name ATLAS, or Association of Latin American Labor Unions.[23]

But the continental labor movement declined rapidly, and Perón's efforts to lead an economic union of South American countries met with little success. Economic treaties were signed with Bolivia and, more important, with Chile in 1953, but these nations hardly became satellites of Argentina. Democratic Uruguay successfully resisted Peronist influence, and remained a haven for those who fled the Argentine dictatorship. Only Paraguay, the smallest and weakest of South American nations, fell within Perón's sphere of influence. Although Perón aided in the reelection of Getulio Vargas in Brazil in 1952, his hopes for close collaboration with that dictator were never fulfilled. In fact, the suicide of Vargas in August, 1954, spelled not only the end of Argentine hopes for collaboration with a Brazilian dictatorship, but also "one of the first tremors of the earthquake that was to shatter Perón's regime."[24]

Perón's rapprochement with the United States, then, was carried out in the gloomy aftermath of his failure to create a Greater Argentina. Although this "diplomatic revolution," as Professor Arthur P. Whitaker has referred to the new policy toward the United States, was never publicly announced or admitted by Perón, it began with a more friendly attitude in his references to Washington. After a visit by Milton Eisenhower in 1953, came more concrete evidence of the new friendship. Perón accepted a $60-million loan from the Export-Import Bank. United States businessmen, congressmen, and army officers began to make frequent visits to Argentina. Finally, on March 29, 1955, it was announced that Perón had signed an agreement with a subsidiary of the Standard Oil Company of California for the exploitation of petroleum reserves in Patagonia. Climaxing Perón's movement into

[23] Robert J. Alexander, "Peronism and Argentina's Quest for Leadership in Latin America," *Journal of International Affairs* 9 (1955): 51–55.
[24] Arthur P. Whitaker, *Argentine Upheaval*, pp. 98–99.

what army nationalists called the dollar orbit, the oil contract set off a wave of anti-Yankee protest in Argentina.[25] For the army, the oil contract was the final sign of Perón's failure to deliver a powerful, united, self-sufficient industrial nation. A clause in the oil agreement authorized Standard Oil to establish airfields in Patagonia. This led to rumors in the army that these airfields would eventually become United States military bases on Argentine soil.[26] Here was another reason for the alienation of the army and the Catholic nationalists. By 1955 the polarization of popular integral nationalism, through alienation of the army and labor at the same time, was running its swift couse. His economic policies were despised by the *descamisados*, nurtured on more than a decade of supernationalism and hatred for the "imperialists."

Outside the Peronist structure, general discontent was rife. Argentines of all political persuasions were alienated by inflation, depression, government scandals, and widespread corruption. Representatives of the democratic middle class—the Radicals, Socialists, and Progressive Democrats—had always maintained a harried but determined resistance to Perón. Now their opposition to his regime was spiced by cries of economic sell-out. Furthermore, a sense of national shame spread across the land as evidence of moral decay became manifest. In 1953, the suspicious suicide of Perón's secretary, Juan Duarte, who was Eva's brother, set off rumors of governmental intrigue and corruption. There was also Perón's new love life, his attraction to the fourteen-year-old Nélida Rivas, for which the army, after the revolution of 1955, would condemn him for behavior "unworthy of an officer and a gentleman."[27]

Public opinion was closely connected with military rebellion. When in February, 1955, the Catholic nationalist Mario Amadeo discussed the possibility of revolution with General Justo León Bengoa, commander of the third army division, he was given an interesting lesson in military uprisings. They could only succeed, General Bengoa stated, if the minister of war collaborated in the plot, or, better, if public

---

[25] *Ibid.*, pp. 99–101.
[26] George Pendle, "The Revolution in Argentina," *International Affairs* 32, no. 2 (April, 1956): 169.
[27] Tad Szulc, *Twilight of the Tyrants*, pp. 150–151.

opinion had been aroused to a point of intense hostility that permeated the barracks and drove the military men to action.[28] Since the Ministry of War was under the direction of General Franklin Lucero, a Peronist loyal to the end, the spark of revolt would have to come from the alienation of large sectors of opinion within and without the Peronist structure.

But the army officers proved reluctant rebels. They were, to a large extent, "fat cats," bound to the Perón regime by many ties. Most of the senior officers owed their positions to the dictator. In the wake of conspiracies in the early 1950s, Perón had continually warned them of the purges and the reincorporation of rebels into the high ranks that would inevitably follow his overthrow.[29] In addition, having been given control over state enterprises and the military economy, many of the top officers had engaged in corruption, and feared postrevolutionary exposure.[30] Perón's cordon of security around Buenos Aires also made successful military revolution seem a remote possibility.

A further reason for continuing army loyalty came in 1955, with the "plan to soften the consciences of officers."[31] Just as Perón had bought the support of legislators and union officers with gifts of automobiles, so, too, he tried the same tactic on the armed forces. Kaiser automobiles were to be distributed as outright gifts or at incredibly low prices to all officers who were willing to cooperate with the regime. All these officers need do was come to the Casa Rosada to receive their gifts and, of course, to demonstrate their support of Perón.

Amidst the vacillation in the armed forces, the navy stood out as an unwavering revolutionary force against the regime. Staunchly anti-Peronist, the liberal nationalist navy's resentment of the dictator had smouldered as he lavished funds upon the army, while ignoring the vital necessities of their branch. It was only after 1952, when deep-seated discontent began to emerge in Argentina, that Perón purchased two cruisers from the United States. One year later, he engaged a

[28] Mario Amadeo, *Ayer, hoy, mañana*, pp. 38–39.
[29] García Lupo, *La rebelión de los generales*, p. 62.
[30] Magnet, *Nuestros vecinos argentinos*, pp. 220–221.
[31] Olivieri, *Dos veces rebelde*, p. 83.

Japanese company to construct destroyers and frigates for the navy.[32] But this was too little too late. The time had long passed when Perón, the supreme corruptor, could purchase the loyalty of his naval opposition. On June 16, 1955, the roar of navy planes could be heard over Buenos Aires, signaling the beginning of the revolutionary movement that was to overthrow Perón.

[32] Edwin Lieuwen, *Arms and Politics in Latin America*, p. 72.

7. The Downfall of Perón,
June 16-September 16, 1955

The revolutionary process that toppled Perón began on June 16, 1955, with an unsuccessful naval revolt, and was climaxed exactly three months later by a large-scale and victorious military rebellion known as The Liberating Revolution. This revolutionary process requires analysis from three related standpoints. First, the formation within the military establishment of an uneasy revolutionary alliance of both liberal nationalist and integral nationalist officers. Second, as the revolutionary process increased its pressure upon the regime, internal divisions within the Peronist structure widened, and hastened the downfall of the dictatorship. Third, the actual military operations must be viewed as having sparked political developments within both the revolutionary and Peronist camps. For the Liberating Revolution of September 16, 1955, was far more than just a military rebellion; it was the climax of a larger political process, and must be interpreted in that context.

The ill-fated naval revolt that began the process was doomed by poor coordination and divisive uncertainty within the armed forces. It had the support of most of the liberal nationalist navy under the leadership of Rear Admiral Samuel Toranzo Calderón, included elements of the air force, and, for the vital land support, depended on the aid of army units under General Bengoa, commander of the third division in Entre Ríos. Having served as head of a commission to investigate the suicide of Juan Duarte in 1953, General Bengoa had been quietly exiled from the presidential secretariat to the provincial division. Soon after, he became the leading army officer in what was mainly a naval conspiracy.[1] From the outset the revolutionary process revealed the tendency of the strongly anti-Peronist navy to collaborate with disaffected integral nationalists of the army to obtain the all-important revolutionary backing on land.

Learning that their conspiracy had been exposed by Peronist agents, the naval officers hastily chose to strike on June 16, 1955. But they did so without successfully informing the army conspirators under General Bengoa.[2] The revolt began at 12:45 P.M. with an attack by naval and air force planes on the presidential palace, CGT headquarters, and other government buildings in Buenos Aires. Army pursuit planes were immobilized by naval air attacks on loyal bases in and around the city. Although the rebels dominated the air for a few desperate hours, all ground positions remained loyal under the army. Before the fleet could be called out on behalf of rebellion, it became clear that the uprising lacked the necessary land base.[3]

With the rebellion seemingly suppressed, *descamisados* rallied to the support of the government, and swarmed into the Plaza de Mayo. In a tragic but revealing episode, armed workers of the CGT were gunned down as they moved forward to accept the surrender of rebels in the naval ministry. When class-conscious naval officers had realized who their captors were to be, they had lowered the white flag and proceeded to open fire. Renewed air attacks added to the slaughter and men fell like flies as the deep class hatred seething in the revolution came to the

---

[1] Arturo J. Zabala, *La revolución del 16 de septiembre*, p. 43; Bonifacio del Carril, *Crónica interna de la revolución libertadora*, p. 43.

[2] Zabala, *La revolución del 16 de septiembre*, p. 43.

[3] Arthur P. Whitaker, *Argentine Upheaval*, pp. 20–21.

surface. Although government sources publicly announced that "more than 350" casualties resulted from the revolt, eyewitness reports told of 2,000 graves being dug in the Chacarita Cemetery.[4] At first it seemed as if the navy and air force had rebelled in vain. The 39 planes and 122 men involved in the uprising took flight to Uruguay. Arrests were made among the 588 officers and men of the naval infantry, who had also participated in the revolt. Yet, while the government proclaimed its easy triumph over the rebels, the uprising had produced significant reverberations within the Peronist structure.

The deepened divisions within the military establishment both impeded successful revolution and conditioned Perón's response to the revolutionary process. The navy and air force sought a basic change of government, a revolution to oust Perón and cleanse the nation of his regime. But the army, the most powerful branch, was divided in its support. A small group of high-ranking officers, some active and some retired, supported the navy and air force. But most of the generals, particularly those who owed their positions and personal fortunes to the dictator, desired a gradual change, one that would secure their power in the military against postrevolutionary charges of Peronism. They were, in turn, opposed by lieutenant colonels and junior officers, who, disillusioned with dictatorship and with professional opportunism, favored a thoroughgoing cleanup of the regime and its supporters.[5] These divisions within the armed forces later emerged as basic factors in postrevolutionary politico-military developments.

While these divisions impeded revolution, they also shaped Perón's response to the growing disaffection. All military events of the revolution must be viewed in relation to Perón's desire to maintain the army-labor alliance. The support he received from regiments of the cordon of security around Buenos Aires during the naval revolt increased his dependence on a divided army. Therefore, he attempted at first to placate the army by dropping the war against the church, and by purging the cabinet members most closely associated with that colossal blunder.

---

[4] "Behind the Scenes in Argentina," *America*, August 6, 1955, p. 441.

[5] *Ibid.*, p. 441; Antonio Benedetti, *Péron y Eva: Trayectoria y fin de un régimen*, pp. 210–211.

But this was not enough for the senior officers of the cordon of security. Recognizing that a basic shift in public opinion had occurred against the regime, these officers, led by General José Embrioni, under-secretary of war, pressed for a legal transfer of power. To safeguard their positions in the army, they wanted a constitutional transaction whereby power would be transferred from Perón to a successor who would be responsive to the wishes of the military command.[6]

As pressure from the army mounted, the CGT moved into action. Militant leaders of the CGT began to call upon Perón to fully arm the workers and to form labor militias to defend the regime.[7] Here was evidence of polarization of the army-labor alliance, a situation Perón had sought to avoid at all costs. Each of the two main pillars of the dictatorship was seeking to reconstruct it, but each wanted to alter the balance of power by increasing its own influence.

The swirl of conflicting forces within the Peronist structure goes far to explain the dictator's erratic course in attempting to stem the tide of revolution. Realizing that internal pressures would increase as public opinion shifted against his regime, Perón attempted to conciliate the public. On July 5 he called for a "political truce" and, ten days later, he even made an empty gesture towards resignation. But when this failed to dampen opposition to his regime, he turned to terror. On August 15, hundreds of his political opponents were arrested and Peronist gangs spread terror in the streets of Buenos Aires.[8]

While resorting to fear to squelch opposition, Perón also moved to redress the balance within his regime. He realized that if the *descami-sados* were not aroused in defense of his government, he would become the servant of a divided army. Violence and terror were therefore climaxed by reviving the threat to unleash armed *descamisados*. On August 31, 1955, the *descamisados* poured into the Plaza de Mayo to attend a mass meeting called by Perón and to shout "our lives for Perón" in a manner reminiscent of October 17, 1945. Perón responded with the most incendiary speech of his career, calling for the *descami-*

---

6 Carril, *Crónica interna de la revolución libertadora,* pp. 42–43; Zabala, *La revolución del 16 de septiembre,* p. 45.
7 José Luis Romero in *Ciclo de Mesas Redondas,* p. 120.
8 Arthur P. Whitaker, *Argentina,* p. 147.

sados to "annihilate and crush" opponents of his social program. He concluded with a threat that "when one of our people falls, five of them will fall."[9]

One week after this speech, the executive council of the CGT unanimously proposed the formation of labor militias. This move to the left within the Peronist structure was, of course, resisted by the army. Not even the most loyal Peronist officer would accept such a proposal, for it challenged the military's traditional monopoly of the organized force of the state. It would change the very nature of Peronism, by basing the regime largely on the labor sector, and thus it no doubt sapped the will of the cordon of security to protect the regime. On September 9, 1955, Minister of War Lucero, a thoroughgoing Peronist, flatly declined an offer by the CGT to organize labor militias to support loyal army units. Leaders of the CGT continued to press the issue and the formation of labor militias seemed to have Perón's support.[10] The CGT, which had long possessed small arms, now awaited Perón's decision to open the arsenals to workers. That decision was never to come.

Civilian opponents of the regime were quick to exploit the fears of the military. A famous Catholic nationalist pamphlet, widely circulated in the army, greatly disturbed all military men. It depicted the organization of labor militias as the first step in the formation of a Popular Syndicalist State of the New Argentina. After basing the state on labor support, the pamphlet continued, Perón would launch a vast purge in the armed forces, reorganize the comands, take weaponry away from doubtful regiments, and place power in the hands of the noncoms. Only officers and conscripts of proven loyalty to the Syndicalist State would be allowed to serve in the army.[11]

This was effective propaganda, but in reality Perón sought a restoration of the army-labor balance rather than the formation of a syndicalist state. Although he paid loud lip service to the formation of labor militias in order to intimidate both his restless army backers and his revolutionary opponents, he was very reluctant to fully arm the *descamisados*. According to Perón himself, he was fearful of a blood bath similar to

[9] Whitaker, *Argentine Upheaval*, pp. 20–21.
[10] Alejandro Magnet, *Nuestros vecinos argentinos*, p. 246.
[11] Felix Lafiandra, ed., *Los panfletos*, pp. 314–315.

the Spanish Civil War.[12] Furthermore, he brought to demagoguery the habits of the army officer, concerned, above all, with social order rather than revolution by the masses. Finally, the formation of labor militias would perhaps change the nature of his regime, making him the servant rather than the master of labor. As always, maintenance of balance was Perón's aim.

The threat to create labor militias spurred the formation of revolutionary alliance between liberal nationalist and Catholic nationalist elements within the armed forces. As conspiracy spread within the army, liberal nationalist naval officers, totally committed to revolution and supported by most of the air force, seemed now to be assured of a land base. However, army conspiracy was uncoordinated and still rent by personal and ideological divisions. Army garrisons in Córdoba were conspiring without contacts with the revolutionary networks under Generals Bengoa, Pedro Eugenio Aramburu, and Raul Uranga in Buenos Aires. Separate plots were also being hatched by General Lagos in Cuyo and by General Videla Balaguer in Río Cuarto. Combination of the naval conspiracy with the army plot of General Bengoa had failed in the June uprising. Hence the navy later shifted its support to General Aramburu, the liberal nationalist who was emerging as the leader of the revolution in Buenos Aires.[13]

That neither Bengoa nor Aramburu nor Uranga had command of troops in the province of Buenos Aires is a significant point. The Buenos Aires conspiracies, especially those in the cordon of security, were representative of only a small minority of the officer corps, for most of the army commands were under military men still committed to the dictatorship. It was the officers of the Córdoba garrison, linked to civilian Catholic nationalists, who furnished the navy its revolutionary land base. In mid-August, these officers had made contact with the Aramburu conspiracy in Buenos Aires, requesting that a leader be sent out to Córdoba from the capital. The officer who undertook this mission was a retired general, Eduardo Lonardi, longtime conspirator against the Perón regime.[14]

---

[12] Juan D. Perón, *La fuerza es el derecho de las bestias*, p. 87.
[13] Carril, *Crónica interna de la revolución libertadora*, pp. 208–210.
[14] Luis Ernesto Lonardi, *Dios es justo*, pp. 24–26.

Lonardi had entered the revolutionary network against the will of Aramburu. When in early August, Lonardi, the Catholic nationalist, had offered his services to Aramburu, the liberal nationalist, he was bluntly rebuffed. Aramburu stated that he "neither conspired nor would conspire."[15] That a conspiracy actually was in the making in Buenos Aires was confirmed to Lonardi by Colonel Arturo Ossorio Arana, the officer assigned to lead the Cordobese revolutionaries. Both Colonel Ossorio Arana and General Lonardi went to Córdoba. Because of General Lonardi's superior rank, Colonel Ossorio Arana turned the command over to him.[16]

After Lonardi assumed command of the revolution in Córdoba, contacts were made with Colonel Eduardo Señorans, chief of staff of the Aramburu conspiracy in Buenos Aires. Señorans, aware of the weakness of the Buenos Aires plot, welcomed Lonardi and the Cordobese garrison into the fold.[17] Although strengthened by this union, the revolution nevertheless seemed to face insuperable obstacles. With each passing day, intense government vigilance took more conspirators into custody. The conspiracy in Córdoba was uncovered, support in the littoral provinces was lacking, and not one important unit in Buenos Aires was sworn to revolution. Under these conditions, on September 4, General Aramburu made a historic decision—the revolution must be postponed for at least a year.[18]

General Lonardi was incensed by this decision. He contended that postponement of the revolution meant its end. Delay would afford the dictatorship enough time to root out conspiracy and make arrests. Young officers, who had staked their careers on the success of the revolution, would be the chief victims of postponement. The spark of resistance within the army would be smothered, perhaps forever. Lonardi therefore decided to assume the leadership of the revolution. He was certain that if Córdoba created a nucleus of rebellion for forty-eight hours, the revolution would spread throughout the nation. The date

[15] *Ibid.*, p. 23.
[16] *Ibid.*, pp. 25–26.
[17] *Ibid.*, p. 27.
[18] *Ibid.*, pp. 35–37.

set for the outbreak of revolution, not to be postponed under any conditions, was September 16, 1955.[19]

Having made this decision, Lonardi sought the support of the liberal nationalist navy and the remnants of the Aramburu conspiracy in the army. The liberal nationalist navy really had no choice but to accept Lonardi's leadership. Naval rebellion was doomed without a land base, and General Lonardi seemed prepared to provide this essential element. Furthermore, the participation of army units was essential to symbolize the union of the armed forces in rebellion against the dictatorship. Without the army's participation, the rebellion would appear to be a confrontation between the two major branches of the military establishment. Accordingly, the leader of the naval conspiracy, Captain Ricardo Palma, placed his forces under the command of General Lonardi. When Colonel Señorans and other Aramburu supporters also pledged themselves to the rebellion, it meant that an uneasy revolutionary alliance of liberal nationalist and Catholic nationalist officers had been, at least temporarily, forged by the necessities of the moment.[20]

Even after the union of these disparate forces, the revolution was, from the military point of view, a great gamble. And at first the outlook for success seemed decidedly grim. General Uranga, encharged with raising in rebellion the Colegio Militar and first infantry of Buenos Aires, failed in his efforts and took flight to the Escuela Naval. General Bengoa, who was assigned the chore of spreading subversion in the littoral provinces, was imprisoned, escaped, and, deciding that his escape had annulled the factor of surprise, remained in Buenos Aires. General Aramburu, who had belatedly followed Colonel Señorans into the Lonardi uprising, went out from Buenos Aires to raise the garrison of Curuzú Cuatía in rebellion but failed in his efforts and was forced to flee the province of Corrientes.[21] This spelled the end of hopes for a second land base for the revolution.

The revolution did, however, succeed on three crucial fronts: the

---

[19] *Ibid.*, p. 40.
[20] *Ibid.*, pp. 45–46.
[21] The failure in Curuzú Cuatía is analyzed in Rolando Hume, *Sublevación en Curuzú Cuatía.*

Córdoba garrison, which provided the necessary land base; the second army of the garrison of Cuyo, which, since it faced Chile and the Andes, prevented Perón from surrounding the land base at Córdoba; and the naval bases of Puerto Belgrano and Puerto Madryn.

At dawn on September 16, 1955, General Lonardi, accompanied by junior officers, took over the artillery school of Córdoba. The revolution was initiated as shells were lobbed from there into the loyalist infantry school. Quick cannon fire was necessary to avert a charge by the well-equipped infantry. Colonel Guillermo Brizuela, head of the infantry school, answered the artillery with mortar shells, and the firing rang out all through the day. In the late hours of the night, after a discussion with Lonardi, Brizuela surrendered; his troops were accorded all military honors by the artillery. Lonardi then moved his troops to the aviation school on the outskirts of the city of Córdoba.[22]

The revolutionary land base was won; but could it be held? The revolution had been defeated in the army garrison of Curuzú Cuatía and the naval base of Río Santiago. Only the artillery and aviation schools of Córdoba were in the rebel camp. The rebels of Córdoba lacked infantry forces and were threatened from every side. Loyalist troops were marching on Córdoba from Alta Gracia and the eleventh and twelfth infantry, under the loyalist Miguel Iñiguez, were closing in from Santa Fe. Furthermore, the "command of repression" of the Perón regime had ordered the convergence on Córdoba of all garrisons surrounding that central province. Troops from the capital and from Cuyo were to be concentrated at Río Cuarto in a pincers operation aimed at Lonardi in Córdoba. How long could the Lonardi force, even though bolstered by Catholic nationalist civilians, hold the land base?

Then on the night of September 17, 1955, came good news for the rebels. The second army of Cuyo had rebelled and so had naval forces at Puerto Belgrano. The rebellion of the Cuyo garrison, under the leadership of its ex-commander, General Julio A. Lagos, was a turning point in the revolution. With these regiments of western Argentina in the rebel camp, a third front had been opened against the Perón regime

[22] For an eyewitness account of revolutionary operations in Córdoba, see Lonardi, *Dios es justo*, pp. 63–118.

—one that made encirclement of the Córdoba land base impossible.[23] Now with the garrison of Cuyo sealing off the western border and with the navy beginning its blockade of the coastline, loyalist Argentina was largely cut off from the outside world.

The final blow to the Perón regime came from the navy, united under the command of Rear Admiral Isaac Rojas. The navy had been in rebellion since the afternoon of September 16. Navy rebels had been forced to evacuate the naval base of Río Santiago, but by September 17 all naval forces were united under Admiral Rojas and were preparing to proceed to Buenos Aires. On that day, Admiral Rojas declared a blockade of all Argentine ports.[24]

The first naval ships appeared at the entrance of the Río de la Plata on the afternoon of September 18. When by the following morning the whole fleet had assembled there, Admiral Rojas issued a warning that unless the government surrendered, he would order the bombardment of Buenos Aires.[25] It was well known that Admiral Rojas was a man quite capable of ordering such a bombardment of the great portcity. He had already shown the fire power of the navy in bombarding and capturing the Mar del Plata port.

By September 19, two pockets of army rebellion had bought the time necessary for the navy to bring its power to bear on the Perón regime. The outbreak of military hostilities left Perón dependent on the loyalist army for support. With the army-labor balance gone, Perón delegated his presidential functions to a military junta on September 19, 1955. The junta members reflected the views of the Embrioni faction within the army and held to the position known as the subtle line. In the hope of preserving their positions in the armed forces, they sought to impose themselves as mediators between the Peronist and anti-Peronist sectors into which the nation was divided. They convinced Perón that the time had come to negotiate with the rebels.[26]

Significantly, it was Minister of War Lucero who read the document

23 For an eyewitness account of revolutionary operations in Cuyo, see Carril, *Crónica interna de la revolución libertadora*, chap. 2.
24 Text of Rojas communiqué in Lonardi, *Dios es justo*, p. 123.
25 *Ibid.*, p. 124.
26 Carril, *Crónica interna de la revolución libertadora*, pp. 104–105.

signed by Perón and dealing with pacification. The document encharged the army "with the situation, with the order, with the government, to seek the pacification of Argentines before it is too late, employing for this [purpose] the most adequate and temperate form."[27]
Perón had no doubt that his forces could suppress the rebellion, but he
feared the price in human lives that this would involve.

The document was a model of ambiguities. It did, however, bolster
the determination of rebel forces to seek an unconditional surrender.
Both Generals Lonardi and Lagos distrusted Perón and his loyalist
generals, and they were determined not to deal with them for only a
truce. General Lonardi responded to Lucero's pleas for a truce and a
conference with a demand for the resignation of Perón.[28]

By September 20 Perón knew he could not suppress the revolution.
The forces sent from Santa Fe to quell the rebellion in Córdoba had
been defeated at La Calera, and were retreating in disorder. Artillery
and infantry units sent from Buenos Aires against Córdoba had joined
the rebel force. The gendarmerie, concentrated around the Campo de
Mayo garrison as part of Perón's cordon of security, refused to obey
orders from the government. Actively against the regime, along with
the army regiments in Cuyo, Patagonia, and Córdoba, were the forces
of Bahía Blanca and Mar del Plata to the south. The city of Buenos
Aires was isolated from the rest of the country, for civilian guerrillas
had destroyed all the powerful radio antennae around the metropolis.
The rebels commanded the naval and air force planes. Civilian guerrillas, drawn from nearly all anti-Peronist political sectors, had reenforced the Córdoba garrison, and more than ten thousand were concentrated in Buenos Aires, awaiting orders to neutralize police forces in
the capital city. Perón could command the loyalty of only some of the
regiments of Buenos Aires. Yet if he decided to entrench himself in the
capital city, he was trapped, for he had neither the air force nor can-
nons to fight against the navy's long-range artillery.[29]

---

[27] Text of Perón declaration in Lonardi, *Dios es justo*, pp. 119–121.
[28] *Ibid.*, p. 126.
[29] Summary of situation facing Perón from Dr. Germán O. E. Tjarks, Argentine
historian and participant in the revolution of 1955.

And so, Perón, who had promised the CGT to fight to the death, assigned to the military junta the chore of negotiating a transfer of power. He then boarded a ship for Paraguay, whence he later moved to Nicaragua. The revolution was over; popular integral nationalism was overthrown.

PART IV
THE LEGACY: A DIVIDED ARMY
IN A DIVIDED NATION, 1955-1966

The traditional-modern dichotomy of values within the army was submerged in a tide of postrevolutionary revulsion against Peronism. After the Liberating Revolution, the central and burning question confronting the armed forces was what to do with the lusty remnants of Peronism? Perón was gone, but his shadow continued to haunt Argentina. The Peronists continued to control labor, the largest and most coherent voting bloc (30 to 40 per cent of the voters). Within the army, nearly all active officers had, at one time or another, cooperated with the dictatorship for the purposes of professional advancement. Who, then, was Peronist and who was not? These considerations explain why General Lonardi, who ruled Argentina during the first two months after the revolution, was backed by a majority of army officers. Lonardi represented those military men who wanted to take a moderate line toward Peronism in the army, and to reintegrate Peronist labor into the political system as soon as possible.

But the course of postrevolutionary politico-military history was determined by a coalition of the staunchly anti-Peronist navy in league with a militant minority of the army. The minority in the army was comprised of the vengeance-seeking rebels of 1951 and ambitious junior army officers. This anti-Peronist coalition in the armed forces ousted Lonardi and installed in his place General Pedro E. Aramburu. Under Aramburu (1955–1958), the process of de-Peronizing every social institution, including the army, was speeded to a climax. The armed forces became committed, through a combination of liberal nationalist idealism, genuine revulsion, and professional opportunism, to a staunchly anti-Peronist position.

Since 1958 the major dichotomy within the army has not stemmed from established institutional values as it did previously, but has arisen in response to the overriding issue of Peronism. For officers who had staked their careers and lives in campaigns against the followers of the ex-dictator, a Peronist resurgence might carry vengeance in its wake. One side of the new dichotomy—those uncompromisingly anti-Peronist—was known first as the Gorillas, later as the Interventionists, and today is known as the *colorados* ("reds"). Descended from the vengeance-seeking faction of 1951, this group, in league with the navy, has tried steadfastly to exclude the Peronists from all participation in politics. Some of the most fanatic have even favored a military dictatorship that would stamp out Peronism once and for all. Under Aramburu, the Gorillas supervised the de-Peronization of the armed forces and other institutions. During the administration of Arturo Frondizi (1958–1962), the Interventionists blocked all efforts made by the president to integrate the Peronists into his party. When in March, 1962, the Peronists scored breathtaking victories in gubernatorial and congressional elections, the Interventionists led the way in overthrowing Frondizi.

During the Frondizi administration, another coalition, which became known as the Legalists, began to emerge within the army. (This group bore no relationship to the anti-Uriburu Legalists of the 1930s.) Defenders of constitutionality and civilian rule, the Legalists attempted during the Frondizi years to limit military intervention in politics. After reluctantly assenting to the ouster of Frondizi in March, 1962, the Legalists became known as the *azules* ("blues"). It was the *azules* who blocked the *colorados'* efforts to establish a military dictatorship after Frondizi was overthrown. During the interim regime of José María Guido (1962–1963), the *azules* avowed their support of civilian rule, the ultimate removal of the army from politics, and the gradual integration of the Peronist masses into political life by a process subject to electoral restraints. In a series of contests for power with the *colorados* of both the army and navy, the *azules* emerged as the dominant coalition in the armed forces. Their victory paved the way for the election in 1963 of Arturo Illía, presidential candidate of the moderate Popular Radicals.

The *azul* tradition proved extremely fragile. The commitment of the armed forces to legalism came to an abrupt halt on June 28, 1966, when, after thirty-two months in office, President Illía was ousted by a military coup. Once again, it was the inflammatory issue of resurgent Peronism that led to military action against a constitutional regime. Illía had adopted a policy to permit the integration of neo-Peronists into the institutional structure of Argentina. For army officers, major election victories by the Peronists, combined with the weakness of the Illía regime in the face of economic crisis and the supposed rise of left-wing extremism, proved intolerable. Even ardent *azules* had come to view Illía's do-nothing regime as a dangerous power vacuum. Illía was accordingly overthrown, and the armed forces installed retired General Juan Carlos Onganía, an officer who, ironically, had dedicated the last decade of his career to the defense of constitutionality.

For more than a decade after Perón, then, the armed forces, torn by the crucial issues of Peronism and the role of the military in Argentine society, have been a divided power factor in a divided nation. Despite its divisions, the influence of the military in Argentine society and politics has continued to expand. Guns and organization do not alone explain this condition. The political power of the military has grown because of the acute fragmentation of Argentine society and the failure of the political parties as effective carriers of public opinion and civilian power. During the years from 1955 to 1963, the Argentine political spectrum was represented by an alliance of the right-wing armed forces with the upper class—an alliance determined to concede little to the Peronist bloc; a sharply divided middle class, with no one of its political parties capable of ruling the nation alone; and a politically marooned Peronist mass that, lacking legal outlets, turned to terror and labor strife to voice its demands.

The military alliance with elites and the upper middle class came about through its staunch anti-Peronist stand and its return to the liberal nationalist, or conservative, tradition. During the Perón era, the army had gambled on big government and big labor, and got its fingers burnt. After Perón's fall, military men, wanting to rid their institution of the taint of collaboration with the dictatorship, adopted values diametrically opposed to those held in the past. Reacting against totalitarian statism, the officers turned to economic individualism. Against the demagogic promotion of social welfare, they supported a society that left the solution of such problems to the free interplay of economic forces. Except for economic resources vital to national defense, such as petroleum, the officers were prepared to go along with the concepts of a free economy, private enterprise, and the opening of the nation to foreign investments.[1] This meant abandoning their statist nationalism for new and freer roads to economic reconstruction. For the Peronist masses, these values indicated the return of the military to the Justista tradition of alliances with the conservative elites and the foreign economic interests. Hence, the army was pitted against Peronism.

The alliance between the armed forces and business and landowning elites gave these social sectors political influence out of proportion to their number of members. This despite the fact that the conservatives were both weak and divided. The Democratic party, which gave political support to General Aramburu, drew 337,479 votes in 1957 and polled only 77,796 votes in the presidential elections of February, 1958. This party was also weakened by the defection of a group called the Popular Conservative Democratic party, which sought, unsuccessfully, to align itself with the Peronists and to prove that the upper class could draw popular support. In November, 1958, the Democratic party and other conservative elements united to form the National

---

[1] Sergio Bagú, "Diagrama político de la Argentina de hoy," *Cuadernos Americanos* 90 (November–December, 1956): 49–50.

Federation of Parties of the Center. Conservatives, especially business-men, also gave some support to the Independent Civic party organized by Alvaro Alzogaray in 1957. The traditionalist Catholic nationalist sector of the oligarchy expressed itself through the Federal party, organized in 1958 and closely associated with the newspaper *Azul y Blanco*.[2]

Significantly, the large though inchoate Argentine middle class, which might have ruled the nation effectively, was hopelessly divided in the years from 1955 to 1963. Although comprising roughly one-half the Argentine population, the middle class has, since the turn of the century, been rent by basic social divisions. Along with many subdivisions, there have been two main wings, called the "old" and the "new" middle class. The "old" middle class of professionals, businessmen, and independent farmers of moderate means has been more closely allied with the oligarchy than with the "new" middle class. The "new" middle class, comprised of bureaucrats, technicians, white-collar workers, small shopkeepers, and artisans, became, in turn, divided after 1955 by the crucial issue of Peronism.[3]

In 1957, the Radicals, heirs of Yrigoyen, split into two rival organizations: the Intransigent Radical Civic Union (UCRI), and the People's Radical Civic Union, or Popular Radicals (UCRP). The break was partly personalistic, involving a power struggle between Intransigent leader Arturo Frondizi and Popular Radical leader Ricardo Balbín. However, basic social and ideological divisions in the "new" middle class fostered this significant split.[4] A part of the middle class, especially the urban intellectuals, supported the Intransigents as the more left wing of the two Radical sectors. The Intransigents preached an intense Radical nationalism and supported the integration of the Peronists into political life. They tended to look upon Peronism as a

2 An excellent article on postrevolutionary political alignments and factionalization is Robert A. Potash's, "Argentine Political Parties," *Journal of Inter-American Studies* 1 (October, 1959): 515–524.

3 Jeanne Kuebler, "Argentina and Peronism," *Editorial Research Reports*, May 15, 1963, p. 383.

4 This split and others are analyzed in Ismael Viñas, *Orden y Progreso: La era del frondizismo*, pp. 47–49.

force in Argentine life that really antedated the dictator and that would also survive him. Intransigent leader Frondizi believed that the Peronist masses needed only another vehicle (the Radical Intransigents, for example) to bring them within the democratic structure.

The more moderate Popular Radicals represented the sector of the middle class, especially the upper stratum, that feared gains in power made by the lower-class Peronist bloc. Many Popular Radicals supported the liberal nationalist stand of Aramburu and the army. Members of this wing tended to look upon Peronism as a unique national tragedy. Unrepentant Peronists, they believed, must be reeducated. The intransigent trade unions, which they equated with Peronist fanatics, must be forced to see reason and to understand the dire economic realities of the nation.[5]

From 1955 to 1963, Argentina had something of a mixture between a two-party and a multi-party system. The two sectors of the Radicals, the Intransigents and the Popular Radicals, were the only serious contenders in the national elections and they shared between them most of the seats in Congress. However, there were also a number of smaller parties of some importance which vied for the votes of a divided middle class. The Argentine Socialist party, its membership of some 500,000 largely from the city and province of Buenos Aires, also split after 1955 over the significance of Peronism. The faction of Américo Ghioldi, disillusioned by the traitorous working class for having sold out to the dictator, was willing to witness the loss of much of the lower-class social base of the Socialist party. The Ghioldistas supported the stern anti-Peronist measures decreed by the Aramburu government, and later opposed Frondizi's policy of integration.

Pitted against the Ghioldistas within the Socialist party, was the wing led by Ramón Muñiz and Alicia Moreau de Justo, widow of the party's founder. This wing sought to win lower-class support for the Socialist party by defending social gains made under Perón. It favored the reinstatement of trade-union leaders and was tolerant of efforts to incorporate the masses into accepted political chanels. The Muñiz-Moreau

---

[5] "Argentina Two Years after Perón," *World Today* 14 (December–January, 1958): 20.

faction opposed the policies of the Aramburu regime, and adopted a wait-and-see policy toward Frondizi in 1958.[6]

Along with the divided Radical and Socialist forces, there were other parties attempting to claim the allegiance of the Argentine middle class. The Progressive Democrats, a leftist, anticlerical, and anti-imperialist organization in the provincial tradition of Lisandro de la Torre, was supported by about 140,000 votes. Most of these supporters came from the city of Rosario and the surrounding area of Santa Fe province, where a large middle sector of farmers and merchants had developed. Some middle-class Argentines also gave support to a new moderate centrist party, the Christian Democrats, who polled an impressive 420,606 votes in 1957 and 289,245 votes in the presidential elections of 1958.

When the Peronist party was outlawed in November, 1955, the fundamental dilemma of Argentine politics emerged: how to run a democracy in a nation in which the single largest sector of the electorate (about 2.5 million votes) retained its devotion to a dictatorial symbol —Perón; and, in which also, the military, the most influential power factor, was determined that no Peronist should hold office. The quick reinstatement of the idea of Perón as the champion of the under-privileged was partly due to the conservative nature of the Aramburu regime. His government was regarded as an agent for the restoration of the oligarchy and Yankee imperialism and as a threat to the social gains the workers had made under Perón. The fact is that the workers had made very concrete social gains under Perón. "Despite vagueness and debate over statistics," writes James W. Rowe, "the best evidence is that even by late 1955 the wages of Argentine skilled and unskilled workers had more than outpaced the inflated cost-of-living when compared with 1943, not to mention the fringe benefits amounting to some 40 to 50 per cent of wage costs."[7] Furthermore, Peronism's "participation revolution" had given the workers a new sense of dignity and power. For the Peronist masses, the conservatism of the postrevolu-

---

[6] Robert J. Alexander, "Argentine Socialism after Perón," *Socialist Call* 26, no. 10 (October, 1958): 12–14.

[7] James W. Rowe, *Argentina's Durable Peronists: A Twentieth Anniversary Note*, p. 21.

tionary regimes, at a time when their parties were proscribed, confirmed Perón's warning that his overthrow would mean political reaction spearheaded by the corrupt alliance between the oligarchy and foreign economic interests.

Therefore, the proscription of outright Peronist party activity from 1955 to 1963 created a lump in the body politic which, far from dissolving with time, grew and grew in the warm light of martyrdom. In 1958, after three years of political suppression under Aramburu, Peronism chose to support Arturo Frondizi and the Intransigents as a second best alternative. However, in 1960, Peronism returned to its 1957 position and cast blank protest ballots against what it deemed to be betrayal by the Frondizi regime. In 1962, the Unión Popular, the party most closely representing Peronism, was permitted to present candidates, though its subsequent victories were nullified by the overthrow of Frondizi. By 1963, in the aftermath of victories by the *azules* in the armed forces, the neo-Peronists were finally allowed to participate in congressional elections and to take seats in the Chamber of Deputies. In line with his policy of gradually integrating the Peronists, Illía legalized the participation of the Unión Popular in the elections of March, 1965.

These March elections involved more than half of the seats in the lower house. The results of the election were of striking significance. They revealed a grouping of votes unknown since the decade between 1946 and 1955, when the nation was divided into two vast Peronist and anti-Peronist sectors. With the left consolidated into Peronist ranks, the middle represented by the strengthened Popular Radicals, and a third force mobilizing on the conservative right, it seemed as if Argentina was moving toward an effective political alignment.[8] But the large Peronist vote alarmed the military and converted Legalists into activists. As the military men looked ahead to future elections, they feared even greater Peronist victories and this concern was translated into action in the military coup that ousted Illía.

Like other sectors of Argentine society, in 1965 the Peronists were

8 Peter Ranis, "Peronismo without Perón: Ten Years after the Fall (1955–1965)," *Journal of Inter-American Studies* 8 (January, 1966): 120–122.

also divided. First and most important of the three visible Peronist factions was the syndicalist wing, dominated by leaders of the influential metallurgical and textile unions. Peronist control over the labor movement was also tightened in 1965. While the backbone of Peronist strength was, and is, in the Buenos Aires area, they have become strong also in other industrial centers, such as Rosario and Córdoba, and in the agricultural centers of northern Argentina. Peronists have come to wield control over the metalworkers union, which has jurisdiction over steel production, metal fabrication, automobiles, electrical and all other appliances. Their influence has also become dominant in the packinghouse workers, the light and power workers, the textile makers, and the movement has gained the support of workers in numerous other unions of CGT.[9] The syndicalist wing believed in placing both the vast mass support and the great financial resources of the CGT at the disposal of Peronist leadership. The syndicalists were the inflexible Peronists, nurtured on a decade of supernationalistic dictatorship and hardened by still another decade of military suppression. Unswerving, die-hard Peronists, they wished to recover the benefits of bygone days. The second faction, comprised of the political Peronists, gained their support from the capital and the provincial cities of Córdoba and Rosario. They were not trade unionists, but middle-class professionals (mainly lawyers), who were the intellectual leaders of Peronism. In their ranks were academicians, ex-Socialists, and disenchanted idealists. The third group, known as the neo-Peronists, drew its support from the provinces. It was essentially rural, moderate, and nationalistic, though it lacked a hardened ideology. Politically, it ran the spectrum, for it was the least class-conscious wing of Peronism. Its leadership was drawn from the provincial middle class and there were even some aristocrats who were members of this wing. The grass-roots support of the neo-Peronists was found in the provinces of Mendoza, Tucumán, Chaco, Jujuy, Salta, and San Juan.[10]

The syndicalist wing developed a concrete political program. In the economic sphere, it supported the nationalization of the banking sys-

[9] Morris A. Horowitz, "The Legacy of Juan Perón," *Challenge* 12, no. 1 (October, 1963): 30.
[10] Ranis, "Peronismo without Perón," p. 124.

tem, a freeze on prices and rents, extensive urban renewal, and basic land reform. Politically, it proposed a universal amnesty, meaning the return of "exiled" Peronist politicans and the reincorporation of purged military men into the armed forces.[11] Hence, this program was a direct challenge to those officers who risked their careers in purges against their Peronist colleagues in the armed forces.

The political Peronists and neo-Peronists subscribed to this program, but acted as restrainers on the syndicalists. During the Aramburu and Frondizi years, Peronist syndicalism became associated with violence and inflammatory declarations. The other two wings considered that the perpetuation of these practices would threaten the movement's efforts to win a place as a democratic organization in the political structure.

Their years of suppression and illegality have made ex-dictator Perón a martyr in the eyes of his followers, and bolstered his role as their charismatic leader. The unique feature of the Peronist movement was and is its unprecedented allegiance to a long-deposed dictator. "Juan Perón still represents the single most important cog within the *peronista* movement. He remains *de jure* leader if not in *de facto* control of the movement's day-to-day policies." Through clever political manipulating and enduring mass popularity, Perón keeps the "movement within the range of his veto, if not control."[12] While Peronism has striven to prove that it can take its place as a democratic party, it retains its allegiance to a dictatorial symbol.

Judgments of the Peronist movement differ. Some observers see it as the major product of moral corrosion in Argentina. "Scratch the average Peronist 'thinker' in Argentina, . . ." writes Keith Botsford, Latin American correspondent for the *New Leader*, "and you will find a third-rate writer, a worker who doesn't care to work, an army officer in search of quick promotion, or an intellectual *manqué*." Peronism is "the product of acute demoralization, not of thought." It tends to "destroy institutions at the base, corrupting individuals all the way down the line by providing them with a semblance of power, and none of the responsibility." It creates "conditions of such vulgarity (as under

---

[11] *Ibid.*, p. 125.
[12] *Ibid.*, pp. 114, 125–126.

Perón) that nothing of value, democracy included, can survive." It tends to "sap all the structures of a rational society."[13]

But Peter Ranis, another skilled observer, has given a different picture of Peronism. While conceding that Peronists still retain their devotion to a dictatorial symbol, Ranis depicts the movement as having "become more moderate and conciliatory." Peronist leaders have given up the claim that their movement is synonymous with the whole national will. After the 1965 elections, they cooperated in the Chamber of Deputies, conferred with military men, and did their utmost to convince business of the movement's nonrevolutionary character. The Ranis position implies that the Peronists could take their place as a legitimate, and perhaps constructive, left in the Argentine political spectrum.[14]

The backdrop for this whole panorama of politics has been continuing economic crisis. Economic conditions have aggravated the political situation continuously and have, in turn, been fostered by the failure to evolve a national political consensus. The administrations that followed Perón inherited serious economic problems: a large foreign debt, an almost empty treasury, and an acutely unfavorable balance of trade. Agricultural and livestock production had declined, and the nation faced serious problems in the development of industry. During the ten years of Perón's rule, the population increased by three million, or 15 per cent, while per capita productivity had increased by only 3.5 per cent.[15]

There were good reasons for the decline in the export earnings of agriculture and livestock during Perón's regime. First, landowners, lacking in incentives, failed to apply modern techniques to raise production and to increase surpluses for export. By using export profits to finance his industrial program, Perón had discouraged improvements in agriculture and livestock. In addition, the terms of Argentine trade had declined since 1950, creating an adverse balance and pointing up the vulnerability of the agrarian-based economy. And also, the growth in population and the rise of urban labor's standard of living had led to

---

[13] Keith Botsford, "Paralysis in Argentina," *New Leader*, October 15, 1962, p. 16.
[14] Ranis, "Peronismo without Perón," pp. 117, 123.
[15] Raúl Prebisch, *La situación económica del país*, pp. 5–6.

an increase in the domestic consumption of products like meat, and thereby reduced the amounts available for export. The value of Argentine exports, in million United States dollars, sank from 1,613 in 1947 to 929 in 1955. Foreign exchange reserves declined from about $1,700 million in 1946, to $457 million in December, 1955.[16]

Besides this decline in export earnings, there were other obstacles to industrialization. From the standpoint of resources, power, and transport facilities, Argentina was not well-equipped for industrialization. She lacked iron, coal, strategic metals, and the available petroleum. Sources of hydroelectric power were far from the industrial cities. Although Argentina had ample petroleum reserves, in the years following the downfall of Perón, she still imported 60 per cent of her requirements at a cost of $250 to $300 million per year. With regard to transport facilities, the capital assets of the costly railroads, purchased from the British in 1948, had depreciated nearly to the point of being worthless. The trains were moving scraps of metal and wood that barely managed to handle shipments of agricultural and industrial produce. Argentina's highways had also fallen into serious disrepair.

The decline of exchange-earning exports and the inability of industry to replace basic import requirements resulted in severe economic difficulties. The peso declined, inflation grew and the cost of living soared. Using the depression year, 1953, as 100, the cost of living rose to 124 in December, 1955, to 275 in December, 1958, and to 482 in June, 1959.[17] Economic crisis and continuing inflation form the backdrop to the political disturbances in Argentina down to this day.

The architect of Argentina's post-Perón economic policies was Raúl Prebisch, an Argentine economist who served as the executive secretary of the United Nations Economic Commission for Latin America (ECLA). First hired by Lonardi and retained by Aramburu, Prebisch prescribed the bitter pill of austerity as the remedy for Argentina's economic woes. His recommendations for recovery included such measures as the removal of price and exchange controls, the return to private ownership of many state enterprises, the reduction of the swollen bureaucracy, and the affiliation of the nation with the World Bank and

16 George Pendle, *Argentina*, pp. 146–147.
17 *Ibid.*, p. 148.

the International Monetary Fund. He also proposed that foreign capital should again be welcomed into Argentina. Above all a sound currency should be established, a necessary adjunct being a realistic devaluation of the peso in international exchange. Moreover, inflation should be curbed by granting wage increases only to the lowest paid workers, and these small increases should derive from increased profits rather than from the consumer. The cycle of inflation, wage hikes, and then more inflation should be resisted.[18]

Political obstacles prevented Aramburu from the consistent and strict application of the Prebisch proposals. Aramburu devalued the peso, agricultural exports increased, and foreign investment grew. But the name Prebisch became anathema to Peronist labor. They called violent strikes against the imposition of economic austerity and the Aramburu administration was forced to grant large wage increases to labor. The failure to hold the line on wage hikes kept the inflationary cycle in continuous motion.

In spite of his fiery campaign in 1957 for economic nationalism, Arturo Frondizi, once installed in the presidency, embarked upon a neo–liberal nationalist economic program. This included the establishment of the free convertibility of the peso with the United States dollar; the acceptance of hundreds of million dollars in loans from the International Monetary Fund, the United States, and other foreign governments; and the active encouragement of foreign investment in Argentina, a trend climaxed by multi-million-dollar contracts with foreign petroleum companies. Beginning in January, 1959, Frondizi also attempted to institute his own austerity program. In an attempt to increase productivity, he freed the oligarchy and industrialists from many government restrictions. Feather-bedding was reduced in state-owned enterprises. An attempt was made to resist wage increases. All of these measures were adopted on the assumption that orthodox methods would increase productivity and capital accumulation, which, in turn would lead to an economic revival capable of healing the social and political fissures in Argentina.

Like Aramburu, Frondizi failed in his unpopular attempt to pull

---

[18] See Prebisch's speech to the military in his *La situación económica del país*.

Argentina out of the economic doldrums. The economy continued to slide into deep depression. As was expected, the workers' share of national income decreased, and this intensified social and political unrest. The petroleum policy did reduce the quantity of oil imports from $250 million in 1957 to $40 million in 1963, but it aroused nationalistic opposition in nearly all quarters. Inflation pressed on relentlessly as the cost of living rose by 323 per cent between 1958 and 1962. And despite the devaluation of the peso, agricultural export earnings dropped in the period from 1960 to 1962. This was a severe blow to the Frondizi administration since it had gambled on that sector for economic recovery. Significantly, the gross domestic product of Argentina was 10 per cent less in 1962 than it had been in 1948, one of Perón's best years. By the close of 1962, the public foreign debt had mounted to $2.7 billion, while the private foreign debt was $800 million. This left Argentina with a debt service for the remainder of this decade of between $300 million and $500 million per year.[19]

Under Illía (1964–1966) economic conditions in Argentina continued generally to deteriorate, although there were some improvements. In 1962 the cost of living increased by 28 per cent; in 1963, 24 per cent; in 1964, 22 per cent, and it continued to soar in 1965. The rate of unemployment was 8 per cent. The acreage devoted to agricultural produce continued to be smaller than it had been twenty years previous. However, by the end of 1965 the gross national product had expanded by 7.8 per cent while per capita income had risen by 6 per cent. Argentina also began to roll up trade surpluses. But the upsurge of 1965–1966 lifted the economy only to where it had been in 1961. Furthermore, the upsurge, which reflected pent-up demands after a sharp recession in 1962–1963, was marred by continued inflation. While industrial output rose by 11 per cent in 1965, production costs shot up by 30 per cent. The budget deficit was so staggering that the Illía government kept "solvent" by the continuous printing of more money; the money supply increased by 39 per cent in 1964 and 26 per cent in 1965.[20]

[19] Thomas F. McGann's *Argentina: The Divided Land*, pp. 62–65, gives an excellent account of postrevolutionary economic developments.

[20] *U.S. News & World Report*, July 11, 1966, p. 59.

Illía's failure to curb inflation alienated the Argentine business community, and thus the military. Despite its professed goal of holding wage increases to 15 per cent during 1966, the Illía regime failed, and businessmen were angered by the wide gap between Illía's promises and his performance. The economic failures of the regime were important factors in precipitating the military coup that brought Onganía to power.

8. Lonardi: Neither Victors nor Vanquished

After Perón was overthrown there was the important
question of who would wield political power. Despite
the fact that the navy had played the key role in the Liberating Revolution, that institution acceded to the traditional army-navy formula in
military power arrangements. To the army, as the most powerful
branch of the military establishment, would go the office of provisional
president, and to the navy would go the post of vice-president. Although there were many army candidates, the presidency went to the
Catholic nationalist General Lonardi, inspirer, if not recognized leader,
of the Liberating Revolution. Aside from Lonardi's key role in the
revolution, his emergence to the provisional presidency was determined
by the fact that, as leader of the conspiracy of 1951, he had been
among the first army officers to break openly with Perón.[1] The vice-
presidency went to Rear Admiral Isaac Rojas, commander of naval
forces during the Liberating Revolution. This was second place, but
did not mean that the liberal nationalist navy, having tasted real power,
was about to relinquish its newly won influence.

[1] *Ciclo de mesas redondas*, pp. 121–122.

For Lonardi, the provisional presidency was to prove a tragic climax to a long career as army officer and anti-Peronist conspirator. Born in Buenos Aires on September 15, 1896, he was the son of an Italian immigrant who rose from music teaching to the post of band leader for the Argentine army. After graduating from the Colegio Militar in 1916, as second man in his class, Lonardi became an artillery lieutenant and began the long and arduous climb up the military ladder of a peacetime army. Lonardi was the immigrant's boy who socially "made good"; the army proved the vehicle of social mobility. In 1924, while on maneuvers in the province of Córdoba, Lonardi met and married Señorita Mercedes Villada Achával, the daughter of a prominent Cordobese family. Lonardi's father-in-law was Clemente Villada Achával, who was to become identified with Catholic nationalism in Córdoba, the stronghold of that movement. From the very outset of his provisional presidency these associations made Lonardi suspect in the eyes of liberal nationalist and masonic officers. After teaching briefly at the Colegio Militar, Lonardi served as professor in the Superior Technical School and the Superior War College. He later became a general staff officer and a chief of an anti-aircraft unit. In 1938 he was sent to Chile as a military attaché, in the wake of a scandal involving espionage activities by his predecessor, one Major Juan Perón. From 1942 to 1948, Lonardi represented his nation in Washington on the Inter-American Defense Board. Upon his return, he was named commander of the important army garrison in Rosario. There, with other officers, he was among the first to plot against the Perón regime in the conspiracy that failed when General Menéndez chose to move prematurely against the dictatorship. Deeply implicated as a leader of the conspiracy, Lonardi resigned from the army. He moved to Buenos Aires, and there he continued to conspire against Perón. For such activity, he was imprisoned for almost a year. He was released by Perón in December, 1953, having been deemed harmless. But in 1955 he proved to be the man of the hour in sparking the Liberating Revolution.[2]

As provisional president, Lonardi adopted the slogan Neither

[2] Tad Szulc, "The Quiet Man Who Overthrew Perón," *New York Times Magazine*, October 23, 1958, pp. 17, 25.

Victors nor Vanquished. His regime, admittedly a caretaker government, was to be devoted to national reconciliation. Peronism was to be decapitated, but not uprooted. Its vigorous remnants, purified at the top, were to be used as instruments of the regime. The two strongest Peronist forces—the army and the CGT—were to be treated with utmost caution. In the army, nearly all of whose officers were tinged by Peronism, only those military men who had actively supported the dictator down to the very end were to be purged. Thus, in the early days of the regime twenty generals were arrested and, shortly thereafter, forty-three generals and ten admirals were forced into retirement.[3] The higher ranks were shaken up, but no effort was made to dig below the surface. With regard to labor, Lonardi sought the support of Peronist leaders of CGT.[4] Much of the dismay of democratic union leaders, he cooperated with the Peronist leaders of CGT.[5]

Lonardi's policy of national reconciliation was, however, shattered by power struggles within the provisional government and within the military. The explosive issue of Peronism, and Lonardi's softness toward it, came to the foreground and opened deep divisions. The uneasy, liberal nationalist–Catholic nationalist alliance that had executed the Liberating Revolution broke down.

To Lonardi's credit, he approached the presidency with an outlook that transcended his Catholic nationalist antecedents and affiliations. True, the Catholic nationalists who were close to him, Mario Amadeo and Clemente Villada Achával, backed the policy of national reconciliation and they were undoubtedly influential in the government. But Lonardi himself sincerely believed that the nation needed a healing period of national reconciliation, and that pressing the issue of Peronism would be opening a Pandora's box of woes for Argentina. Peronism, even though corrupt and authoritarian, had won real social gains for the workers, and these had to be respected. In the army Peronism was only a matter of degree, for nearly all officers had identified them-

---

[3] Alejandro Magnet, *Nuestros vecinos argentinos*, pp. 248–249.

[4] Bonifacio del Carril, *Crónica interna de la revolución libertadora*, p. 128.

[5] Francisco Peréz Leiros, Secretary General of Unión Obreros y Empleados Municipales, to Robert Alexander in personal interview, Buenos Aires, May 19, 1956. Used by permission of Professor Alexander.

selves with the dictatorship at one time or another. Yet, if Lonardi attempted to transcend partisan politics, his policy was doomed by the political necessities of a caretaker government. As provisional president, he was obligated to give representation to all the divergent anti-Peronist forces in postrevolutionary Argentina. These forces brought him down.[6]

One important force in the Lonardi provisional regime was Catholic nationalist in orientation. It emanated from the presidential secretariat, under the control of Villada Achával and Amadeo. These men believed that the Liberating Revolution had been fought to correct the errors and excesses of Peronism, not to dismantle the Peronist structure. They and Lonardi agreed on national reconcilation and not pressing the issue of Peronism.

The second force had its power base in the Ministry of the Interior and represented the views of the minority democratic parties (Socialist, Progressive Democrat, and Conservative). Having been scorned by Perón as politically inept and weak, these politicians wanted a regime that would be tough on Peronism and would favor them politically. The most influential figure in the Ministry of the Interior was Eduardo Busso, a liberal Conservative.

The third force, based in the Ministry of the Navy, was largely controlled by Captain Arturo H. Rial, the undersecretary. Rial was responsive to Américo Ghioldi's Socialist group and to Miguel Zavala Ortiz's Radical group. Both of these opposed the Lonardi regime and wanted to reorient Argentine government toward a tough anti-Peronist policy.

The fourth force was entrenched in the presidential military staff, and was comprised of the revolutionaries of 1951. Having suffered imprisonment, torture, and exile at the hands of the dictatorship, this faction was bent on a vengeful policy toward Peronism. Led by Colonel Bernardino Labayru, the faction of 1951 was to turn on its former leader, General Lonardi, and to play a key role in his ouster. Peronism, they argued, must be rooted out of the national body politic.

The fifth force might have acted as a counterweight to the faction

[6] The postrevolutionary political divisions are described in detail in Carril, *Crónica interna de la revolución libertadora*, especially pp. 152–153, 157–158.

of 1951. It was based in the Ministry of War under General Bengoa. Long identified with the Perón regime before he turned to conspiracy, Bengoa had many friends in the army who were Peronists. He was not disposed to press the issue of Peronism, for he realized what difficulties were involved. Bengoa was a loyal servant of Lonardi and his policies.

The largest sector of the army officer-corps shared Bengoa's views, that is, most officers were willing to fraternize with the Peronists, and certainly had no wish to persecute them. They were known as neutrals. However, in addition to this majority there were roughly three other sectors of opinion in the army in 1955. One sector, a decided minority of about 10 per cent, was made up of diehard Peronists. A second second sector consisted of those officers who had executed the Liberating Revolution and who were therefore anti-Peronist in outlook, although this did not mean that they were desirous of large-scale purges against the followers of the ex-dictator. In the third and most important sector were the militant and numerous members of the faction of 1951, those who had suffered by virtue of their participation in the Menéndez, Lonardi, and Suárez conspiracies. The faction of 1951 was also supported by junior officers seeking to move into the higher echelons of the army hierarchy as it was purged of Peronists.[7]

The faction of 1951 and the junior army officers found allies within the liberal nationalist navy, which, having lived through its first successful revolutionary experience, was determined to flex its new muscles against Peronism. These three groups united behind the leadership of General Aramburu, the liberal nationalist who was serving as chief of staff of the army. This alliance forced the resignation of Minister of War Bengoa and thereby struck a blow at the neutral position. The alliance considered Lonardi too soft on Peronism and subject to the influence of Catholic nationalism. When it became known that he was suffering from cancer, they successfully forced his resignation from the presidency and backed Aramburu as his successor. On November 13, 1955, Aramburu became provisional president, inaugurating a new era in Argentina's politico-military history.[8]

[7] Magnet, *Nuestros vecinos argentinos*, p. 248.
[8] Carril, *Crónica interna de la revolución libertadora*, pp. 159, 167–170, 174–175.

Lonardi was embittered by his ouster. He denounced the leaders of the faction of 1951, Colonels Bonnecarrere, Labayru, and Lanusse, all of whom had once been his friends and collaborators.[9] To the press, Lonardi declared: "I wish to make it known through you that it is not true that I have presented my resignation, not [true] that my health had anything to do with my retirement from Government House. This act has been produced exclusively by the decision of a sector of the armed forces."[10]

Yet, Lonardi was mortally ill and his removal anticipated fate by only a few weeks. Embittered though he was at the end, Lonardi left an enduring mark upon Argentina. His policy of national conciliation, the cardinal principle of his regime, was destined to be revived by President Arturo Frondizi in 1958. In fact, Frondizi, the Radical nationalist, would one day sing the praises of the Catholic nationalist General Lonardi, thus dramatizing their shared objective.[11] And there is evidence that even if Lonardi had survived, national reconciliation would have been difficult to achieve. Lonardi was the first to seek the economic advice of Raúl Prebisch, who prescribed economic austerity, free enterprise and a welcome to foreign investors as steps the nation must take to recover from Peronist economic blunders and corruption. The fact that Frondizi tried to combine reconciliation with such economic measures was a key reason for the weakening of his regime. Hence, the same frustrations might have resulted from similar efforts by the Lonardi regime.

[9] *Ibid.*, p. 179.

[10] *Buenos Aires Herald*, November 14, 1955, p. 1.

[11] In Félix Luna, *Diálogos con Frondizi*, p. 82, Frondizi, while denouncing the officers who overthrew General Lonardi, refers to him as that "blameless man of extraordinary purity."

9. Aramburu and the Liberal Nationalist Restoration, 1955-1958

After Lonardi's ouster, Argentina was ruled for the next two and a half years by a five-man military junta. True to the traditional army-navy formula, it was headed by General Aramburu, as provisional president, and Admiral Rojas, retained as vice-president. The other three members were the chiefs of the army, navy, and air force. Politicians were given a voice through places in the National Consultative Council, but it served only in an advisory capacity. Real power was vested in Aramburu and the junta, which ruled the nation by decree. Congress remained dissolved and the reconstituted Supreme Court offered no opposition to the will of the military men who ruled the nation.

Aramburu was a virtual unknown to the nation. However, amidst an unspectacular record of army promotions, two outstanding characteristics of his career could be noted at the outset. First, Aramburu was one of the few generals untainted by graft during his service under Perón, indicative of a fundamental personal honesty that even his worst enemies have never denied.[1] Second, although the new provisional president had served the dictator with apparent loyalty for many years —rising to the rank of brigadier general in December, 1951, and major general in December, 1954,—he was associated with those officers in whom the bitter experience with Peronism had produced a revulsion. He was therefore in favor of restoring democracy to Argentina, and the armed forces to their nonpolitical status.[2] In the record of Aramburu was written the fundamental dilemma of the military man in confronting Peronism: how to obey elected civilian authority and safeguard one's career, while a majoritarian dictatorship was eroding the democratic traditions of Argentina. Although distrustful of perpetual military conspirators, Aramburu had, albeit belatedly, turned toward revolution in the twilight years of Perón's dictatorship.

In terms of ideology, the Aramburu regime represented a revival of the liberal nationalist and masonic traditions within the armed forces. His regime was to end the liberal nationalist–integral nationalist (Catholic nationalist and Peronist) dichotomy within the military establishment, but it would give birth to new divisions that plague the armed forces to this day. In the political sphere, Aramburu's objectives were to restore the forms and liberties of republican democracy, transfer authority to the civilians, and remove the armed forces from politics. Economically, his views represented a liberal nationalist fusion of military emotions and the harsh demands of the economy, as outlined by Prebisch. Prebisch's call for the freer economy and increased foreign investment fitted well the new thinking on liberty within the purged armed forces. A decade of experience with Peronist statism had disgusted the officers of the armed forces. They now preferred economic individualism, laissez faire, and the free economy, to totalitarian statism. In foreign policy, they did not agree with integral nationalist hostility toward the United States and Great Britain, and true to liberal nationalist tradition, sought instead to draw closer to the western powers. Their new political values were supported by the old oligarchy, rich businessmen, and sectors of the upper middle class.

Aramburu's policies were, however, shaped more by the pressures of

[1] *New York Times*, January 26, 1957, p. 12.
[2] Arthur P. Whitaker, *Argentina*, p. 155.

historical forces than by any fixed ideology. In addition to attempting to fulfill his political aims, his regime had to struggle with two other demanding situations. First, the need to de-Peronize Argentina and still survive against the lusty remnants of dictatorship. Second, the necessity of satisfying those forces that had brought him to power; that is, the faction of 1951, the junior army officers, the navy, and the democratic politicians.

The first stage of Aramburu's rule combined a struggle for survival with one for intense de-Peronization. No sooner had he come to power, than he was confronted with a general strike by the CGT. This first challenge to his regime was met decisively by full use of the armed forces and the police. Aramburu stopped the strikers' pay, arrested hundreds of labor leaders and kept many of them in jail for the next six months. The strike was weakened by the fact that the non-Peronist unions of the CGT, the independents, numbering about one-third of the total—refused to support it. Once having broken the strike, Aramburu "intervened" the CGT and its member unions, placing them under government administrators. Significantly, he chose a naval captain as intervenor of CGT, evidence of his abiding faith in that branch.

Once in control of the labor sector, Aramburu moved towards the de-Peronization of the other political forces, including the military. Some three hundred business firms, both individual and corporate, were placed under interventors. Both Peronist parties, male and female, were outlawed. Peronists were barred from public office and participation in political activities. Evidences of corruption were sought in Peronist bank accounts and other records.[3]

The process of de-Peronization was also extended to the armed forces, with Aramburu greatly intensifying the process begun by Lonardi. Like de-Peronization in other areas, it was spurred in the armed forces by the faction of 1951, the junior army officers, and the liberal nationalist navy. These officers were, at first, known as the Gorillas, or vigilantes of the revolution, and they were determined to cleanse the nation of Peronism. Mingling anti-Peronist revulsion with professional opportunism, they demanded and got from Aramburu large-

[3] *Ibid.*, pp. 154–155.

scale purges of the senior officers, of scores of officers of lower rank, and of many of the Peronist noncoms. When the Gorillas became dissatisfied with General Alberto Lagos, the commander in chief who was considered too lenient on Peronism, they successfully moved for his ouster in May, 1956. But soon they also grew dissatisfied with his successor, General Francisco Zerda, and pressed insatiably for more purges. By June, 1956, these purges had reduced the number of generals to a quarter of the required figure, the number of colonels had been cut down from 168 to 73, and of lieutenant colonels from 320 to 198.[4] Disaffection and fear spread through the army. Opponents of the Aramburu regime were also embittered by the fact that the navy had played a key role in army purges, a development that aroused both professional and social hostilities.[5]

On June 9 and 10, 1956, Catholic nationalists and Peronists in the army moved against the Aramburu regime. Led by two purged Peronist officers, General Raúl Tanco and General Juan José Valle, the rebels struck while Aramburu was on an official visit to Rosario. The poorly coordinated uprising erupted in the city of Buenos Aires, where Peronist noncoms and civilians seized an arsenal, and spread to La Plata, capital of Buenos Aires province, and to Santa Rosa, capital of the southcentral province of La Pampa. The rebels issued proclamations calling for a government of recuperation built on the same social doctrines as those of the Perón regime. The proclamations also demanded immediate amnesty for all political and trade-union prisoners, the restoration of trade unions to the power they wielded under Perón, and general elections within 180 days.[6]

Acting in the absence of President Aramburu, Vice-President Rojas quickly suppressed the revolt through the use of air power. Order was restored in the city of Buenos Aires, and rebel positions in La Plata and Santa Rosa were bombarded. Upon his arrival to Buenos Aires, Aramburu declared martial law. This decree made prisoners liable under

---

[4] *The Economist*, June 16, 1956, p. 1079.
[5] Carlos Cossio, *La política como conciencia: Meditación sobre la Argentina de 1955*, pp. 132–133.
[6] *New York Times*, June 11, 1956, pp. 1, 3.

military law to sentences of death by firing squads.[7] In a move unprecedented in all Argentine politico-military history, President Aramburu had twenty-seven of the rebel leaders court-martialed and shot. This move violated the tacit rules of the politico-military game, for not even Perón had dared to order the execution of military men. But it had the desired effect. Never again was Aramburu's hold over the government seriously challenged.[8]

Yet Aramburu was not done with unprecedented acts. In November, 1956, he forced the retirement of eighteen generals, nearly all those in active service. Included in the group was General Francisco Zerda, commander in chief of the army. The audacious move not only opened the upper ranks of the army to the faction of 1951 and other Gorillas, but it removed all resistance to Aramburu's plans to restore civilian rule.[9] Furthermore, Aramburu had served notice, once and for all, that he would brook neither palace intrigues nor active opposition within the armed forces. In February, 1957, Rear Admiral (formerly Captain) Arturo Rial was separated from the government. One month later Commodore Ricardo Krause, leader of the air force in the Liberating Revolution, was forced into retirement.[10]

Having consolidated his hold over both the government and the military, Aramburu announced his Political Plan of the Liberating Revolution. It called for general elections by the end of 1957, an event later postponed until February 23, 1958, owing to a constitutional convention. The plan also set May 1, 1958, as the date for the transference of power to civilian authorities.

The Political Plan of the Liberating Revolution created a new dichotomy within the armed forces. Gone was the liberal nationalist–integral nationalist dichotomy—it had been largely resolved by massive purges. But in 1957, while secret lodges proliferated within the armed forces, three currents of opinion emerged in response to the plan. First, *que-*

---

[7] *Ibid.*, June 12, 1956, p. 12.

[8] Whitaker, *Argentina*, pp. 154–155.

[9] Bonifacio del Carril, *Crónica interna de la revolución libertadora*, pp. 185–186.

[10] Mariano Montemayor, "Siete días de política," *Azul y Blanco*, April 3, 1957, pp. 1, 4.

dantismo, or the belief in delaying presidential elections to permit the complete extirpation of Peronism from the body politic. Second, *continuismo*, or support of the manipulation of elections in order to guarantee the transference of power to civilian groups acceptable to military leaders. Third, Fair Play, or insistence on honest elections as scheduled by the government and the transference of power to any legal organization that won. This division contained the seeds of a dichotomy that has persisted in the armed forces down to the present.[11] The first two sectors rallied around Admiral Rojas and were the forerunners of the later coalitions known first as the Gorillas, then as the Interventionists, and today as the *colorados*. These coalitions favored a hard-line approach to Peronism, and some of their members supported the establishment of military dictatorship to destroy all remnants of Peronism in Argentina. The Fair Play sector, led by General Aramburu, later evolved into the coalition known first as the Legalists, and today as the *azules*. They were to become the coalition in the military that supported civilian rule, constitutionality, and the gradual integration of the Peronists into the political system.

Despite the revival of opposition within the armed forces, Aramburu was determined to execute his political plan. This decision, however, involved the larger question of to whom political power was to be transferred. Aramburu also had the problem of satisfying all of the civilian political forces that had backed his rise to power. These forces —the democratic parties—were divided into those parties with few votes and those with many. The minority democratic parties (Conservative, Progressive Democrat, and Socialist) favored a constitutional convention with the purpose of adopting proportional representation. This reform would translate their few votes into actual power. On the other hand, the Radicals, who had substantial backing, opposed proportional representation and favored the retention of the incomplete list used under the Sáenz Peña Law. This list gave control of the government to the two parties with the most votes.[12]

---

[11] James W. Rowe, *Argentina's Restless Military*, pp. 11–12.
[12] Carril, *Crónica interna de la revolución libertadora*, pp. 186–187.

The permanent split of the Radical party into two separate organizations in 1957—the Intransigents and the Popular Radicals—complicated the situation. As has been stated, the position of the moderate Popular Radicals (UCRP) equated intransigent trade unionism with Peronist fanaticism. Hence, the views of the Popular Radicals proved congenial to the military regime and this shaped Aramburu's response to the political situation. He first chose to satisfy the minority political parties by calling a constitutional convention in 1957, but later, behind the scenes, supported the succession to power of Balbín and the Popular Radicals.[13]

However, when the convention was assembled in July, 1957, it dealt a disastrous blow to the plans of Aramburu and the military. As expected, both Radical organizations withdrew from the convention after bitter debate, and the minority parties remained to trade windy oratory. More important, the convention provided an electoral preview that established Perón as the arbiter of the presidential elections of 1958. Roughly one-fourth of the 8.7 million votes went to the minority parties. The left-wing Intransigents polled 1.8 million and the Popular Radicals drew 2.1 million votes. The blank votes of the Peronists totaled 2.1 million, or a crucial one-fourth which held the balance of power.[14] The Popular Radicals were by then identified with the Aramburu government and its policies, and could never hope to gain Peronist support. Frondizi's Intransigents, on the other hand, could gain such support only at the cost of a deal with the fallen dictator.[15]

If Frondizi needed Perón at the time, Perón also needed Frondizi. One month before the Argentine presidential elections of February, 1958, the dictator Marcos Pérez Jímenez was overthrown in Venezuela and Perón was forced to seek refuge in the Dominican Republic. For Perón's less affluent political lieutenants, amnesty and a return to Argentina now became a pressing necessity. This was one major concession made by Frondizi to Perón in a deal that assured victory for the Intransigent Radicals in 1958. Frondizi also promised that along with a general amnesty and the return of confiscated property, the Peronist

---

[13] *Ibid.*, pp. 189–190.
[14] George Pendle, *Argentina*, pp. 143–144.
[15] Carril, *Crónica interna de la revolución libertadora*, pp. 190–193.

party would be legalized and granted the right to run candidates in future elections.[16]

Less than three years after his overthrow, Perón was again a power to reckon with in Argentine politics. Furthermore, his hold over the *descamisados* had been strengthened by Aramburu's de-Peronization campaigns and economic policies. The *descamisados* resented the fact that Aramburu's advisers on economic matters included representatives of business but not of labor. They were incensed by the whole Prebisch approach to economic issues, with its emphasis on private enterprise, foreign investments, and economic austerity. The Prebisch program not only aroused their fiery nationalism, but struck at their wage-earning capacity. Wage raises instituted in late 1955 were supposed to compensate the workers for the price hikes that resulted from the devaluation of the peso, but the workers complained that they failed to do so and that wage raises lagged considerably behind soaring prices. As the workers' grievances mounted, they seemed to confirm a warning constantly repeated by Perón during his dictatorship. He had warned that his overthrow would mean a restoration of the old alliance between the liberal nationalist oligarchy and foreign economic interests, with a consequent loss to the workers of past social gains.

The revival of Peronist power loomed as a threat to those military men who had staked their positions and even their necks on campaigns against Perón's followers. This explains why Aramburu's hopes for removing the military from politics were to prove illusory. Although he had destroyed Catholic nationalist–Peronist power in the military, the Gorillas were dissatisfied. Rallying around Admiral Rojas, these officers complained that even Aramburu had been too easy on the Peronists. Now, in 1958, they were about to witness an alliance of the Radical Intransigents with the hated Peronists. They were, to say the least, enraged by this development.

The presidential campaign was a preview of Frondizi's political tactics. Running on a program of flaming Radical nationalism, he denounced the Prebisch program and the encroachment of foreign economic interests. Playing to the nationalist sentiment of the Argentine

---

[16] Juan de Onís, "Argentina Tested by Economic Realities," *Foreign Policy Bulletin*, July 15, 1959, p. 162.

people, he set forth a view of the future Argentina as a nation with great industries based on fuel and energy from state monopolies free of foreign influence. Having gained Peronist support through a deal with the exiled dictator, Frondizi and the Radical Intransigents won the election by a landslide, obtaining 4.1 million votes to 2.6 million polled by the Popular Radicals.[17]

The Gorillas, infuriated by Frondizi's catering to the Peronists, pleaded with Aramburu to refuse to turn the reins of government over to the Intransigents. But Aramburu, true to his promise and the liberal nationalist goal of civilian rule, permitted Frondizi to be inaugurated on May 1, 1958.[18] In his inaugural address, Frondizi declared that "the revolutionary period has terminated. Henceforth the armed forces do not decide. Now the representatives of the people decide."[19] Promising them full satisfaction of the material needs of the armed forces, Frondizi requested that officers return to their barracks.

This request went unheeded, for in the eyes of the Gorillas Frondizi's acceptance of Peronist support was a cardinal sin never to be forgiven. According to Frondizi himself, the Gorillas began plotting against him on the night of April 30, 1958, only hours before he took office. After listening to Frondizi's inaugural address, Aramburu and Rojas departed with a haste meant to remind the president that he ruled under the sufferance of the military. As early as May 18, Gorilla officers and their political allies met at the Naval Club and agreed that the Frondizi government should be closely scrutinized and blocked from taking any step unacceptable to the military.[20] It was clear that stormy days lay ahead.

---

[17] Pendle, *Argentina*, p. 144.

[18] Carril, *Crónica interna de la revolución libertadora*, p. 196.

[19] Ministerio del Interior, *Mensaje de pacificación y desarollo nacional, leido ante la asamblea legislativa por el presidente de la nación Dr. Arturo Frondizi al inaugurar su período constitucional el 1° de mayo de 1958*, pp. 52–53.

[20] Rowe, *Argentina's Restless Military*, p. 12.

10. Frondizi: The Florentine on a Tightrope, 1958-1962

Arturo Frondizi was an immigrant's son, a doctor of law, and a student of economics. He had risen to the leadership of the Intransigent wing of the Radical party from being head of a leftist populist-nationalist faction that was comprised largely of younger politicians. During the Perón regime, Frondizi and his followers were steadfast opponents of the dictator. Their opposition was coupled with a bid for labor support and so they made heated assaults on the "corrupt alliance" between the liberal nationalist oligarchy and the foreign economic imperialists. When in 1955 Perón signed a contract with Standard Oil for the exploitation of Patagonian reserves, Frondizi led a savage campaign against the move. After Perón was overthrown, Frondizi and his backers made an all-out effort to win the Peronist bloc of votes by pledging themselves to the protection of the workers' social gains against a restoration of rule by the oligarchy and foreign imperialism. He continued to stress labor's rights and economic nationalism in his driving campaign for the presidency and, as has already been related, this and his deal with Perón secured for him the Peronist support needed to win the 1958 election.

Once in office, however, Frondizi acted in a manner diametrically opposed to his former political positions and campaign promises. Confronted by economic crisis, he embarked upon neoliberal policies. Branded as a betrayal, these policies alienated the Peronists, melted Frondizi's popular support, and left him dependent upon his political wiles to survive pressures from the military. For his Machiavellian maneuvers, Frondizi was named the Florentine. During four stormy years this fox of a politician survived no less than thirty-four politico-military crises. Then, in March, 1962, the lions of the military, aroused by a Peronist resurgence, clawed the fragile tightrope upon which he was balanced so precariously and Frondizi came tumbling down. In the end, few of his political enemies were willing to defend civilian rule as represented by Frondizi, a sad testimony to the wide social fissures his regime had engendered. Yet Frondizi was no mere political opportunist, bent on maintaining power at all costs. After his four years in office, a pattern had emerged that may explain his political behavior.

Frondizi personified the almost mystical belief Intransigents shared in the righteousness of their cause. As part of this simplistic mystique, Frondizi seems to have believed that he had hit upon the one and only solution to all of Argentina's ills. His solution lay in the pursuit, at all costs, of economic revival. He believed that his unpopular economic policies would lead to an economic resurgence that would heal the deep social splits and answer his outraged opposition in Argentina. Like many other leftist intellectuals in Latin America, Frondizi had come to believe that democracy, social welfare, and national unity depended upon *prior* economic development. Hence, long-range political ideals and campaign promises must be subordinated to immediate economic requirements.[1] This narrow view ignored the important fact that it was the absence of political consensus, a condition aggravated by Frondizi's maneuverings, that tended to impede economic reconstruction.

If Argentina had entered the road to economic recovery, Frondizi and the Intransigents would have undoubtedly returned to economic nationalism. But, meanwhile, political honesty and principles must be

[1] Kalman H. Silvert, *Economics, Democracy, and Honesty: An Assessment of the Frondizi Regime*, p. 7.

sacrificed at the altar of economic revival. In line with such thinking, Frondizi, in July, 1958, began a series of contracts with foreign companies (mainly in the United States, but also European) for the exploitation of Argentine petroleum resources. The action recalled the last days of Perón, when, attempting to break the petroleum bottleneck, the dictator entered into a contract with Standard Oil of California, and thus contributed significantly to his downfall. Now, Frondizi, forsaking his campaign promises, was executing the same policy, carrying it out by what appeared to be illegal decrees. Frondizi argued that the terms of the contracts safeguarded national interests, and that they would serve the cause of national economic independence by converting Argentina from a heavy importer into an exporter of petroleum products. But all nationalists except the liberal school denounced the move as a sell-out cloaked in the banner of nationalism.

Frondizi took an even more controversial step in December, 1958. He entered into a stabilization agreement with the International Monetary Fund as a basis for long-range economic development plans involving commitments to free enterprise, foreign capital investment, and economic austerity. The aims of the far-reaching stabilization-and-development program were to combat inflation, to create financial stability through austerity, and to heighten productivity and so raise the standard of living. On January 1, 1959, most government subsidies and price controls were dropped, restrictions were placed on imports, and the government announced that all wage hikes would be linked to corresponding increases in productivity. Simultaneously, the Argentine peso was devalued. The first effect of this program was a tremendous increase in the price of foodstuffs.

Like the oil contracts, the stabilization-and-development program was in direct contradiction of Frondizi's campaign promises. For Peronist labor, this sudden dose of liberal nationalism from a leader elected by virtue of their support was especially repulsive. They were convinced, and rightly so, that they would be forced to bear the burdens of austerity. Hence, Frondizi's reversal on economic matters spelled disaster for his second major objective: the integration of the Peronists into the political system under the banner of the Radical Intransigents. In the early days of his administration, Frondizi had attempted to fulfill his part of the deal with Perón. After ordering a general wage increase of 60 per cent, he had granted amnesty to exiled and imprisoned Peronists, and even permitted some followers of the ex-dictator to regain posts in the labor unions and the judiciary. But his economic betrayal ruled out a restoration of the labor counterpoise to the armed forces, and meant that a potentially strong buffer between the government and the military had been dissolved.

Frondizi, however, never yielded in his efforts to promote integration. In selecting presidential advisers, he drew from a vast assortment of political shadings, ranging from noncommunist Marxists to neo-Peronists to anticommunist Catholics. Their one common denominator was populism, that is, a belief in the rapid integration of the Peronist masses into political life. What Frondizi hoped to accomplish by such diverse appointments is not clear. Perhaps he was attempting to maintain his links to the Peronist leadership in the hope that, in the wake of an economic resurgence, he would lead a popular movement against the military.[2] In any case, the appointments issue became the alleged grounds for continuous military intervention during the Frondizi years.

The alienation of the Peronist bloc and the decline of popular support determined Frondizi's third major policy. He had to search for new sources of power, to provide the political leverage necessary for survival. As early as September, 1958, a law was passed that gave degrees granted by Catholic and other private educational institutions equal standing with those granted by public institutions. For many Argentines, this was a violation of Argentina's long-established tradition of secular education, but for practicing Catholics, it came as a long-awaited step toward real educational freedom. Frondizi probably saw this as the addition of another power factor to his weakened alignment. Perhaps he hoped that the church, favored by the military and safely anticommunist, would lend a degree of respectability to his regime.

For further support, Frondizi reached outside the traditional Argentine power forces. As part of his effort to assume the mantle of world

[2] *Ibid.*, pp. 6, 11.

statesman, he sought the support of the United States, which was already committed to aiding his stabilization-and-development program. The bonds between Frondizi and the United States were strengthened as the threat of Fidelism loomed on the horizon. While the United States needed Argentine support to bolster its hemispheric policy, based too heavily on the smaller republics, Frondizi needed the United States as the sponsor of the economic showcase he hoped Argentina would become as a result of his policies. His major bargaining point with the United States would have been lost, however, if he had acceded to the demands of the Argentine military to sever relations with Castro's Cuba. Frondizi sought to play the role of mediator between the United States and Cuba, and soon after the Alliance for Progress was launched at Punta del Este, he granted an interview to Che Guevara. This interview incensed Argentine military leaders who successfully applied pressure for the severance of relations between Argentina and Cuba. Yet Frondizi's search for international recognition and aid had taken him to many far off places including the United States, Canada, India, Greece, and Japan. For a time he had succeeded in his efforts to play the statesman's role as he explained Latin America to these other countries and other countries to Latin America.[3]

Despite the quest for respectability and new sources of power, Frondizi remained a president ruling without effective popular support. The political scientist, K. H. Silvert, has explained with striking perception how the average Argentine citizen felt about Frondizi in 1960.

It was little more than a year after Frondizi had become the first freely elected civilian to take office since 1928, and democracy seemed a "fraud." Once an ardent anti-Peronist, Frondizi had attempted to turn over union leadership to Peronists. Once an anticlerical, Frondizi had guided a bill through Congress allowing the establishment of Catholic institutions of higher learning. Once an anti-imperialist, Frondizi had signed contracts with foreign companies which allowed them "to suck out the riches of the subsoil." Once an anti-Yankee, Frondizi took Argentina into the North American camp and paid tribute "to the raven-

---

3 Kalman H. Silvert, *The Annual Political Cycle in Argentina: A Jaundiced Retrospective*, p. 7.

ing Colossus of the North on its home grounds." Once a proponent of the welfare state, Frondizi had become the champion of free enterprise on the advice of the International Monetary Fund. Once a friend of the people, Frondizi's policies had caused rampant inflation. "Ay, Frondizi."[4]

Without popular support, Frondizi's greatest source of strength lay in the divisions within the enemy camp. In shrewd fashion, he pitted faction against faction, party against party, resolving individual crises but doing nothing to broaden the political consensus in Argentina.[5] Time must be bought for an economic revival and, after all, his enemies were already divided. On the right, squabbling conservatives were convinced that Frondizi was at heart a communist, but some were nevertheless attracted by his economic orthodoxy. On one day, Frondizi would court conservative opinion; on the next, he would lash out at the reactionary mossbacks. In the middle, the Popular Radicals, their thunder stolen by Frondizi's economic policies, moved toward an intense economic nationalism and called for the president's overthrow by the military. The splintered Socialists were torn between their allegiance to civilian rule and their hatred for Frondizi and his policies. On the left, frustrated and violent Peronists were confounded by the Florentine who preached integration, acted like a reactionary, and seemed forced by military pressures into harsh acts against labor. And, then, there was the military, divided, but still the most powerful of all of Frondizi's enemies.

Discontent with Frondizi had seethed within the armed forces from the early hours of the administration and, as has been shown, it was only reluctantly that the Gorillas allowed him to take over the reins of government. Yet amidst the many secret lodges in the armed forces after the downfall of Perón, there was one that had given its support to Frondizi. This secret lodge was known as the Green Dragons, and it was headed by Colonel Manuel Raimundes. The Green Dragons were sworn to the defense of civilian rule, the removal of the armed forces from politics, and the propagation in the army of social consciousness

---

[4] Silvert, *Economics, Democracy, and Honesty*, pp. 3–4.
[5] James W. Rowe, "The Argentine Elections, III: The Reluctant Coup," pp. 5–6.

toward the laboring masses. It had been organized from London, where Colonel Raimundes served as military attaché during the Aramburu regime. When Frondizi was installed in the presidency, Raimundes was named undersecretary of war, an office he used in attempts to win converts within the army to his cause.[6] Another Green Dragon, General Héctor Solanas Pacheco, was named minister of war by Frondizi.

Military protest against Frondizi's policies and appointments erupted during the first days of his administration. In July, 1958, Rear Admiral Arturo Rial, commander of the Río de la Plata naval region and president of the Naval Club, opened verbal fire upon the Frondizi administration for the appointment of Peronist judges and civil servants. His protest was backed by naval Captain Francisco Manrique, former chief of Aramburu's military staff. Once again, the issue was appointments and the infiltration of Peronist influence into political life. This same issue led to the resignation of Supreme Court Justice Alfredo Orgaz, who had been appointed by President Aramburu.[7]

Still enjoying popular support at that time, President Frondizi met this first crisis with decisiveness. With his backing, the naval minister, Admiral Adolfo Estévez, successfully disciplined Rial. Following this show of strength, Frondizi delivered a speech in which he declared that Peronism would never return to Argentina. He praised the armed forces for "interpreting the will of the Argentine people" in overthrowing Perón and in later restoring the government to the civilians, and he urged the armed forces to aid him in carrying forward a program of constitutionality, pacification, and national development. However, he reminded them that he was commander in chief and that he would exercise his authority "with maximum energy" in order to maintain "rigid principles of discipline and hierarchy" in the services.[8]

Two months later, rebellion in the air force tested the president's will on this very issue. In September, 1958, Frondizi restored Commodore Ricardo Krause to active duty. Krause had been forcibly retired

---

[6] Rogelio García Lupo, *La rebelión de los generales*, p. 62; Edwin Lieuwen, *Generals vs. Presidents: Neomilitarism in Latin America*, p. 13.
[7] *New York Times*, July 9, 1958, p. 5.
[8] *Ibid.*

during the Aramburu regime for having led a protest rebellion in favor of Fair Play. The reinstatement, ordered by the pro-Frondizi air minister, Commodore Roberto Huerta, resulted in a wave of protest climaxed by the refusal of air officers to allow Krause entry to his offices. Frondizi, after initially supporting his air minister, decided to accept his resignation and named Brigadier Ramón Abrahim in his place. Although confined to one branch, this crisis set an important precedent. The Frondizi administration had backed down, and had thereby sanctioned the insubordination of commanders against both military hierarchy and civilian authority. The administration attempted to salvage its dignity by calling the affair a "military crisis of nonpolitical and strictly institutional character."[9] But a precedent for military defiance of civilian authority had been set.

So long as Frondizi ruled with effective popular support, his regime could withstand many of the pressures of the military. However, when he announced in mid-1958 that he was embarking upon his neoliberal economic programs, the popular base began to dissolve. In November, 1958, and January, 1959, labor responded to his betrayal with a series of strikes. The extent to which these swept the nation indicated that Frondizi had lost Peronist support.[10] The armed forces could then impose their will upon the regime, since it was dependent upon them for the military force necessary to maintain order.

Thus it was that six months after the army had turned power over to the civilians, it returned to play a major role in government decisions. In November, 1958, it executed what one correspondent called "almost a bloodless coup," that removed from government nearly all of those Frondizi advisers who favored integration with the Peronists. One of those whose resignation the military demanded and got was Rogelio Frigerio, secretary of economic and social affairs and a leading proponent of integration. More than seven hundred Peronists, communists, and Catholic nationalists were brought into custody. The Peronist weekly *Norte* was seized by the police.[11]

[9] James W. Rowe, *Argentina's Restless Military*, p. 13.
[10] John J. Kennedy, "Accountable Government in Argentina," *Foreign Affairs* 37 (April, 1959): 457.
[11] *New York Times*, November 12, 1958, p. 1.

But even these moves were not enough for the Gorillas and Interventionists of the army, who were intensely suspicious of lingering Peronist influence in the government. In June, 1959, the Interventionists, led by Generals Raúl Poggi and Florencio Yornet, began another protest rebellion. Minister of War Solanas Pacheco retaliated with an order for their arrest. However, resistance to this step, led by retired General Arturo Ossorio Arana, spread like wildfire among the interior army garrisons. The Interventionists were especially powerful in the fourth army division in Córdoba, which had led the Liberating Revolution. Having mobilized their power, the Interventionists demanded the resignation of the Green Dragons, Solanas Pacheco and Raimundes. The resignation of Raimundes was received in mid-June, but the administration tried to counter with orders for the arrest of Ossorio Arana and other officers. These orders proved unenforceable, and on June 22 the entire Frondizi cabinet resigned. Frondizi's capitulation became complete when, on July 1, Minister of War Solanas Pacheco turned in his resignation. The Green Dragons had been routed by the Gorilla-Interventionists.[12]

Shortly thereafter, Frondizi suffered yet another serious setback in the military—a defeat that was to cost him the support of the minister of the navy, Admiral Adolfo Estévez, who had been considered the most pro-Frondizi of all of the military hierarchy. Anti-Frondizi agitation in the navy was led by retired Admirals Arturo Rial and Samuel Toranzo Calderón, both of whom had been leaders of the Liberating Revolution of 1955. Orders for their arrest brought a wave of mass resignations in the navy along with open insubordination. Again Frondizi capitulated, by accepting the resignation of Admiral Estévez. These two rebellions, erupting almost simultaneously, signaled the reestablishment of the 1955 anti-Peronist alliance between army garrisons in the interior and naval stations on the coast.[13]

Leadership of the Interventionist alliance fell to General Carlos Severo Toranzo Montero, commander in chief of the army. An ardent Gorilla, Toranzo Montero had for years been a stormy figure in Argen-

---

12 "Green Dragons and Gorillas," *The Economist*, September 26, 1959, p. 1032.
13 Rowe, *Argentina's Restless Military*, p. 14.

tine affairs. From the advent of Peronism in the 1940s, he had begun criticizing the army for its role in bringing the dictator to power. During the Perón regime, Toranzo Montero stayed at the bottom of the promotion list. In 1950, when he was only forty-eight years old, he retired embittered, as a lieutenant colonel. A year later, as conspiracy against Perón spread within the army, he was jailed. Released in 1953, he left his native Argentina for neighboring Uruguay, but when the Liberating Revolution erupted, Toranzo Montero joined the rebel forces in Córdoba. After victory was achieved, he was reincorporated into the army as a general.[14] Having suffered professional disgrace, imprisonment, and exile at the hands of the dictatorship, Toranzo Montero the Interventionist was prepared to stake all against a resurgence of Peronism.

In September, 1959, Toranzo Montero spearheaded an army rebellion against the Frondizi administration. Frondizi's new minister of war, General Elbio C. Anaya, was elderly, dignified, and politically neutral. When he attempted to punish Toranzo Montero's insubordination by having him relieved from duty on September 3, Toranzo Montero refused to retire, and proceeded to set up rebel headquarters at the army mechanical school, whence he rallied the Interventionists, including fifteen generals, to his support. As loyalist troops and tanks started moving from the Campo de Mayo garrison toward the city of Buenos Aires, the Interventionist fourth army division in Córdoba marshalled ten thousand troops and was also prepared to march. At this critical juncture, Frondizi again decided to "avoid bloodshed." In two days, Toranzo Montero was restored and Anaya resigned, his post going to General Rodolfo Larcher.[15]

Bolstered by his victory, Commander in Chief Toranzo Montero began to overreach himself. As the leader of the Interventionists, he proclaimed a doctrine of almost total military vigilance over civilian government, a political stance that could easily slip into a coup d'état. In line with this doctrine, he presented three demands to the Frondizi government in October, 1960: first, the removal of Minister of Economy

---

[14] *New York Times*, October 15, 1960, p. 8.
[15] Rowe, *Argentina's Restless Military*, p. 14.

Alvaro Alsogaray, who, though he had been installed by the army, was becoming too outspoken on military expenditures; second, the elimination of the lingering influence in the government of ex-Peronist Rogelio Frigerio, former minister of economy; and third, the replacement of several governors considered to be too tolerant of Peronism. Minister of War Larcher supported President Frondizi, who defended his regime in a radio address to the nation. In this address, Frondizi charged that a "minute sector" of the armed forces wanted to assume power, and, before the whole nation, he held the military responsible for any interruption of civilian rule. Eighteen Interventionist generals resigned in protest against the speech, but the outcome of the crisis was a draw. Although Frondizi again sacrificed his minister of war, General Larcher, the policies of his regime survived intact.[16] The crisis, however, did reveal the weakening position of Toranzo Montero and the Interventionists, and it was also indicative of basic changes within the armed forces.

Toranzo Montero's partial defeat was attributable to the rise of a new coalition within the military. Although his regime had been rocked by serious crises, Frondizi still had one ace-in-the-hole—an important sector of the military did not want to seize direct control of the state. Still dedicated to a semblance of civilian rule and constitutionality, these officers were willing to exchange a commanding position for a strong bargaining position within the state.[17] By 1960, these officers feared that the Toranzo Montero doctrine of total military vigilance would turn into outright revolution. Descended from the coalition that supported Fair Play in 1958, they were unwilling to sacrifice civilian rule and constitutionality for the sake of fanatic anti-Peronism. They formed the coalition known as the Legalists, which was prepared to defend civilian rule and which, at the outset, believed that the Peronists should be restrained for an indefinite period by electoral controls. The Legalists thus took an intermediate position between the Green Dragons and the Interventionists.[18]

Whereas the Interventionists drew their strength from the army in-

16 *Ibid.*
17 Kennedy, "Accountable Government in Argentina," pp. 457–458.
18 Lieuwen, *Generals vs. Presidents*, p. 14.

fantry and engineering sectors in league with the Gorillas of the navy, support for the Legalists came from the powerful Campo de Mayo garrison and from the cavalry, which controlled motorized units including tanks. At the outset of the Frondizi regime, most officers of the armed forces were Interventionists. Having been given electoral support by the Peronists, Frondizi began his term by waving the Peronist banner under the noses of the military. Peronists were amnestied and key posts in the government went to the pro-Perón supporters of Rogelio Frigerio, the *eminence gris* ("man behind the scenes") of the administration. The Interventionists then applied heavy pressure upon the administration to alter its course. These pressures were applied at a time when Frondizi embarked upon neoliberal economic policies that alienated the Peronists. When the Peronists replied with terror and violence, Frondizi became dependent on military force for domestic order. By March, 1960, the state of siege was reenforced by the Plan Conintes, under which the government by decree ceded to the military broad authority to deal with crimes against the security of the state.[19] As Frondizi became dependent on the military for both order and survival, he began to toe the army line and to purge Peronist influence from his government.

As fears of Frondizi's integration policies subsided in the army, the Legalists began to expand their strength and by 1960 they were forced to test their power against the Interventionists. At that time, the Interventionist position had slipped imperceptibly into an attitude favoring a coup d'état. The Interventionists demanded that the Frondizi government had to follow the army's wishes on every issue or risk being overthrown by armed force. For the Legalists, this was dangerous *golpismo*, the very negation of their dedication to civilian rule. Thus it was that in the crisis of October, 1960, the growing coalition of Legalists, spurred into action by Frondizi's pleas, thwarted the plans of Toranzo Montero and the Interventionists. Toranzo Montero's plan called for the resignation of Frondizi and for a new presidential election within ninety days. That Toranzo Montero succeeded only in

[19] On the Plan Conintes see Rafael Cuesta, "Normas integrantes del derecho de guerra aplicables para casos de acción subversiva," *Revista de la Escuela Superior de Guerra* 38, no. 338 (July–September, 1960): 386–389.

gaining the resignation of Minister of War Larcher, revealed that in the face of rising "legalism," his position had weakened.[20] Needless to say, the shrewd Frondizi adroitly manipulated these divisions within the military.

The decisive collision between the Legalists and the Interventionists came in March, 1961. It was triggered by Frondizi's offer to mediate United States–Cuban differences. This move was distasteful to the staunchly anti-Fidelist military, opposition being led by the new minister of war, General Rosendo Fraga. However, Fraga was a moderate in political affairs and would brook none of Toranzo Montero's *golpismo*. When in late March, 1961, Commander in Chief Toranzo Montero, strengthened by three consecutive Intransigent defeats in provincial elections, again demanded the resignation of Frondizi, Minister of War Fraga was ready to do battle. Marshalling all of his Legalist support, Fraga led a group of thirty-six generals in voting to maintain Frondizi in office and to accept Toranzo Montero's resignation.[21] The Legalists had achieved their first clear-cut victory. An Interventionist revolt seemed likely when ex–Vice-President Rojas, leader of the navy Gorillas, announced his public support for Toranzo Montero. But this failed to materialize, and Frondizi emerged from the crisis stronger than ever.

It is clear, then, that during the Frondizi regime a basic split occurred in the armed forces, the divisions personified by the Legalist ex-President Aramburu, and by Interventionist ex–Vice-President Rojas. What measure of independence Frondizi enjoyed as president depended, largely, upon these divisions. So long as the military was divided, that fox of a politician was able to outmaneuver the officers. When it was united, he was forced to accede to its demands.

In late 1961, foreign policy became the leading issue in Frondizi's confrontation with the military. At this time, the navy having replaced the army as the major intervening force, the pattern was one of silent, steady military pressure rather than spectacular troop movements. Earlier there had been rumblings in the military over Frondizi's offer

---

[20] The Legalist-Interventionist conflict is traced historically in the *Buenos Aires Herald*, April 2, 1961, p. 2.
[21] *Ibid.*

to mediate the United States–Cuban crisis. Still playing the role of international statesman, Frondizi met secretly with Che Guevara, the Argentine-born Cuban minister of finance, on August 18, 1961. The military, always discontented by Argentina's tolerant position on Cuba and communism, viewed this secret interview as proof that Frondizi was some sort of radical wolf in neoliberal fleece. It was at this juncture that the navy became convinced that Frondizi must go.[22] The navy's determination to raise a political tempest was fueled in February, 1962, by Argentina's abstention in the vote to exclude Cuba from the Organization of American States. Within a few days, the three branches of the military, firmly united on this issue, forced Frondizi to sever relations with Cuba.

His position weakened by his show of military unity, Frondizi decided to gamble on an audacious move that might strengthen his position within the state. In what Professor Arthur P. Whitaker has called his "crowning blunder,"[23] the president legalized the participation of the Peronist parties in upcoming elections. Hitherto, the Peronist mass could vote effectively only by throwing their support to candidates approved by the ex-dictator, or by casting blank ballots in protest. Now the Peronists were to be permitted to organize, present a platform, and name candidates. As usual, there was a tricky logic to the president's great gamble. His dramatic gesture was based on three assumptions. First, an election held under the continuing terms of Peronist abstention would probably be won by the Popular Radicals— this would be a serious blow to his faltering regime. Second, by permitting Peronist participation, Frondizi expected to cause a polarization of the electorate. The contest would be seen as a choice between the Intransigent Radicals representing legality, and the Peronists representing chaos through labor strife and certain military intervention. Third, if as the campaign developed, it seemed that the Peronists might win, the military would force the government to proscribe their parties, in which case he and his Intransigents could point to the officers as the

[22] Rowe, *Argentina's Restless Military*, p. 15.

[23] Arthur P. Whitaker, "Left and Right Extremism in Argentina," *Current History* 44 (February, 1963): 86.

culprits in the affair.[24] This, then, was the Intransigent strategy, and they clung to it down to the elections of March 18, 1962. Military proscription did not take place, but Frondizi remained confident to the end that the polarization of the electorate would occur.

Much to Frondizi's dismay, the results of these elections represented a breathtaking victory for the Peronists. Nationally, the Peronist vote totaled more than 2.5 million. The Peronists won nine of the fourteen governorships and forty-seven of the ninety-six seats at stake in the Chamber of Deputies. The Intransigent Radicals polled a little more than 2 million votes, and the Popular Radicals a total of 1.7 million.[25]

The reaction to the election was immediate crisis. The ministers of war, navy, and the air force, their undersecretaries, and the three commanders in chief, held a full-dress conference in the air ministry. At this meeting, the navy, through its minister, Admiral Gastón Clement, demanded the immediate resignation of Frondizi. But the moderation of Legalists of the army and air force prevailed. Instead, the armed forces drew up a list of demands that the Frondizi regime must meet in confronting the Peronist resurgence. The military chieftains demanded the formation of a coalition government of national union, the complete annulment of Peronist victories, the proscription of all Peronist political activity, the elimination of all "integrationists" from the government, and the intervention of all provinces that had voted Peronist pluralities. Frondizi's failure to meet these demands would mean their demand for his resignation, and, if he refused to resign, a military coup.[26]

Frondizi met the crisis with typical political craftiness; once again, however, he outsmarted himself. To maintain legality and to steal the military's thunder, Frondizi, on his own initiative, ordered the intervention of five Peronist-won provinces: Buenos Aires, Tucumán, Santiago del Estero, Rio Negro and Chaco. The move was an attempt to pacify the military and to win the time necessary to rally the forces of constitutionalism. But again Frondizi miscalculated. His intervention

24 Rowe, "The Argentine Elections. III," pp. 5–6.
25 Karl M. Schmitt and David D. Burks, *Evolution or Chaos: Dynamics of Latin American Government and Politics*, p. 188.
26 James W. Rowe, "The Argentine Elections. II: The Votes," pp. 3–5.

decrees failed to satisfy the military and, also, caused a bitter reaction from the democratic civilian forces who viewed them as a complete negation of the political processes.[27] From all sides, political pressure was exerted against the tottering government.

At this point, Frondizi reaped the bitter fruits of the political discord he had sown for four years. Of the seven parties invited to discuss a cabinet of national union with the president, only three would even talk the matter over. The rejection by the Popular Radicals came as no surprise in view of their hatred for Frondizi but the refusal by the Conservatives was a powerful blow against the reeling regime. Only the small Independent Civic party, the Christian Democrats, and Frondizi's own Intransigents would talk with him of national union. One after another, the opposition parties demanded his resignation as a condition for collaboration. But Frondizi, "close to being the most unpopular man in Argentina," refused to resign.[28]

By March 23, Frondizi had found only four prospects for a coalition cabinet, all of them of Radical origin. Frustrated, he then called upon Legalist leader, ex-President Aramburu, to act as mediator in the crisis. But Aramburu, also thwarted in his efforts to organize a coalition cabinet under Frondizi, then concluded that Frondizi must resign. This sealed Frondizi's fate. On March 29, 1962, the military arrested the protesting president and he was banished to the island of Martín García.

The ouster of Frondizi was one of the most reluctant military coups in Latin American history. Most of the higher-ranking military did not want to seize direct control of the government. Legalists hoped, down to the very end, for an acceptable solution that would enable Frondizi to remain in office. When this was ruled out, the military pressed for the peaceful resignation of Frondizi so that a constitutional succession would take place. However, when Frondizi refused to resign, the military was forced, albeit reluctantly, to depose him.[29]

The crisis did prove one obvious point about the political posture of the military. Under no circumstances, would the military accept a

---

[27] *Ibid.*, p. 4.
[28] *Ibid.*, p. 5.
[29] Rowe ,"The Argentine Elections. III," p. 9.

sudden and intensive resurgence of Peronism. Officers who had staked their careers and their lives on anti-Peronism were not about to allow the followers of the ex-dictator to gain a significant foothold in the government. Some Legalists might favor the very gradual and piece-meal integration of the Peronists, but even their views barred a full-scale resurgence. Such a resurgence would quickly turn Legalists into Interventionists.

11. Guido, Illía, and Militarism Resurgent, 1962-1966

After Frondizi was overthrown, the two major coalitions of the Argentine military were known as the *colorados* ("reds") and the *azules* ("blues"). The *colorados* supported attempts by the commanders in chief of the armed forces to assume direct control of the nation through the establishment of a military junta. The *azules* insisted that the transference of power be executed in accordance with constitutional norms. Having conceded that the ouster of Frondizi was irrevocable, the *azules* were determined to prevent his overthrow from ending in military dictatorship. It was they who thwarted efforts by army commander in chief, General Raúl Poggi, to head a ruling military junta. The *azules* quickly swore in as president of the nation José María Guido, president pro tempore of the Senate. This lightninglike action was taken before General Poggi could have himself sworn in. With one bold stroke, the *azules* managed to preserve civilian rule and a semblance of legality. The Argentine constitution stipulates that in the absence of the chief executive, the leader of the Senate shall assume the presidency. With the president deposed and the vice-presidency vacant, Guido, as president pro tempore of the Senate, became the legal heir to power.[1]

Since the *azul-colorado* split shapes subsequent politico-military developments, an analysis of these rival coalitions is in order. As has been stated, the *azules* were descended from the Legalists of the Frondizi years. They were inclined to support civilian rule and the withdrawal of the armed forces from politics, and were considered less violently anti-Peronist than their *colorado* rivals. The *azules* drew their military support primarily from the Campo de Mayo garrison, and from the cavalry. Their undisputed leader was Brigadier General Juan Carlos Onganía, laconic, unostentatious, and deemed to be a man without political ambitions. Regarded as a highly professional officer, Onganía commanded wide respect in the army and surrounded himself with capable aides. Other *azul* leaders were Generals Benjamín Rattenbach, Julio Alsogaray and Pascual Pistarini, and Colonels Alejandro Lanusse, Julio Aguirre, and Juan Guglialmelli.

The *colorados*, on the other hand, were considered to be the adamant anti-Peronists. Their military strength was primarily in the infantry and artillery, and they were especially powerful in the provincial garrisons. Although both the *colorados* and the *azules* participated in the overthrow of Frondizi, the former coalition played the key role. Like the *azules*, the *colorados* came from varied antecedents, mainly the middle, and lower middle, class. However, the *colorados* subscribed to ultraconservative (or staunch liberal nationalist) economic views, and so intense were these views that it was alleged that many of these officers were involved with business and banking interests in Argentina. Along with economic laissez-faire and staunch anti-Peronism, the *colorados* espoused a simplistic anticommunism which Argentines labeled as *macartismo*. Some *colorados* were in favor of a period of military dictatorship "to straighten the country out, break the back of peronism and achieve real democracy."[2] During his brief interim administration, Guido was caught in the swirl of power conflicts between these rival

---

[1] Thomas M. Millington, "President Arturo Illía and the Argentine Military," *Journal of Inter-American Studies* 6 (July, 1964): 406.

[2] James W. Rowe, "Argentina: Reds, Blues and the New Year, II," pp. 1–2.

coalitions. His regime was really nothing more than the tool of the divided Argentine military. In the first days of the military-controlled Guido government, Congress was dissolved, the Peronists were proscribed politically, and all of the March election results were annulled. Interventors were appointed to investigate the affairs of all political parties, and all party activity was ordered suspended. Meanwhile, party documents and assets were seized by the government.

But after these initial tough measures, the Guido regime was beset by continuing military crises. In April, 1962, the first *azul-colorado* war scare shocked the nation. A tank column from the Campo de Mayo garrison sped toward downtown Buenos Aires, where the troops of *colorado* leader General Poggi were digging in. In a move reminiscent of the Frondizi years, Guido chose to avoid a bloody showdown. He replaced the minister of war, Carreras, and the commander in chief, Poggi, with an officer acceptable to both coalitions. This officer, a moderate, General Juan Bautista Loza, was to serve as both minister of war and interim commander in chief. His appointment to both posts represented an inconclusive truce.[3]

Despite the strict policies of the Guido regime, the *colorados* soon grew restless. In mid-August, 1962, *colorado* General Federico Toranzo Montero, younger brother of the retired Interventionist leader, and commander of the fourth army corps in Salta, rebelled against the Guido government. His objective was the replacement of moderate General Loza by a strong anti-Peronist. The Guido administration sacrificed Loza, replacing him in the Ministry of War by General Eduardo Señorans. Señorans, loyal to civilian rule, sought an immediate showdown with the *colorados*, and the Campo de Mayo garrison offered him support. But when the *colorados*, backed by the navy, refused to allow Señorans to enter the War Ministry building, Guido surrendered to their pressures. The impotency of the presidency was then dramatized in a tragic spectacle in which the *colorados* took over the key posts in the army. By the end of August, 1962, *colorados*, most of whom favored military dictatorship, were in control of the Ministries of Interior, Defense, Foreign Relations, and War. *Colorado* generals took over the posts of minister of war, commander in chief, and chief of staff. It seemed as if the Guido government was slipping the noose around its own neck. The *colorados* made no secret of their plans to impose a military dictatorship, postpone all elections, proscribe the political activities of all leftist organizations, and purge the Peronist-controlled labor movement.[4]

Then in September, 1962, the *azules* struck back. Along with the backing of the Campo de Mayo, the *azules* had the support of forty out of fifty army generals. The air force, still adhering to balance-of-power politics, threw its support to the *azules*. On the other hand, the navy refrained from supporting the army *colorados*. Apparently, the navy was, at this point, reluctant about involving itself in the quarrels of army coalitions. The actual armed conflict between the *azules* and the *colorados* began on September 18, 1962, and ended five days later on September 23. The outcome was a decisive triumph for the *azules*.[5] General Onganía was named commander in chief of the army, placing it under the firm control of the *azules*.

In the wake of their victory, the *azules* issued the famous Communiqué No. 150, stating the ideological basis for their action. Dated at the Campo de Mayo, September 22, 1962, this communiqué merits quotation in full.

The great drama experienced in recent days has been the culmination of the efforts and anxieties of those men who believe that before anything the nation should re-orient itself along the path of the constitution.

Our objective in the national sphere is to maintain the existing executive power and to assure it sufficient and necessary freedom of action, insofar as its duty may lead to the fulfillment of the commitments contracted with the people of the nation, to achieve in the shortest possible time the rule of the constitution.

In the military field we seek the reestablishment of justice and discipline, respect for the laws and regulations, without discrimination in their application.

We believe, above all, that the nation should return as soon as possible to the full reign of the constitution bequeathed to us by our elders. In it,

[4] Millington, "President Illía and the Argentine Military," p. 407.
[5] Rowe, *Argentina's Restless Military*, pp. 16–17.

and only in it, will all of us Argentines find the bases of internal peace, or national union and prosperity, which have been seriously compromised by those who showed that they had no other right than force nor other aim than seizure of power.

We maintain that the principal guideline of constitutional life is the sovereignty of the people. Only the popular will can give legitimate authority to the government and majesty to the presidential office.

We favor, therefore, the holding of elections under a regime which will assure to all sectors participation in the national life; which will prevent any of them from obtaining, through electoral methods which do not accord with the norms of the country, an artificial monopoly of the political life; which will require of all of the parties democratic organization and principles; and which will insure the impossibility of a return to the past; which will not leave out of the political solution truly Argentine sectors which, erroneously and tendentiously led in the past, can today be incorporated honestly into the constitutional life.

On this basis of concord we must achieve political stability and fruitful coexistence among all Argentines, who want only to work in peace for the grandeur of the country and for their own welfare.

We believe that the Armed Forces should not govern. They should, on the contrary, be subordinate to civilian power. That is not to say that they should not influence the institutional life. Their role is, at one and the same time, silent and fundamental. They guarantee the constitutional pact left to us by our ancestors and have the sacred duty to prevent and contain any totalitarian movement which arises in the country, whether it be from within the government or from the opposition.[6]

Beneath this statement of high-minded professionalism, constitutionalism, and civilianism, surged the fundamental dilemma of the *azul* position. The crucial Communiqué No. 150 had proclaimed two major, and perhaps contradictory, principles: first, "the holding of elections under a regime which will assure to all sectors participation in the national life"; second, "the impossibility of a return to the past." This apparently meant that the Peronists would be allowed ample participation in the electoral processes, but that a return to rule by Perón or a Peronist-dominated regime was out of the question. Sup-

---

[6] Text of Communiqué No. 150 in Rowe, "Argentina: Reds, Blues and the New Year, II," pp. 9–10.

pose, however, that the Peronists made a full-scale resurgence that gave them great influence in the government. How, then, would the *azules* reconcile their commitments to the democratic processes and to the prevention of a Peronist-controlled regime? Was it possible to reconcile the two major principles of the idealistic Communiqué No. 150?[7]

In the months after the communiqué was issued, Argentine politics became a virtual see-saw, as the primacy of one and then the other of these two principles was asserted. When in January, 1963, the electoral court recognized the legality of three neo-Peronist parties, the air force led the way in an anti-Peronist interpretation of the communiqué. That branch issued a statement demanding that "the Executive Power take all necessary steps to insure the full force and effect of existing legislation to prevent a Peronist return to power." Confusion reigned and on February 8, 1963, Minister of War Rattenbach issued the following statement: "In the Army we distinguish clearly between two things, *peronismo* and *justicialismo*. *Peronismo* is the group of men who continue addicted to Perón. *Justicialismo* is that mass which sustains a combination of ideas which deserve the most respect."[8]

By late March, 1963, the two apparent inconsistencies of the *azul* position brought the nation to the brink of crisis. Retired Admiral Rojas, the personification of the *colorado* position, openly voiced his opposition to the Rattenbach distinction. Rumblings of opposition in the navy, the rise of *colorado* discontent in the army, and general confusion—all of these caused the Guido regime to harden its policy toward Peronism. Arrest warrants were issued for labor leader Andrés Frámini and other Peronists. The air was charged with controversy and at dawn on April 2, 1963, a storm broke.[9]

On that day, the navy staged the Little Revolution of April, 1963. It was an attempt by the *colorados* of the navy to make a comeback with the aid of retired army and air force officers. The revolution came after weeks of deep-seated political tensions over the forthcoming July presidential election and the role the Peronists would be allowed in it.

---

[7] James W. Rowe, "Election Eve Again," p. 4.
[8] *Ibid.*
[9] *Ibid.*, p. 5.

The figurehead of this poorly executed military upheaval was an aging, perennial rebel, retired General Benjamín Menéndez. However, the real leaders of the rebellion were retired Admirals Jorge Palma and Isaac Rojas, along with most of the senior naval officers on active duty, and retired *colorado* leader General Federico Toranzo Montero. Describing the Guido government as "fraudulent, undemocratic, and undermining the nation's institutions," the *colorados* of the navy called for its overthrow.[10] The *colorados* also hoped, however, that if victory turned out to be beyond their reach, negotiations would nevertheless bring tougher anti-Peronist policies. The Little Revolution lasted four days, and brought only light casualties. The rebels took several radio stations and parts of downtown Buenos Aires, but the navy made no effort to bombard the city. Nor was there a major military encounter between the large rebel force of 17,000 at Puerto Belgrano and an advancing loyalist force of 25,000. After four days of light fighting the navy capitulated.

The Little Revolution of April, 1963, had significant repercussions, however. It demonstrated that the *colorados*, although they had suffered a setback in the outcome, were still a strong force in the military. It proved once again that the navy could not mount a successful revolt without the cooperation of another branch to furnish the land base, and marked the end of the navy's significant role in postrevolutionary politics. On April 16, 1963, the number of admirals was reduced from twenty-seven to two, and to ensure against future naval revolts, the strength of the naval marines, who had done much of the fighting, was cut from 8,000 to 2,500.[11] Finally, the revolt proved that Commander in Chief Onganía and the *azules*, no matter how poorly defined their position, were well in control of the army and determined that the presidential elections would be held in July.

After the revolt, however, the army's position on Peronism stiffened. Communiqué No. 200 was issued, which declared "resolute opposition to the return of the Peronist regime or the implantation of any other kind of totalitarianism or extremism." It defined Peronism as "the plan

[10] Rowe, *Argentina's Restless Military*, p. 17.
[11] Jeanne Kuebler, "Argentina and Peronism," *Editorial Research Reports*, May 15, 1963, p. 370 n. 19.

systematically carried out by the deposed dictator and his henchmen for the purpose of provoking disruption and deformation of the traditional way of life of our people as evidenced by the spread of moral and intellectual corruption, the denigration and dissolution of our country's basic constitution, the removal of political adversaries by means of extortion, physical violence and the limitation of fundamental freedoms provided for in the Argentine Constitution."[12]

Following this sweeping condemnation, the army began to whittle down the scope of legal Peronist political expression. First came a decree-law that reinstated strict controls on the propaganda of Peronist parties. This was followed on May 17, 1963, by a crucial decree that struck down the Unión Popular. This largest of the Peronist parties was to be limited to elections involving local and legislative offices, and barred from presidential and gubernatorial contests. The explanation for such action was the failure of the Unión Popular to prove that it was no longer under Perón's control. When Peronists tried to enter a newly formed Frente Nacional y Popular, comprised of the Intransigent Radicals, Christian Democrats, and the Unión Popular, the military again moved into action. In June, 1963, the Guido government decreed that all national candidates of the Frente must come from parties other than the Unión Popular. Furthermore, no person with even a remote connection with the Unión Popular would be allowed to run for any executive office. The decree also warned that any party running candidates connected with the Unión Popular would have its entire list of candidates banned. Under such pressures, there occurred a massive Peronist exodus from the Frente, and that coalition was dissolved.[13] Hence, on the eve of the election the *azules* resolved their basic dilemma by placing severe restraints on Peronism. As some Argentines remarked, the democratic *azules*, or blues, had turned a royal purple as the election approached.

By imposing eleventh-hour restraints on Peronism, the army aimed at forcing that bloc to return to its pre-1961 tradition of abstention through blank protest ballots. Furthermore, it was hoped that the votes

12 Rowe, "Election Eve Again," p. 6.
13 Peter Ranis, "Background to the 1965 Argentine Elections," *World Today* 21 (May, 1965): 201.

of those not abstaining would be divided between the two Radical parties, with only a light turnout for the provincial neo-Peronist parties. The army's strategy proved successful, although it marred the mandate produced by the election.

The Peronists entered the contest divided, confused, and obviously ruffled. Two days before the election of July 5, 1963, Perón, in Madrid, ordered his followers to cast blank ballots. This marked a sudden shift from the policy of supporting the Frente Nacional y Popular, and many confused Peronists simply abstained. Others, to the amount of 600,000 votes, disobeyed the official line and voted for provincial neo-Peronist parties. The result of division and confusion was that the election marked the first contest since 1946 in which the Peronists did not emerge as the leading political force in Argentina.[14] However, blank votes did total nearly 19 per cent of the presidential vote, more than those gained by any candidate except Arturo Illía of the Popular Radicals. If the neo-Peronist vote was included with the blanks, the total mounted to 24 per cent.

With 25.1 per cent of the vote, Arturo Illía, candidate of the Popular Radicals, emerged as the victor in the presidential contest. This meant that Illía was a distinctly minority president, but, unlike Frondizi in 1958, he came to office with a straightforward plurality and no alliances with Peronists, Catholic nationalists or communists. His position was strengthened by the division of the Radical Intransigents into two wings under rival leaders Oscar Alende and Arturo Frondizi. And, his Popular Radicals had secured consistent pluralities in congressional and provincial elections.

After the 1963 election Argentina breathed a sigh of deep relief. The nation had avoided a military dictatorship on the one hand, and a massive blank Peronist vote on the other. The disobedience of many Peronists toward the official line of the ex-dictator was viewed as a victory for democracy. Furthermore, the neo-Peronists of the interior, who had disregarded the official line, had accounted for 6.5 per cent of legislative ballots, and would send sixteen representatives to the Chamber of Deputies. The military also seemed reasonably satisfied by the

---

[14] *Ibid.*, p. 202.

outcome of the election. "After many years of political convulsion, the nation opted, as if by instinct, for the least spectacular remedy available."[15]

The new president, Arturo Illía, personified the nation's desire for a political breathing-spell. He brought to the presidency a reputation for honesty and conciliation, and, as a newcomer to politics, he had made few enemies and compromises. A small-town physician who had won the governorship of Córdoba in the annulled elections of 1962, Illía, at sixty-three, projected a kindly and fatherly image that fitted the mood of the Argentine people. The platform of his party, the Popular Radicals, a heterogeneous, middle-of-the-road organization, promised few surprises for the nation. Like other parties, the Popular Radicals had promised to cancel Frondizi's petroleum contracts, and they promptly did so. However, the fulfillment of two other political promises remained to be seen. Illía was sworn to a broad amnesty, lifting the state of siege, and the subordination of the military to civilian authority.

Within the military, the *colorado-azul* conflict burned with lingering intensity as Illía took office. In October, 1963, President Guido had granted a general amnesty that included the *colorado* insurgents. But Illía, once in office, threw all of his weight against the *colorados*. With the consent of the Senate, he pushed through a series of military promotions that filled the vacancies in command and also shut the door once and for all on the question of reincorporation of the *colorados*. This step climaxed the victory of the *azules* over the *colorados* in the struggle for control of the army.[16]

During the first eighteen months of the Illía regime, the major issues in Argentine political life were the role of Peronism, the petroleum question, and the general state of the economy. This period witnessed a promising abatement of the burning issue of Peronism. The Illía regime followed a policy of deemphasizing ideological distinctions and emphasizing inter-party cooperation within a Popular Radical framework. An important extension of this policy was the

---

[15] James W. Rowe, *Argentina: An Election Retrospect*, p. 13.
[16] Millington, "President Illía and the Argentine Miliary," p. 409.

effort to gradually integrate the Peronists into the institutional framework of Argentina. The regime voided anti-Peronist decree-laws, and took pride in the initial integration of sixteen neo-Peronists into the Chamber of Deputies. The behavior of the neo-Peronists in Congress dispelled many illusions as to their irresponsibility; indeed, there was a general concurrence between the Popular Radicals and the neo-Peronists on basic issues. Meanwhile, the *azul*-controlled army, still dedicated to the official doctrine of "professionalization, dedication to specific tasks, and subordination,"[17] looked on, and quietly watched and waited to see how far and how fast integration would go.

The lull in the Peronist controversy was almost shattered when on December 2, 1964, the ex-dictator, traveling on the Spanish Iberia Airlines from Spain, made an attempt to reach Argentine soil via Brazil. It is difficult to believe that Perón himself counted on landing in Argentina without being detected. More than likely his flight was an attempt to perpetuate the Perón myth. Having promised that 1964 was the year of return, he probably felt the need to make a token effort. In any case, he was detained and returned by Brazilian authorities within forty-eight hours of his landing in Rio de Janeiro. When Perón's abortive return became public knowledge, the CGT staged a two-day general strike on December 17 and 18. The response was less than 50 per cent successful, "the most unhappy example of peronista-worker solidarity in a decade."[18] In fact, many of the Peronist leaders were happy at the outcome, for they cherished the new legal gains made by their movement under Illía. They could see a hopeful political future for Peronism if Perón remained in far-away Madrid while they adopted realistic programs of reform. Their tactic was also to play down the movement's dictatorial associations, curb the excesses of the syndicalist wing, and promote an image of the movement that would show its fitness to take its place in a democratic structure.

In the economic sphere, right-wing opponents severely criticized Illía for canceling the foreign oil contracts made under Frondizi. The

[17] James W. Rowe, *A Note on Argentina: Change, Stagnation, and Unrealized Promise*, p. 20.
[18] Peter Ranis, "Peronismo without Perón: Ten Years after the Fall (1955–1965)," *Journal of Inter-American Studies* 8 (January, 1966): 119.

hard economic fact was that the nation was unable to take up the slack in production that resulted from the withdrawal of foreign capital and technicians. Increased petroleum imports, resulting from the cancellation of the foreign contracts, acted as a drain upon the depleted treasury. With industrial and consumer demand for petroleum rising by 6 per cent annually, YPF production, which had been rising by only 3.8 per cent annually, fell far short of the mark. Petroleum imports, as a percentage of production, had fallen to 7 per cent by 1963; one year later, after cancellation, they had risen to about 20 per cent. By 1964, the value of petroleum imports rose to $55 million, and it continued to rise in the following years. However, many of the Popular Radicals claimed that the cancellation of the foreign contracts was based not on economic considerations, but on campaign promises and moral-legal principles concerning the improper manner in which Frondizi undertook negotiations.[19] After all, Illía was no Frondizi.

The budget deficit, aggravated by increasing petroleum imports, tended to deepen the financial crisis in Argentina. The antiquated railroads continued to be the biggest drain upon the treasury. In despair, the Illía government resorted to inflationary financing. This brought the peso's free value down from 170 pesos to the United States dollar in December, 1964, to about 225 to the dollar in March, 1965. In an effort to halt inflation, speculation, and corruption, legislation was passed in a special session of Congress in February, 1964, giving the Illía administration extensive powers to regulate the production, distribution and sale of basic commodities. Under this law, the government attempted, albeit unsuccessfully, to maintain reasonable prices for basic commodities. For the military, the Illía government was a do-nothing regime since it was unable to cope with serious economic disorders. Despite bumper wheat and beef production in 1964, Illía was not able to remedy the nation's economic distress. His inability to curb inflation caused costs of industrial production to shoot sky-high, alienating business elements and their military associates.

As the elections of March, 1965, approached, the Illía government presented a platform based on two achievements: first, domestic peace

19 Ranis, "Background to the 1965 Argentine Elections," p. 204.

—the absence of military interventions, stage-of-siege conditions, and disruptive general strikes; second, advances in political democracy as evidenced by the legalization of the Unión Popular and other neo-Peronist parties, and by the absence of political prisoners.

The results of the election exhibited a polarization of the Argentine electorate unseen since the days of Perón when the nation was divided into two large sectors, Peronist and anti-Peronist.[20] Election figures indicate that support of the Popular Radicals was viewed as the only alternative to a massive Peronist vote. The Peronist Unión Popular received 31 per cent of the vote, indicating the heaviest popular support of the movement since the Perón dictatorship. Other neo-Peronist parties polled 7 per cent of the vote; hence, the combined Peronist vote totaled 38 per cent. The governing Popular Radicals received 30 per cent of the vote as compared to 25 per cent in 1963, thus representing the other pole in the division of the electorate. Frondizi's new Movimiento de Integración y Desarrollo (MID), which had split from the Radical Intransigents after 1963, polled 7 per cent of the vote. All other parties, including the Radical Intransigents, received all-time lows of under 5 per cent each.

At stake in the elections were ninety-nine seats in the Chamber of Deputies. Although Popular Radical representation there was reduced from 72 to 70, that party also controlled 25 out of 46 seats in the Senate and so retained its legislative leadership. The Peronist Unión Popular soared from no representation to a 36-member bloc in the Chamber of Deputies. The provincial neo-Peronist parties maintained their representation of 16 deputies. Hence, the combined neo-Peronist and Popular Radical representation was more than 70 per cent of the lower house, with 122 out of 192 members. This meant a virtual political emasculation of the splintered minority parties.

The 1965 elections thus represented a significant step towards an effective biparty system in Argentina, with perhaps a third force mobilizing on the conservative side.[21] The political left and the antigovernment forces had consolidated into the ranks of the Peronists, thus ending any vague hope that a leftist democratic party would some day serve

[20] *Ibid.*, p. 207.
[21] *Ibid.*, p. 208.

as the vehicle for the integration of the Peronists. Quite the contrary, the election showed that the Peronists were absorbing the Argentine left. On the other hand, the Popular Radicals had absorbed votes from the centrist and conservative parties, reflecting fears in these right-wing groups of a strong Peronist comeback.

This momentous Peronist victory sent tremors through the Argentine military. Judging from their success in March, 1965, the Peronists might well capture the major governorships, as well as more congressional strength, in the elections of 1967. There was also the possibility that they might gain a Peronist victory in the presidential election of 1969, and so accomplish a return to full power through legal channels.[22] For the military, this was a nightmare possibility. After the elections of March, 1965, rumblings of military discontent became progressively stronger.

The first overt sign of a break between the military and the Illía regime came in June, 1965, when Under Secretary of Foreign Affairs Ramón J. Vásquez resigned his post. He charged the Illía government with vacillation in the support of the United States effort in the Dominican Republic, and, more important, with weakness in the face of communist and Peronist subversion in Argentina. His views reflected those of important military men, who wanted the immediate "repression of the burgeoning Peronist movement."[23]

By November, 1965, an open breach emerged between the military and the Illía regime. General Onganía resigned as commander in chief of the army, marking the most serious crisis since Illía came to power on October 12, 1963. The resignation was triggered by the appointment to the Ministry of War of Brigadier General Eduardo R. Castro, a move made by Illía without consulting Commander in Chief Onganía. But Onganía's resignation reflected deeper military discontent with the regime's failure to take action against internal subversion by communists and Peronists. Furthermore, Onganía was discontented with Illía's reluctance to support United States proposals for an inter-American peace force to cope with hemispheric subversion.[24]

---

22 *Ibid.*, pp. 208–209.
23 *New York Times*, June 7, 1965, p. 18.
24 *Ibid.*, November 24, 1965, p. 18.

The new commander in chief of the navy was General Pascual Angel Pistarini, an *azul* and considered by *colorados* to be soft on Peronism.[25] But by now, the *azul* tradition of "legalism" had been submerged in the tide of Peronist resurgence. In early June, 1966, General Pistarini forced the resignation of Minister of War Castro and arrested Major General Carlos A. Caro, commander of the second army corps in Rosario. General Caro, the chief supporter of the Illía regime, was accused of meeting with the Peronists, an act that violated army oaths not to do so. For most army officers, this sign of a reconciliation between colleagues and the growing Peronist movement was the last straw. On June 28, 1966, the commitment of the armed forces to "legalism" came to an abrupt halt, when, after thirty-two months in office, President Illía was ousted by a military coup.[26]

The overthrow of Illía demonstrated the fragility of the Legalist tradition in the army. In the face of a full-scale Peronist resurgence, military men refused to stand by and accept the lackluster Illía regime as the only alternative to future Peronist victories. The military proceeded to install retired Lieutenant General Onganía as president of Argentina. Ironically, Onganía had built his reputation in the military as a thoroughgoing Legalist. Now, aided by a three-man junta representing all branches of the armed forces, Onganía had been placed at the helm of a military regime that openly declared the civilians incompetent to rule.

[25] *Ibid.*, November 26, 1965, p. 12.
[26] *Ibid.*, June 28, 1966, pp. 1, 15.

Postscript: A Guide to Current Politico-Military Crises

There are three considerations that guide the historian through the labyrinthine course of current politico-military history in Argentina. The first is concerned with who actually wields power, what military faction and civilian allies control the nation. The second deals with what social sector bears the burden of economic recovery in Argentina. The third, and final, consideration focuses on what is done about Peronism, a political force that attracts from 30 to 40 per cent of the Argentine electorate.

Onganía came to power in 1966 on the wave of a profound disillusionment with the workings of democracy in post-Perón Argentina. Influential Argentines, civilian and military, were fed up with the whole system of parties, political divisions, and leadership during the period of 1955 to 1966.[1] This, in part, explains the transformation of Onganía from a Legalist defender of the constitution and civilian rule into an authoritarian proponent of integral nationalism. Behind

[1] James W. Rowe, *Onganía's Argentina: The First Four Months*, pp. 4–6.

the façade of a "new politics," the 1966 military revolt represented a revival of the integral nationalist tradition in Argentina. It was a return to the authoritarian, statist, Catholic, and traditionalist brand of nationalism.

The reasons for the transformation of the *azules* from the civilianist and constitutionalist military faction into right-wing nationalists are suggested in a study made by Philip B. Springer. In comparing the *azules* with the *colorados*, Springer writes that the *azules* tended to be more nationalistic, more Catholic, and more pro-Franco than the *colorados*. Furthermore, the *azules* tended to be more interested in industrialization than were the *colorados*.[2] This observation suggests that the *azules*, like Onganía their chief, harbored certain right-wing views that did not surface until they actually wielded power.

Elements in the Argentine military have always dreamed that, given authoritarian powers, they could rule the nation according to a patriotic, objective national interest. This dream emerges whenever the professional politicians and the republican-democratic system fails in Argentina. As usual, the 1966 coup was a coup to end all coups by changing the political system. Having sensed the need for basic change, Onganía consolidated his power with acts that exceeded even those of Perón. All political organizations were outlawed. The members of the Supreme Court were ousted and replaced. Governors of all provinces were replaced by interventors. Congress was dissolved. Troops were sent into the universities, violating the traditional autonomy of these institutions. Although Onganía declared his regime to be nonpolitical, some key posts in the government went to integral and Catholic nationalists.[3]

Like those of Uriburu in 1930, the authoritarian acts of the Onganía regime tended to dissolve some of the dictator's civilian support. But Onganía had learned the lessons of history; he knew that without broader civilian backing his regime might be ousted or lose power to

[2] Philip B. Springer, "Disunity and Disorder: Factional Politics in the Argentine Military," in *The Military Intervenes: Case Studies in Political Development*, ed. Henry Bienen, pp. 150–152.

[3] David C. Jordan, "Argentina's New Military Government," *Current History* 58 (February, 1970): 85.

the liberal nationalists. After all, this is what had happened to Uriburu in 1930 and to Lonardi in 1955. Thus in late December, 1966, six months after the revolution, Onganía reshuffled his cabinet, bringing in liberal nationalists to share political power.[4] This integral and liberal nationalist combination was retained throughout the four years of rule by Onganía. It meant that the oligarchy and upper middle class again ruled Argentina in league with the military. The liberal nationalist sector of the oligarchy, defenders of democratic forms and free enterprise, had made its peace with a regime that promised no return to the established institutions of Argentina.

This compromise was later extended to the army. In 1967, the post of commander in chief of the army went to Major General Julio Alsogaray, a liberal nationalist.[5] In the wake of labor strife and disorders in May, 1969, Onganía again appointed a liberal nationalist, General Alejandro Agustín Lanusse, to serve as commander in chief of the army.[6] Lanusse has become a power in recent Argentine history.

With the army and the oligarchy in control of Argentina, economic progress was made the primary objective of the Onganía regime. This brings us to the second consideration: what social sector would bear the burdens of economic progress. During the Onganía regime, Argentina made solid economic progress. Production in vital industries soared. Inflation was curbed. The Argentine peso became one of the strongest currencies in Latin America. Gold and foreign exchange holdings rose to over a billion dollars in 1968, four times Argentina's holdings in 1966. The federal deficit decreased from 25 per cent in 1966 to 5 per cent in 1968.[7] But while Onganía's hard-peso policy attracted foreign investment, it created mass discontent over lagging wages.[8] Once again labor, which had prospered under Perón, was told that it must bear the cost of economic development—economic development fomented and supervised, that is, by the two sectors of the nation's elite.

[4] *Ibid.*, p. 88.
[5] Alvin Cohen, "Revolution in Argentina," *Current History* 53 (November, 1967): 287.
[6] Jordan, "Argentina's New Military Government," p. 116.
[7] *Ibid.*, pp. 85–86.
[8] *New York Times*, June 10, 1970.

During the Onganía regime, labor was deeply divided. The unions most hostile to the dictatorship began to organize on March 28, 1968. They elected as their secretary general Raimundo Ongaro of the Peronist Printers' Union, and he moved into the leadership of the opposition to Onganía. At this point, there were two opposing general confederations of labor, one led by Augusto Vandor, which was cooperating with the government, and the other, which opposed, led by Ongaro. Furthermore, the cooperative labor bloc was itself divided into two major groups: participationists and dialogists. While the participationists actively cooperated with the dictatorship, the dialogists, led by Vandor, communicated with and refrained from active opposition to the government.[9]

Labor unrest spread throughout the nation in 1968. This discontent was attributed to the government freeze on wages, a measure meant to check inflation. The Ongaro wing of the CGT took the offensive against the government's economic measures, declaring in April, 1969, that "after three years of this government we now know who really controls the country: the monopolies, the oligarchy, the old heads of the governing class."[10]

In his policy toward labor, Onganía was caught in a profound dilemma. Right-wing integral nationalism was marked by a tradition of populism, using social welfare as a bridge between the elite and the working class. For example, upon seizing power, the Catholic nationalist Lonardi sought to align himself with Peronist labor. In 1968, Onganía was caught between his desire to conciliate labor and the requirements of economic progress. Furthermore, it is likely that liberal nationalist civilians and military men, now the allies of Onganía's far-right nationalists, were critical of the government's desire to deal with labor, a bastion of Peronism.

By 1969, Ongaro's defiance had spread throughout the labor movement. Rank-and-file members, no matter what their union leaders had said about cooperation, rallied to the cause of Ongaro. They were joined by the students, who opposed the government's strict controls

---

[9] Jordan, "Argentina's New Military Government," p. 89.
[10] *Ibid.*, p. 90.

on the university system, the low budget for education, and Onganía's Catholic morality. Finally, there was a growing number of Catholic priests who attacked social injustices in Argentina.[11]

This undercurrent of unrest surfaced violently on May 15, 1969, when university students in Corrientes demonstrated against an increase in cafeteria prices. One student was shot to death by a policeman, which set off a nationwide wave of student protest. Workers joined the student protests as Ongaro seized the opportunity to call a general strike. This strike proved successful and it ignited civil insurrection in the city of Córdoba. There police fired on a group of workers who were marching toward the governor's mansion. In general, the military overreacted to the upheaval: fifteen people were killed and about fifty were wounded. Military law was imposed on both the cities of Corrientes and Córdoba. Sentences of from three to ten years were meted out to four trade union leaders. Ongaro was arrested and imprisoned.[12]

As violence spread throughout the land, the military's confidence in Onganía waned. On June 30, 1969, terrorists murdered Vandor, head of the Metal Workers Union and leader of the moderates within the labor movement. Hours later, General Onganía imposed a state of siege, limiting all constitutional guarantees. To placate labor, he agreed to a general wage increase. But the violence continued and the nation's democratic leaders, including the liberal nationalist ex-President Aramburu, called for a return to democratic forms of government. The kidnapping of General Aramburu proved to be the last straw. On June 8, 1970, nearly four years after Onganía's assumption of power, he was deposed by the commanders in chief of the armed forces.

After the ouster of Onganía, high-ranking military leaders spoke in contradictory terms. Soon after the coup, the three commanders promised elections and a return to civilian government. However, they gave no date.[13] The commanders chose as president Brigadier General Roberto Marcelo Levingston, fifty-year-old former military attaché to Washington. Five days after he took office, on June 23, 1970,

[11] *Ibid.*
[12] *Ibid.*
[13] *New York Times*, June 10, 1970.

Levingston delivered a speech which, while affirming his belief in a return to constitutional rule, indicated that elections were still far off.[14]

Underlying the seeming contradictions among military men was the problem of Peronism in Argentina. This brings us to the third and final consideration of this postscript: what will be done about Peronism. Liberal nationalist military men, like Commander in Chief Lanusse, may avowedly favor democracy and a return to civilian rule, but they strongly oppose the group most likely to win in a free election—the Peronists. Owing to intense factionalism in Argentine politics, the party that can win one-quarter of the votes usually gains the presidency. Peronists can usually poll one-third of the votes and are by far the strongest, most cohesive voting bloc. If the Peronists ever come to power in Argentina, they might purge the military of high-ranking officers who risked their positions and necks in ridding the officer corps of followers of the ex-dictator. Furthermore, a victory by the Peronists would strengthen organized labor as a power factor in competition with the military.

At the outset of his nine-month rule, Levingston attempted to compromise with labor. A congress of CGT delegates, held in August, 1970, elected José Rucci to the key post of secretary-general of the organization. Rucci was a Vandorista, a follower of Augusto Vandor, the moderate who had been assassinated. Like his late leader, Rucci propounded the doctrine of "Peronism without Perón," which subordinated loyalty to the distant dictator to bread-and-butter union issues. As a conciliatory gesture, Levingston deferred appointment of his minister of labor until the CGT made its decision. After the election of Rucci, Levingston chose as minister of labor Juan Alejandro Luco, a former Justicialista (Perón party) whip in the Chamber of Deputies. His role was to smooth differences between government and labor.[15]

But like his predecessors, Levingston attempted to make labor bear the burden of economic recovery in Argentina. As inflation returned to Argentina, Levingston placed a limit of 19 per cent on wage raises for

[14] *Ibid.*, June 24, 1970, p. 8.
[15] *Christian Science Monitor*, August 11, 1970, p. 6.

1971.[16] Levingston also adopted nationalistic economic policies reminiscent of Perón. He attempted to force the landed oligarchy to share in the fight against inflation. By sharply increasing taxes on ranchers in order to force them to sell livestock, Levingston attempted to keep the cost of living from soaring. This move is reported to have depleted the country's cattle herds. Since beef is the staple of the Argentine diet, the cattle shortage sent prices soaring.[17] In Argentina, beef consumption averages four pounds a week per person, and therefore high beef prices can bring down a government.[18]

High prices and wage ceilings again stirred labor strife in the explosive city of Córdoba. Strikes were called by the outlawed Córdoba branch of CGT in March, 1971. Looting and gunfire became widespread throughout the city. This breakdown of law and order was a direct challenge to Levingston. He declared Córdoba an emergency area and appointed the eighth governor of the province in four and a half years of military rule.[19]

Córdoba was not, however, the only scene of civil strife. Guerilla terror spread throughout Argentina as the radical left Castroites fused with the radical right Peronists.[20] Guerilla groups claimed responsibility for the assassination of Vandor and the kidnapping and murder of Aramburu. Their acts of violence prompted Levingston to state that "international subversion has chosen our country as the camp for its international operations."[21] But Levingston seemed unable to stem the tide of terrorism in Argentina.

On March 23, 1971, after nine months in office, Levingston was deposed by the commanders in chief of the armed forces. As of this writing, General Lanusse, commander in chief of the army, has emerged as the political strongman in Argentina. He will serve as president for one year and then be followed by Admiral Pedro Alberto José Gnavi, the navy commander, and Brigadier General Carlos Al-

[16] *New York Times*, March 25, 1971, p. 15.
[17] *Ibid*.
[18] *Ibid*., March 28, 1971, The Week in Review, p. 6.
[19] *Ibid*., March 19, 1971, p. 14.
[20] *Ibid*., February 19, 1971, p. 2.
[21] *Ibid*.

berto Rey, the air force chief, for like periods.[22] General Lanusse is a member of one of Argentina's most important landowning and business families. An ex-member of the faction of 1951, which led the way in purging Peronists from the military after 1955, Lanusse is a liberal nationalist. He believes in creating the conditions necessary for a return to constitutional and civilian rule.[23]

Whereas the *azul-colorado* cleavage seems to have dissolved, it has been replaced by a renewal of the struggle between liberal nationalists and integral nationalists.[24] The liberal nationalist officers want a return to civilian rule, democratic forms, and free enterprise. Liberal nationalists also favor creating the conditions for national elections to be held as soon as possible.

General Lanusse has even invited Perón to return from Spain, perhaps in an effort to dissolve the charisma of the ex-dictator. Early in April, 1971, the military government of Lanusse made conciliatory gestures toward Perón and proposed an agreement on the conditions under which he might return to Argentina. Perón has not responded to this offer. Perhaps he realizes that his presence in Argentina might result in his wielding less influence over the Peronist movement than he is able to exert by remote control from Spain.[25] Although at the time of this writing it is impossible to assess this development, it may be that a new day is dawning in the labyrinth of Argentine politics.

[22] *Ibid.*, March 26, 1971, p. 3.
[23] *Ibid.*, March 24, 1971, p. 3.
[24] Peter G. Snow, *Political Forces in Argentina*, p. 143.
[25] *Christian Science Monitor*, June 12, 1971, p. 6.

BIBLIOGRAPHICAL ESSAY

I. *General Histories of Modern Argentina.* The definitive history of modern Argentina in English has yet to be written. Impressive contributions have, however, been made, especially by Professor Arthur P. Whitaker. His *The United States and Argentina* (Cambridge, Mass.: Harvard University Press, 1954) and *Argentina* (Englewood, N.J.: Prentice-Hall, 1964) are essential introductions to and analyses of modern Argentine history. Still one of the best one-volume works in English is Ysabel Fisk [Rennie's] *The Argentine Republic* (New York: Macmillan Co., 1945). Brief but valuable is George Pendle's *Argentina*, 2nd ed. (London: Oxford University Press, 1961). James Scobie's *Argentina, a City and a Nation* (New York: Oxford University Press, 1964) is a brilliant socio-economic interpretation of pre-Perón Argentina. An excellent history by a political scientist is H. S. Ferns's *Argentina* (New York: Praeger, 1969). Brief but extremely insightful and well written is Thomas F. McGann's *Argentina: The Divided Land* (Princeton, N.J.: D. Van Nostrand and Co., 1966). Of the many histories by Argentines, Gustavo Gabriel Levene's *La Argentina se hizo así* (Buenos Aires: Librería Hachette, 1960) is the most balanced and lucid. For a revisionist view of modern Argentine history, see Ernesto Palacio, *Historia de la Argentina, 1515–1938* (Buenos Aires: ALPE, 1954).

II. *General Studies of Argentine Militarism.* Much information on Argentina may be gleaned from Edwin Lieuwen's groundbreaking *Arms and Politics in Latin America* published for the Council on Foreign Relations (New York: Praeger, 1961), and his *Generals vs. Presidents: Neomilitarism in Latin America* (New York: Praeger, 1964). The Lieuwen thesis, with its emphasis on the harmful effects of Latin American militarism, may be compared with John J. Johnson, *The Military and Society in Latin America* (Stanford: Stanford University Press, 1964), a brilliant interpretation that emphasizes the potentially constructive role the military may play. S. E. Finer's *The Man on Horseback* (New York: Praeger, 1962) uses many Argentine examples to illuminate the worldwide problem of militarism. His article "The Argentine Trouble: Between Sword and State," *Encounter* 25, no. 3 (September, 1965): 59–61, is a stimulating effort to interpret Argentine militarism through corporate self-interest. See also Marvin Goldwert, "Dichotomies of Militarism in Argentina," *Orbis* 10 (Fall, 1966): 930–939.

An excellent starting point for direct research on Argentine militarism is James W. Rowe's *Argentina's Restless Military*, American Universities Field Staff Reports Service, East Coast South American Series, vol. IX, no. 2 (Hanover, N.H., 1964), which succinctly analyzes over three decades of politico-military trends. Robert A. Potash's *The Army and Politics in Argentina, 1928–1945* (Stanford, Cal.: Stanford University Press, 1969) covers a brief period in detail and with literary skill. Important sociological analyses of the Argentine military are José Luis de Imaz's "Los que mandan: Las fuerzas armadas en Argentina," *América Latina* 7, no. 4 (October–December, 1964): 35–69, and his book *Los que mandan* (Buenos Aires: Editorial Universitaria de Buenos Aires, 1964). A brief left-wing history of Argentine militarism is Jorge Abelardo Ramos's *Historia política del ejército en función de la democracia* (Buenos Aires: Talleres Gráficos Guillermo Kraft, 1958). The army describes its political role in *La historia patria y la acción de sus armas* (1960), published by the Círculo Militar as a special number of the *Revista Militar*, presenting of course a favorable account. For a useful survey of politico-military trends, see Robert A. Potash, "The Changing Role of the Military in Argentina," *Journal of Inter-American Studies* 3 (October, 1961): 571–578.

The role of force in Argentine society is analyzed adeptly in Bonifacio del Carril's *Bajo el imperio de la fuerza* (Buenos Aires: Emecé Editores, 1958). Important reflections on Argentine militarism, by a prodemocratic army officer, are contained in Colonel Roque Lanús's *Al servicio del ejército* (Buenos Aires, 1946). A nationalist's view of the military is presented by Carlos A. Florit in *Las fuerzas armadas y la guerra psicológica* (Buenos Aires: Ediciones Arayá, 1963). Significant insights into modern Argentine militarism may be found also in Rogelio García Lupo, *La rebelión de los generales* (Buenos Aires: Jamcana, 1963). Postrevolutionary civilian thought on Argentine militarism is reflected in Institución de Extensión Universitaria de la Facultad de Derecho y el Centro de Derecho y Ciencias Sociales (FUBA), *Ciclo de mesas redondas: Tres revoluciones (los ultimos veintiocho años)*, (Buenos Aires, 1959).

III. *The Early History of the Professional Army in Argentina.* A useful summary is Augusto G. Rodríguez's *Reseña histórica del ejército argentino, 1862–1930* (Buenos Aires: Dirección de Estudios Históricos, 1964). The crucial role played by Domingo Sarmiento in the formation of the professionalized New Army is told by Augusto G. Rodríguez in *Sarmiento militar* (Buenos Aires: Ediciones Peuser, 1950). The early history of the professional army is described by Colonel Augusto A. Maligne in his "Historia militar de la Argentina" in the special issue of *La Nación* observing the May 25, 1810 centennial (Buenos Aires, 1910). Many articles on the institutional history of the New Army may be found in *Revista Universitaria* 5, (Buenos Aires, 1935), no. 61. Important glimpses into the military way-of-life are contained in Maligne's "El ejército en 1910," *Revista de Derecho, Historia y Letras* 38 (1910): 306–312; and "El ejército en octubre de 1910," *ibid.* 39 (1911): 253–273, 397–425, 557–566. The army as a presidential pretorian guard receives a scorching indictment in A. Belín Sarmiento's *Una república muerta* (Buenos Aires: Imp. "Mariano Moreno," 1892). The only study of secret lodges in the Argentine army is that of Colonel Roque Lanús, "Logias en el ejército durante el siglo XIX," in *La Prensa*, July 1, 1950.

IV. *Radicalism, the Army, and the Revolution of 1930.* Interesting studies of the revolution of 1890 and the birth of the Radical party are found in Mariano de Vedia y Mitre, *La revolución del 90* (Buenos Aires: Talleres gráficos argentinos de L. J. Rosso, 1929) ; Juan Balestra, *El noventa: Una evolución política argentina*, 3rd ed. (Buenos Aires: Fariña, 1959), and the first issue of *Revista de Historia*, 1957, devoted to "La crisis del 90."

The history of Radicalism may be explored through biographies on its leaders: Julio A. Noble, *Cien años, dos vidas* (Buenos Aires: Bases Editorial, 1960); a study of Leandro Alem and Lisandro de la Torre; Álvaro Yunque [pseud. A. Gondalfi Herrero], *Leandro N. Alem: El hombre de la multitud*, 2nd ed. (Buenos Aires: Editorial Americana, 1953); Roberto Farías, *Alem y la democracia argentina* (Buenos Aires: Editorial G. Kraft, 1957); Manuel Gálvez, *Vida de Hipólito Yrigoyen: El hombre de misterio* (Buenos Aires: Talleres Gráficos G. Kraft, 1949) ; Luis V. Sommi, *Hipólito Yrigoyen: Su época y vida* (Buenos Aires: Editorial Monteagudo, 1947); Félix Luna, *Yrigoyen, el templario de la libertad* (Buenos Aires: Editorial Raigal, 1954), and *Alvear* (Buenos Aires: Libros Argentinos, 1958).

A storehouse of information on Radicalism is *Hipólito Yrigoyen: Pueblo y gobierno*, 12 vols. (Buenos Aires: Editorial Raigal, 1956). The Radical party's history has been analyzed in three volumes by Gabriel del Mazo, *El radicalismo: Ensayo sobre su historia y doctrina*, (Buenos Aires: Editorial Raigal, 1951); *El radicalismo: Notas sobre su historia y doctrina, 1922–1952* (Buenos Aires: Editorial Raigal, 1955); and *El radicalismo: El movimiento de intransigencia y renovación, 1945–1957* (Buenos Aires: Ediciones Gure, 1957). A similar study on the Socialist party is found in Jacinto Oddone's *Historia del socialismo argentino*, 2 vols. (Buenos Aires: Talleres Gráficos "La Vanguardia," 1949). Important political memoirs relating to this period are Enrique Dickman, *Recuerdos de un militante socialista* (Buenos Aires: Editorial La Vanguardia, 1949); Federico Pinedo, *En tiempos de la república*, 5 vols. (Buenos Aires: Editorial Mundo Florense, 1946–1948); Juan E. Carulla, *Al filo del medio siglo* (Paraná, Argentina: Editorial Llanura, 1951); and Juan J. Real, *30 años de historia argentina* (Buenos Aires: Ediciones Actualidad, 1962).

The prerevolutionary relationship between the army and the Radicals is described in Enrique J. Spangenberg Leguizamón's *Los responsables: El ejército y la unión cívica radical ante la democracia argentina* (Buenos Aires: Librería "El Ateneo," 1936). Also informative is Nicolás Repetto's *Los socialistas y el ejército* (Buenos Aires: Editorial La Vanguardia, 1946). The rise of military opposition to Yrigoyen and the Radicals is analyzed by Juan V. Orona in "Una logia poco conocido y la revolución del 6 de septiembre," *Revista de Historia*, no. 3 (1958): 73–94.

The starting point for research on the revolution of 1930 is Roberto Etchepareborda's scholarly "Bibliografía de la revolución de 1930," *Revista de Historia*, no. 3 (1958): 156–173. In fact this whole number of the *Revista de Historia*, devoted to "La crisis del 1930," is a monument to Argentine historiography.

The most important work on the revolution of 1930, and one containing an account by Captain Juan D. Perón, is General José M. Sarobe's *Memorias sobre la revolución del 6 de septiembre* (Buenos Aires: Ediciones Gure, 1957). A detailed narrative of the revolution is found in J. Beresford Crawkes's *533 días de la historia argentina: 6 de septiembre de 1930–20 de febrero de 1932* (Buenos Aires: Imprenta Mercatali, 1932). See also Marvin Goldwert, "The Rise of Modern Militarism in Argentina," *Hispanic American Historical Review* 48 (May 1968): 189–205.

V. *The Army in the Infamous Decade (1932–1943).* The Justo period is given detailed treatment in Manuel Goldstraj, *Años y errores: Un cuarto de siglo de política* (Buenos Aires: Editorial Sophos, 1937), and the Justo presidency is also described in Raúl G. Luzuriaga, *Centinela de la libertad: Historia documental de una época* (Buenos Aires: Talleres Gráficos de A. López, 1940). An important memoir, by a conservative nationalist, on this and other periods is *La historia que he vivido* (Buenos Aires: Ediciones Peuser, 1955) by Carlos Ibarguren.

Radicalism in the Infamous Decade is described in the previously cited works by Gabriel del Mazo and in Santiago Nudelman's *El radicalismo al sevicio de la libertad* (Buenos Aires: Editorial Jus, 1947). The important topic of Radical military conspiracies in the 1930s is well dealt with in Colonel Atilio E. Cattáneo's *Entre rejas: Memorias* (Buenos Aires: Editorial "Chango," 1939) and *Plan 1932: Las conspiraciones radicales contra el general Justo* (Buenos Aires: Proceso Ediciones, 1959).

The army's relationship to electoral corruption under Justo is dealt with by General Ramón Molina in the chapter "La subversión institucional de la república, de los últimos años transcurridos—causas y remedios" of his *Defendamos nuestro país* (Buenos Aires: Levante, Depto. Editorial de Proventes, 1940). Scandals in the military during this period are described in Benjamín Villafañe, *La tragedia argentina* (Buenos Aires, 1943). The achievements of the Justo regime, including military reforms, are lauded in *Momento político sudamericano: La obra del gobierno argentino presidida por el General Agustín P. Justo* (Buenos Aires, 1938?).

Fresh insights into this period are contained in a series of articles titled "Un negro cuarto de siglo," *Noticias Gráficas*, November 28, December 2, and December 3, 1955. Nicolás Repetto's memoir *Mi paso por la política: Uriburu a Perón* (Buenos Aires: S. Rueda, 1957) is a helpful Socialist version of political developments, and the rise of integral nationalism in this period is reflected in Juan Carulla's *Genio de la Argentina* (Buenos Aires: Distribuidores R. Medina, 1943). The effects of the Infamous Decade are treated in Ysabel Fisk [Rennie], "Argentina: The Thirteen-Year Crisis," *Foreign Affairs* 22 (January, 1944): 256–266.

VI. *Social and Institutional Dimensions of Argentine Militarism.* On the social and geographic origins of the army officer-corps, see the cited works of Imaz. Important insights into the military way-of-life are contained in the works by the soldier-sociologist, Lieutenant General Benjamín Rattenbach: *Sociología militar: Una contribución al estudio* (Buenos Aires: Librería Perlado, 1958), *Estudios y reflexiones* (Buenos Aires,

1955), and "El sector militar de la sociedad," *La Nación*, November 24, 1963. The "Army's collective personality" is analyzed by James Bruce in chapter 22 of *Those Perplexing Argentines* (New York: Longmans, Green and Co., 1953). Perhaps the most important account of the rise of integral nationalism in the army, by a high-ranking Argentine officer, is General Luis Rodolfo González's "Ideas Contrary to the Spirit of May and Their Repercussion in Argentine Political Life: A Military Opinion at the Service of Definitive Pacification." Translated and annotated by K. H. Silvert and titled "The Military: A Handbook for their Control," it is found in *Letters and Reports Written for the American Universities Field Staff, 1955–1958* (Hanover, N.H., 1958). Interesting comments on military thinking are contained in Colonel Alfredo A. Baisi's *La revolución faltante* (Buenos Aires: Ediciones Ancora, 1959). An idealized version of the army officer's life is described by Lieutenant Colonel Eduardo C. Conesa in "El ejército argentino, escuela de ciudadanía," *Revista Militar* 92 (October, 1951): 1169–1181. The official version of the army conscript's thinking is given by Santiago M. Peralta in *Memorias de un conscripto* (Buenos Aires: Editorial Enero, 1946). "Influencia del ejército en el desarrollo de los valores materiales y morales del pueblo," by Lieutenant Germán R. Teisseire in *Revista Militar* 99 (January–February, 1953): 33–39, describes the values inculcated by military training.

An important two-volume work on the institutions of the Argentine army has been written by a Brazilian ex-military attaché to Argentina, Major Armando Duval: *A Argentina, potencia militar* (Rio de Janeiro: Imprensa Nacional, 1922). See also Colonel Carlos von der Becke's "La République Argentine et l'armée argentine," *Revue Militaire Gènèrale* 4, ser. 2 (Paris, 1938): 443–468. A clear description of the institutions of the Argentine army is Augusto G. Rodríguez's "El ejército argentino" in a special issue of *La Nación* (May 22, 1960) observing the 150th anniversary of May 25, 1810.

There are many works on German influences in the Argentine army. A good introduction to the topic, by a German officer who was prominent in spreading German military influence in Latin America, is General Wilhelm Faupel's "Las relaciones del ejército alemán con los paises ibero-americanos" in his *Ibero-América y Alemania* (Berlin: C. Heymann, 1933). Of utmost importance in the study of German military missions in Argentina is Fritz T. Epstein's "Argentinien und das Deutsche Heer" in *Geschichtliche Kräfte und Entscheidungen* (Weisbaden, Germany: F. Steiner, 1954); and his unpublished manuscript, "European Military Influences in Latin America," at the Library of Congress in Washington, D.C., 1961. German influence in the Argentine army is exposed in Silvano Santander's *Nazismo en Argentina: La conquista del ejército* (Buenos Aires: Pueblos Unidos, 1945) and in T. R. Ybarra's *America Faces South* (New York: Dodd, Mead and Co., 1939).

The works of the Biblioteca del Oficial are helpful in analyzing military thinking in the 1930s and early 1940s. A revealing book is Lieutenant Colonel Ernesto Fantini Pertiné's *Inquietades militares de la época*, Biblioteca del Oficial vol. 220 (1937). The army's views on economic growth are described in Colonel Eduardo A. Grimaldi's *Industria siderúrgica argentina: Antecedentes y comentarios*, Biblioteca del Oficial vol. 352 (1947). On the army and economic development, see also Lieutenant Colonel Julio Sanguinetti's *Nuestro potencial económico industrial y la defensa nacional*, Biblioteca del Oficial vol. 331 (1946). A liberal nationalist's approach to this topic is General José M. Sarobe's *Política económica argentina* (Buenos Aires: Unión Industrial Argentina, 1942). The integral concept of preparation for war is defended by Colonel Juan Lucio Cernadas in *Estrategia nacional y política de estado* (Buenos Aires: El Ateneo, 1938). The most detailed military lamentation of the plight of an economically dependent nation is Lieutenant Colonel Mariano Abarca's in "La industria y la independencia nacional," *Revista de Economía* 43 (May, 1944): 66–67. Growing army sympathy for foreign fascism is reflected by Auditor de División Ricardo Sacheri in "El nuevo orden económico en Europa," *Revista Militar* 79 (October, 1942): 727–773.

A defense of the army as an institution, showing its contributions to Argentine society, is General Laureano Orencio Anaya's *El ejército: Factor ponderable en el desenvolvimiento económico, social y político de la nación* (Buenos Aires: Círculo Militar, 1949). An attempt to reconcile military expenditures with social needs is made by Lieutenant Colonel Matías Laborda Ibarra in "La conciliación de intereses sociales, económicos y financieros de la nación, con la organización y desarrollo de la fuerza ejército," *Revista de la Escuela Superior de Guerra*, no. 324 (January–May, 1957): 71–78.

A standard work on navy history, that stresses the early periods, is *Historia naval argentina* (Buenos Aires: Emecé Editores, 1944) by Captain Teodoro Caillet-Bois. See also Manuel Zumaran Lavalle's *Evocación histórica de la marina* (Buenos Aires, 1949). Important social data on the navy are contained in "La escuadra y la escuela naval: Breve reseña histórica" in *Los viajes de la "Sarmiento"* (Buenos Aires: Ediciones Argentinas,

1931). A more recent study is Lieutenant Carlos Enrique Zartmann's "The Argentine Navy," in *United States Naval Institute Proceedings* 86, no. 7 (July, 1960): 82–101.

VI. *The Argentine Revolution of 1943 and the Rise of Perón.* On the revolution of 1943, a complicated affair, citations of utmost importance may be found in Américo Ghioldi, *Historia crítica de la revolución del 43* (Buenos Aires, 1950), pp. 351–355. Other very valuable information is found in the series "Documentos para la historia," in *La Vanguardia,* July 17, 1945, September 25, 1945, October 2, 1945, and October 9, 1945. For insightful North American views of the revolution and the military dictatorship that followed, see *Argentine Diary* (New York: Random House, 1944) by Ray Josephs and *Revolution before Breakfast* (Chapel Hill: University of North Carolina Press, 1947) by Ruth and Leonard Greenup. See also Felix Weil's *Argentine Riddle* (New York: John Say Co., 1944).

On the organization of GOU and the rise of Perón, see Gontran de Guemes's *Así se gestó la dictadura: "El GOU"* (Buenos Aires: Ediciones Rex, 1956), and the previously cited Lanús, *Al servicio del ejército* for early actions by Perón. Also useful on this topic is the previously cited Santander, *Nazismo en Argentina,* and Ernesto Sammartino's *La verdad sobre la situación* (Montevideo, 1951). On the Catholic nationalists and the revolution of 1943, see Saxtone Bradford's *The Battle for Buenos Aires* (New York: Harcourt, Brace and Co., 1943), and Oscar Troncoso's *Los nacionalistas argentinos* (Buenos Aires: Editorial S.A.G.A., 1957).

The military supervision of the elections that brought Perón to power is recorded in a two-volume work from the Ministry of the Interior, *Las fuerzas armadas restituyen el imperio de la soberanía popular: Las elecciones generales de 1946* (Buenos Aires: Imprenta de la Cámara de Diputados, 1946).

VII. *The Perón Era (1946–1955).* The best references on the Perón era are two works by Alejandro Magnet: *Nuestros vecinos justicialistas* (Santiago de Chile: Editorial del Pacífico, 1953) and *Nuestros vecinos argentinos* (Santiago de Chile: Editorial del Pacífico, 1956). George I. Blanksten, *Perón's Argentina* (Chicago: University of Chicago Press, 1953) is especially good for Justicialist doctrine, and Robert Alexander's *The Perón Era* (New York: Columbia University Press, 1951) is informative on matters pertaining to labor. Other excellent analyses of Perón's impact on the labor movement are Samuel L. Baily's *Labor, Nationalism and Politics in Argentina* (New Brunswick, N.J.: Rutgers University Press, 1967), and the previously cited works by Whitaker, Pendle, and McGann. *Why Perón Came to Power* (New York: Alfred A. Knopf, 1968), edited by Joseph R. Barager, is an interesting anthology dealing with this era.

There is no adequate biography on Perón. Helpful for information on his early life is Enrique Pavón Pereyra's *Perón, 1895–1942* (Buenos Aires: Ediciones Espiño, 1953). *The Woman with the Whip: Eva Perón* (Garden City, N.Y.: Doubleday and Co., 1952) by Mary Main (María Flores, pseud.), explores Eva Perón's role and also provides many insights into the role of the army during the Perón era. Ramón J. Lombille's *Eva la predestinada* (Buenos Aires: Gure, 1955) is a study of Eva's political life. Benigno Acossano's *Eva Perón: Su verdadera vida* (Buenos Aires: Editorial Lamas, 1955) is a well-organized, vivid account that is very critical of Juan D. Perón. Finally, there is Eva's own politically inspired memoir, *La razón de mi vida* (Buenos Aires: Ediciones Peuser, 1952).

As Fritz Hoffman describes ("Perón and After," *Hispanic American Historical Review* 36 [1956]: 510–528; and *ibid.*, 39 [1959]: 212–233), the "successful revolution against Perón of September, 1955, loosed a flood of publications." Of these, the most detailed and well organized is Bernardo Rabinovitz's *Sucedió en la Argentina (1943–1956): Lo que no se dijo* (Buenos Aires: Ediciones Gure, 1956). E. F. Sánchez Zinny's *El culto de la infamia: Historia documentada de la segunda tiranía argentina* (Buenos Aires 1958) is based on extensive documentation from the archives of Perón's secretariat. Raúl Damonte Taborda's *Ayer fué San Perón* (Buenos Aires: Ediciones Gure, 1955) is a book by a Radical with some important insights. Important information on the Perón period is also contained in Reynaldo Pastor's *Frente al totalitarismo peronista* (Buenos Aires: Bases, 1959). Ricardo Boizard in his *Esa noche de Perón* (Buenos Aires: Editorial Sedu, 1955) depicts a fun-loving Perón never concerned about the Argentine people. Américo Ghioldi's *De la tiranía a la democracia social* (Buenos Aires: Ediciones Gure, 1956) is interesting for its critical views of the role of Eva. Santiago L. Nudelman's two-volume work *Proceso contra la dictadura* (Buenos Aires, 1953–1955) contains important debates from the Chamber of Deputies. Carlos Cossio, a renowned law professor, gives his view in his *La política como conciencia: Meditación sobre la Argentina de 1955* (Buenos Aires: Abeledo-Perrot, 1957), while Mario Amadeo's *Ayer, hoy, mañana* (Buenos Aires: Ediciones Gure, 1956) gives the Catholic nationalist view. Orestes D. Confalonieri's *Perón contra Perón* (Buenos Aires: Editorial Antygua, 1956), a digest of Perón's lies, contains important documents. Although mainly a summary of official charges against

Perón, *Libro negro de la segunda tiranía* (Buenos Aires: Comisión Nacional de Investigaciones, 1958) is excellent for its simple and direct approach to the topic.

Very useful for this interpretation were the memoirs of the Perón regime by military men. General Franklin Lucero in *El precio de la lealtad* (Buenos Aires: Editorial Propulsión, 1959) defends the position of the minister of war under Perón. Rear Admiral Aníbal O. Olivieri's *Dos veces rebelde: Memorias del contraalmirante* (Buenos Aires: Ediciones Siglo, 1958) is a revealing memoir by the minister of the navy under Perón. Rear Admiral Guillermo D. Plater's *Una gran lección* (La Plata, Argentina: Almafuerte, 1956) is another important naval account of the Perón era.

VIII. *The Decline and Downfall of Perón.* On Perón's relationship with the church, see John J. Kennedy's *Catholicism, Nationalism, and Democracy* (Notre Dame, Ind.: University of Notre Dame Press, 1958); "Church and State in Argentina," *World Today* 12 (February, 1956): 58–66; and, for the Peronist view, Hernán Benítez's "La iglesia y el justicialismo," *Revista de la Universidad de Buenos Aires*, no. 24 (October–December, 1952): 313–360. The best work on Perón's war with the church is Pablo Marsal S.'s detailed account, *Perón y la iglesia* (Buenos Aires: Ediciones Rex, 1955). See also John Murray, S.J., "Perón and the Church," *Studies* 44 (Autumn, 1955): 257–270.

Perón's controversial contract with Standard Oil is given detailed treatment in Adolfo Silenzi de Stagni's *El petróleo argentino* (Buenos Aires: Ediciones Problemas Nacionales, 1955). The Justicialist indoctrination campaign in the armed forces is reflected in "Curso de orientación para jefes de unidad," *Revista Militar*, no. 622 (November–December, 1953): 7–26. Félix Lafiandra in *Los panfletos* (Buenos Aires: Editorial Itinerarium, 1955) has compiled important Catholic nationalist pamphlets that were distributed to the army in 1955.

A useful study of the military revolt that overthrew Perón is Arthur P. Whitaker's *Argentine Upheaval: Perón's Fall and the New Regime* (New York: Praeger, 1956). Compiled by ten Argentine journalists, *Así cayó Perón: Crónica del movimiento triunfante* (Buenos Aires: Editorial Lamas, 1955) is an accurate account of the revolt. Arturo J. Zabala's *La revolución del 16 de septiembre* (Buenos Aires: Ediciones Debate, 1955) gives important biographies of rebel leaders, and Luis Ernesto Lonardi's *Dios es justo* (Buenos Aires: F. Colombo, 1958) is excellent for its description of the planning and operations of the rebellion in the all-important Córdoba garrison. Bonifacio del Carril's *Crónica interna de la revolución libertadora* (Buenos Aires, 1959) is a vital storehouse of information and gives a valuable eyewitness account of the revolution in Cuyo. The failure of the rebellion in Curuzú Cuatía is analyzed by Rolando Hume in *Sublevación en Curuzú Cuatía* (Santa Fe, Argentina: Castellví, 1962). The significant role of the navy in the revolution is described in detail and with anecdotes in Miguel Angel Cavallo's *Puerto Belgrano: Hora cero* (Bahía Blanca, Argentina: Talleres Gráficos de la Nueva Provincia, 1955).

IX. *The Military and Politics after Perón, 1955–1966.* The most revealing analysis of the inner struggles of the military during the Lonardi regime is found in the previously cited work of Carril, *Crónica interna de la revolución libertadora.* Lonardi's efforts on behalf of national reconciliation are described by his son, Luis E. Lonardi, in the previously cited *Dios es justo.* An overview of Argentina during this postrevolutionary period is contained in José Santos Gollán's "Argentine Interregnum," *Foreign Affairs* 35 (October, 1956): 84–94. Army attitudes in this period are examined in Sergio Bagú's "Diagrama político de la Argentina de hoy," *Cuadernos Americanos* 90 (November–December, 1956): 38–57.

Important speeches of the Aramburu regime are contained in *La revolución libertadora* (Buenos Aires, 1956) by General Pedro E. Aramburu and Rear Admiral Isaac F. Rojas. Struggles within the armed forces under Aramburu are described in the previously cited Carril, *Crónica interna de la revolución libertadora.* The role of the armed forces in this period is examined in two works by Mariano Montemayor: *Presencia política de las fuerzas armadas* (Buenos Aires: Ediciones Siglo, 1958) and *Claves para entender un gobierno* (Buenos Aires, 1960). The economic position of the Aramburu regime is analyzed in "Argentina Two Years after Perón," *World Today* 14 (December–January 1958): 18–26.

A detailed interpretation of the Frondizi regime is Ismael Viñas's *Orden y progreso: La era del frondizismo* (Buenos Aires: Editorial Palestra, 1960). See also Daniel Cruz Machado's *Frondizi: una conducta, un pensamiento* (Buenos Aires: Editorial Soluciones, 1957); Nestor Morales Loza's *Frondizi y la verdad* (Buenos Aires: Editorial Urania, 1957); Esteban Rey's *¿Es Frondizi un nuevo Perón?* (Buenos Aires: Ediciones Lucha Obrera, 1957); and Francisco Hipólito Uzal's *Frondizi y la oligarquía* (Buenos Aires: Cía. Argentina de Editores, 1963). Félix Luna's *Diálogos con Frondizi* (Buenos Aires: Editorial Desarrollo, 1963) contains the deposed president's views on military crises during his regime.

Excellent on-the-spot analyses of the Frondizi regime are offered in K. H. Silvert's *Economics, Democracy, and Honesty: An Assessment of the Frondizi Regime*, American Universities Field Staff Reports Service, East Coast South American Series, vol. VII, no. 1 (Hanover, N.H., 1960), and in his *The Annual Political Cycle in Argentina: A Jaundiced Retrospective, ibid.*, vol. VIII, no. 6 (1961). Many of these reports are reproduced in Silvert's penetrating *The Conflict Society: Reaction and Revolution in Latin America* (New Orleans: Hauser Press, 1961).

A favorable estimate of the Frondizi regime, with many insights into the army's position, is John J. Kennedy's "Accountable Government in Argentina," *Foreign Affairs* 37 (April, 1969): 453–461. Another valuable article pertaining to the military during the Frondizi years is David Huelin's "Conflicting Forces in Argentina," *World Today* 18 (April, 1962): 142–152.

On the downfall of Frondizi and the ensuing Guido regime, no source can compare with James W. Rowe's incisive, on-the-spot accounts for the Institute of Current World Affairs in Buenos Aires. His mimeographed reports are on the period from March 11, 1962, to September 15, 1963. As K. H. Silvert's successor on the American Universities Field Staff, Rowe has contributed a number of admirable publications that are a tribute to that organization's work: *Argentina's Restless Military*, AUFS East Coast South American Series vol. XI, no. 2 (Hanover, N.H., 1964), which contains a useful compilation of military crises; *Argentina: An Election Retrospect, ibid.*, vol. XI, no. 1 (1964); *A Note on Argentina, ibid.*, vol. XI, no. 3 (1964); and *Argentina's Durable Peronists: A Twentieth Anniversary Note, ibid.*, vol. XII, no. 2 (1966). Latin American specialists look forward to a forthcoming volume by Rowe on politics in the decade since Perón.

Pleas for military professionalism are contained in two books by Lieutenant Colonel Mario Horacio Orsolini, *La crisis del ejército* (Buenos Aires: Ediciones Arayú, 1964) and *Ejército argentino y crecimiento nacional* (Buenos Aires: Ediciones Arayú, 1965). Military coalitions and struggles during the Illía regime are examined in Thomas M. Millington's "President Arturo Illía and the Argentine Military," *Journal of Inter-American Studies* 6 (July, 1964): 405–424. On Peronism and the deep divisions in Argentine society, see Jeanne Kuebler's "Argentina and Peronism," *Editorial Research Reports* I, no. 19 (May 15, 1963): 367–383. On lingering Peronist control of the labor movement, see Morris A. Horowitz, "The Legacy of Juan Perón," *Challenge* 12 (October, 1963): 27–30.

Probably the best work on Peronism in the postrevolutionary period is Peter Ranis's "Peronismo without Perón: Ten Years after the Fall (1955–1965)," *Journal of Inter-American Studies* 8 (January, 1966): 112–128. Ranis has also contributed an incisive study of the Illía regime and the resurgence of Peronism, entitled "Background to the 1965 Argentine Elections," *World Today* 21 (May, 1965): 198–209.

An excellent analysis of the struggle between *azules* and *colorados* by Philip B. Springer, and titled "Disunity and Disorder: Factional Politics in the Argentine Military," is found in *The Military Intervenes*, edited by Henry Biemen (New York: The Russell Sage Foundation, 1968). The rise of the cavalry to an elite position in the Argentine army is traced in Rogelio García Lupo's "El ejército argentino: Mosaico dominado por la caballería," *Política* 6 (May, 1967): 61–71. An early and perceptive analysis of the Onganía regime is James W. Rowe's, *Onganía's Argentina: The First Four Months*, American Universities Field Staff Reports Service, East Coast South American Series vol. XII, no. 7 (Hanover, N.H., 1966). A detailed and excellent article, favorable to the Onganía regime, is David C. Jordan's "Argentina's New Military Government," *Current History* 58 (February, 1970): 85–90, 116–117. A useful survey of current Argentine politics is contained in Peter G. Snow, *Political Forces in Argentina* (Boston: Allyn and Bacon, 1971).

SOURCES

GOVERNMENT DOCUMENTS

Argentina

Congreso Nacional. *Diario de sesiones de la Cámara de Diputados, año 1927,* vol. IV. Buenos Aires, 1927.

————. *Diario de sesiones de la Cámara de Diputados, año 1946,* vol. I. Buenos Aires, 1947.

————. *Diario de sesiones de la Cámara de Diputados, año 1950,* vol. IV. Buenos Aires, 1951.

————. *Diario de sesiones de la Cámara de Diputados, año 1951,* vol. III. Buenos Aires, 1952.

————. *Diario de sesiones de la Cámara de Diputados, año 1954,* vol. I. Buenos Aires, 1954.

————. *Diario de sesiones de la Cámara de Senadores, año 1949,* vol. I. Buenos Aires, 1949.

Ministerio de Guerra. *Memoria del ministerio de guerra presentada al honorable congreso de la nación, 4 de junio 1946–4 de junio 1947.* Buenos Aires, 1947.

Ministerio del Interior. *Las fuerzas armadas restituyen el imperio de la soberanía popular: Las elecciones generales de 1946.* 2 vols. Buenos Aires: Imprenta de la Cámara de Diputados, 1946.

————. *Mensaje de pacificación y desarrollo nacional, leido ante la asamblea legislativa por el presidente de la nación Dr. Arturo Frondizi al inaugurar su período constitucional el 1° de mayo de 1958.* Buenos Aires, 1958.

————. *La obra de la revolución, reseña sintética de la labor desarrollada.* Buenos Aires, 1931.

Ministerio de Marina. *Memoria del ministerio de marina correspondiente al ejercicio 1936.* Buenos Aires, 1937.

Poder Ejecutivo Nacional, 1932–1938. *Ejército: Ferrocarriles del estado.* Buenos Aires, 1938. [Section on "Construcción militares realizados en el período 1932–1937," vol. VI, no pagination, located in New York Public Library on Fifth Avenue, New York City.]

Presidencia de la Nación, Secretaria Técnica. *Plan de Gobierno, 1947–1951.* 2 vols. Buenos Aires, 1956.

Presidente 1944 (Farrell). *Mensaje y Memoria, 1943–4 de junio, 1944.* Buenos Aires, 1944.

Yacimientos Petrolíferos Fiscales. *Desarrollo de la industria petrolífera fiscal, 1907–1932.* Buenos Aires: Casa J. Peuser, 1932.

United States

Department of State. *Blue Book on Argentina: Consultation among the American Republics with Respect to the Argentine Situation. Memorandum of the United States Government.* New York: Greenberg, 1946.

———. *Papers Relating to the Foreign Relations of the United States, 1934,* vol. IV, The American Republics. Washington, D.C.: Government Printing Office, 1934.

BOOKS AND PAMPHLETS

Alexander, Robert J. *The Perón Era.* New York: Columbia University Press, 1951.

Amadeo, Mario. *Ayer, hoy, mañana.* Buenos Aires: Ediciones Gure, 1956.

———. *La encrujicada argentina.* Madrid: Epesa, 1956.

Arciniegas, Germán. *The State of Latin America.* Translated by Harriet de Onís. New York: Alfred A. Knopf, 1952.

Baisi, Alfredo A. *La revolución faltante.* Buenos Aires: Ediciones Ancora, 1959.

Balestra, Juan. *El noventa: Una evolución política argentina.* Buenos Aires: Fariña, 1935.

Beals, Carleton, Bryce Oliver, Herschel Brickell, and Samuel Guy Inman. *What the South Americans Think of Us.* New York: R. M. McBride and Co., 1945.

Belín Sarmiento, A. *Una república muerta.* Buenos Aires: Imprenta "Mariano Moreno," 1892.

Benedetti, Antonio. *Perón y Eva: Trayectoria y fin de un régimen.* Mexico City: Editores Panamericanos Asociados, 1956.

Beresford Crawkes, J. *533 días de la historia argentina—6 de septiembre de 1930–20 de febrero de 1932.* Buenos Aires: Imprenta Mercatali, 1932.

Blanksten, George I. *Perón's Argentina.* Chicago: University of Chicago Press, 1953.

Boffi, Luis L. *Bajo la tiranía del sable.* Buenos Aires: Talleres gráficos de la Editorial Claridad, 1933.

Bradford, Saxton. *The Battle for Buenos Aires.* New York: Harcourt, Brace and Co., 1943.

Bruce, James. *Those Perplexing Argentines.* New York: Longmans, Green and Co., 1953.

Bucich Escobar, Ismael. *Historia de los presidentes argentinos.* Buenos Aires: Roldán, 1934.

Buezas, Adolfo. *Las fuerzas armadas ante la alternativa: Pueblo o imperialismo.* Buenos Aires: Ediciones "Liberación Nacional," 1959.

Caillet-Bois, Teodoro. *Historia naval argentina.* Buenos Aires: Emecé Editores, 1944.

Carril, Bonifacio del. *Crónica interna de la revolución libertadora.* Buenos Aires, 1959.

Carulla, Juan E. *Al filo del medio siglo.* Paraná, Argentina: Editorial Llanura, 1951.

——. *Genio de la Argentina.* Buenos Aires: Distribuidores R. Medina, 1943.

——. *Latinoamérica en picada.* Buenos Aires, 1947.

——. *Valor etico de la revolución del 6 de septiembre de 1930.* Buenos Aires: Imprenta Belgrano, 1931.

Cattáneo, Atilio E. *Entre rejas: Memorias.* Buenos Aires: Editorial "Chango," 1939.

——. *Plan 1932: Las conspiraciones radicales contra el general Justo.* Buenos Aires: Proceso Ediciones, 1959.

Cernadas, Juan Lucio. *Estrategia nacional y política de estado.* Buenos Aires: El Ateneo, 1938.

Círculo Militar. *Monografía histórica del estado mayor.* Buenos Aires, 1929.

——. *Teniente General D. Pablo Riccheri.* Buenos Aires, 1936.

Columba, Ramón. *El congreso que yo he visto.* 2 vols. Buenos Aires, 1948–1949.

Cossio, Carlos, *La política como conciencia: Meditación sobre la Argentina de 1955.* Buenos Aires: Abeledo-Perrot, 1957.

Damonte Taborda, Raúl. *Ayer fue San Perón.* Buenos Aires: Ediciones Gure, 1955.

Diez periodistas porteños. *Al margen de la conspiración.* Buenos Aires: Biblos Editorial, 1930.

Duval, Armando. *A Argentina, potencia militar.* 2 vols. Rio de Janeiro: Imprensa Nacional, 1922.

El hombre de deber: Una serie de semblanzas del Gral. Manuel A. Rodríguez. Buenos Aires: Librería "La Facultad," 1936.

Etchepareborda, Roberto. *Yrigoyen y el congreso.* Buenos Aires: Editorial Raigal, 1957.

Fantini Pertiné, Ernesto. *Inquietudes militares de la época.* Biblioteca del Oficial vol. 220. Buenos Aires, 1937.

Fillol, Tomás R. *Social Factors in Economic Development: The Argentine Case.* Cambridge, Mass.: M.I.T. Press, 1961.

Fisk [Rennie], Ysabel. *The Argentine Republic.* New York: Macmillan Co., 1945.

Florit, Carlos A. *Las fuerzas armadas y la guerra psicológica.* Buenos Aires: Ediciones Arayá, 1963.

Galíndez, Bartolomé. *Apuntes de tres revoluciones, 1930–1943–1955.* Buenos Aires, 1956.

Gálvez, Manuel. *Vida de Hipólito Yrigoyen: El hombre de misterio.* Buenos Aires: Talleres Gráficos G. Kraft, 1939.

García Lupo, Rogelio. *La rebelión de los generales.* Buenos Aires: Jamcana, 1963.

Germani, Gino. *Estructura social de la Argentina: Análisis estadístico.* Buenos Aires: Editorial Raigal, 1955.

―――. *Integración política de las masas y totalitarismo.* Buenos Aires: Colegio Libre de Estudios Superiores, 1956.

Goldstraj, Manuel. *Años y errores: Un cuarto de siglo de política.* Buenos Aires: Editorial Sophos, 1937.

―――. *El camino del exilio.* Buenos Aires: Librerías Anaconda, 1935.

Greenup, Ruth, and Leonard Greenup. *Revolution before Breakfast.* Chapel Hill: University of North Carolina Press, 1947.

Grimaldi, Eduardo A. *Industria siderúrgica argentina, antecedentes y comentarios.* Biblioteca del Oficial vol. 352. Buenos Aires, 1947.

Guemes, Gontran de. *Así se gestó la dictadura: "El GOU."* Buenos Aires: Ediciones Rex, 1956.

Hernández Arregui, Juan José. *La formación de la conciencia nacional (1930–1960).* Buenos Aires: Ediciones Hachea, 1960.

Hume, Rolando. *Sublevación en Curuzú Cuatía*. Santa Fe, Argentina: Castellví, 1962.

Ibarguren, Carlos. *La historia que he vivido*. Buenos Aires: Ediciones Peuser, 1955.

Institución de Extensión Universitaria de la Facultad de Derecho y el Centro de Derecho y Ciencias Sociales. *Ciclo de mesas redondas: Tres revoluciones (los ultimos veintiocho años)*. Buenos Aires: FUBA, 1959.

Janowitz, Morris. *The Professional Soldier: A Social and Political Portrait*. Glencoe, Illinois: Free Press, 1960.

Josephs, Ray. *Argentine Diary*. New York: Random House, 1944.

————. *Latin America: Continent in Crisis*. New York: Random House, 1948.

Lafiandra, Felix, ed. *Los panfletos*. Buenos Aires: Editorial Itinerarium, 1955.

Lanús, Roque. *Al servicio del ejército*. Buenos Aires, 1946.

Libro negro de la segunda tiranía. Buenos Aires: Comisión Nacional de Investigaciones, 1958.

Lieuwen, Edwin. *Arms and Politics in Latin America*. Published for the Council on Foreign Relations. New York: Praeger, 1961.

————. *Generals vs. Presidents: Neomilitarism in Latin America*. New York: Praeger, 1964.

Liga Patriótica Argentina. *Cuarto congreso nacionalista de la Liga Patriótica Argentina, sesiones del 19, 20 y 21 de mayo de 1923*. Buenos Aires, 1923.

Lonardi, Luis Ernesto. *Dios es justo*. Buenos Aires: F. Colombo, 1958.

Lucero, Franklin. *El precio de la lealtad*. Buenos Aires: Editorial Propulsión, 1959.

Luna, Félix. *Diálogos con Frondizi*. Buenos Aires: Editorial Desarrollo, 1963.

————. *Hipólito Yrigoyen: El templario de la libertad*. Vol. I in *Hipólito Yrigoyen: Pueblo y gobierno*. 12 vols. Buenos Aires: Editorial Raigal, 1956.

Magnet, Alejandro. *Nuestros vecinos argentinos*. Santiago de Chile: Editorial de Pacífico, 1956.

————. *Nuestros vecinos justicialistas*. Santiago de Chile: Editorial del Pacífico, 1953.

Main, Mary [María Flores]. *The Woman with the Whip: Eva Perón*. Garden City, N.Y.: Doubleday, Page and Co., 1952.

Martin, Percy A. *Latin America and the War*. Baltimore: Johns Hopkins Press, 1925.

Martínez, Mariano Reinaldo. *Notas imparciales para la historia del peronismo*. Buenos Aires, 1956.

Matienzo, José N. *Nuevos temas políticos e históricos*. Buenos Aires: J. Roldán, 1928.

Mazo, Gabriel del. *El radicalismo: Notas sobre su historia y doctrina, 1922–1952*. Buenos Aires: Editorial Raigal, 1955.

McGann, Thomas F. *Argentina: The Divided Land*. Princeton: D. Van Nostrand Co., 1966.

———. *Argentina, the United States, and the Inter-American System, 1880–1914*. Cambridge, Mass.: Harvard University Press, 1957.

Monseratt, G. *A través de los tiempos: Estudio historial sobre la equiparación de militares en retiro*. Buenos Aires, 1937.

Olivieri, Aníbal O. *Dos veces rebelde: Memorias*. Buenos Aires: Ediciones Siglo, 1958.

Palacio, Ernesto. *Historia de la Argentina, 1515–1938*. Buenos Aires: ALPE, 1954.

Palacios, Alfredo. *En defensa de los instituciones libres*. Santiago de Chile: Ediciones Ercilla, 1936.

Pastor, Reynaldo. *Frente al totalitarismo peronista*. Buenos Aires: Bases, 1959.

Pavón Pereyra, Enrique. *Perón, 1895–1942*. Buenos Aires: Ediciones Espiño, 1953.

Pendle, George. *Argentina*. 2nd ed. London: Oxford University Press, 1961.

Peralta, Santiago M. *Memorias de un conscripto*. Buenos Aires: Editorial Enero, 1946.

Perón, Juan D. *La fuerza es el derecho de las bestias*. Havana: S. Touriño, 1956.

———. *Significado de la defensa nacional desde el punto de vista militar*. Buenos Aires: Colegio Nacional de la Universidad de La Plata, 1944.

Plater, Guillermo D. *Una gran lección*. La Plata, Argentina: Almafuerte, 1956.

Potash, Robert A. *The Army and Politics in Argentina, 1928–1945*. Stanford, Cal.: Stanford University Press, 1969.

Prebisch, Raúl. *La situación económica del país*. Buenos Aires, 1955.

Quien es quien en la Argentina: Biografías contemporáneas. Buenos Aires: G. Kraft, 1939.

Rabinovitz, Bernardo. *Lo que no se dijo: Sucedió en la Argentina (1943–1956).* Buenos Aires: Ediciones Gure, 1956.

Ramos, Jorge Abelardo. *América latina: Un país.* Buenos Aires: Ediciones Octubre, 1949.

————. *Historia política del ejército argentino.* Buenos Aires: A. Peña Lillo, 1959.

Rattenbach, Benjamín. *Estudios y reflexiones.* Buenos Aires, 1955.

————. *Sociología militar: Una contribución a su estudio.* Buenos Aires: Librería Perlado, 1958.

Repetto, Nicolás. *Los socialistas y el ejército.* Buenos Aires: Editorial La Vanguardia, 1946.

Rivera, Enrique. *Peronismo y frondizismo.* Buenos Aires: Editorial Patria Grande, 1958.

Rodríguez, Augusto G. *Sarmiento militar.* Buenos Aires: Ediciones Peuser, 1950.

Rojas, Ricardo. *El radicalismo de mañana.* Buenos Aires: L. J. Rosso, 1932.

Rowe, James W. *Argentina: An Election Retrospect.* [JWR-1-'64]. American Universities Field Staff Reports Service, East Coast South American Series, vol. XI, no. 1. Hanover, N.H., 1964.

————. *Argentina: The First Four Months. Part I: The "Golpe" in Retrospect.* [JWR-7-'66]. American Universities Field Staff Reports Service, East Coast South American Series, vol. XII, no. 7. Hanover, N.H., 1966.

————. *Argentina's Durable Peronists: A Twentieth Anniversary Note. Part I: Some Preconditions and Achievements.* [JWR-2-'66]. American Universities Field Staff Reports Service, East Coast South American Series, vol. XII, no. 2. Hanover, N.H., 1966.

————. *Argentina's Restless Military: An Analysis of the Role of the Armed Services in Argentine Politics.* [JWR-2-'64]. American Universities Field Staff Reports Service, East Coast South American Series, vol. XI, no. 2. Hanover, N.H., 1964.

————. *A Note on Argentina: Change, Stagnation, and Unrealized Promise.* [JWR-3-'64]. American Universities Field Staff Reports Service, East Coast South American Series, vol. XI, no. 3. Hanover, N.H., 1964.

Salera, Virgil. *Exchange Control and the Argentine Market.* New York: Columbia University Press, 1941.

Sánchez Zinny, E. F. *El culto de la infamia: Historia documentada de la segunda tiranía argentina.* Buenos Aires, 1958.

Sanguinetti, Julio. *Nuestro potencial económico industrial y la defensa nacional.* Biblioteca del Oficial Vol. 331. Buenos Aires, 1946.

Santander, Silvano. *Nazismo en Argentina: La conquista del ejército.* Buenos Aires: Ediciones Pueblos Unidos, 1945.

Sarobe, José María. *Memorias sobre la revolución de 6 de septiembre de 1930.* Buenos Aires: Ediciones Gure, 1957.

————. *Política económica argentina.* Buenos Aires: Unión Industrial Argentina, 1942.

Savio, Manuel N. *Ley de Fabricaciones Militares: Conceptos que fundamentaron su proyecto.* Buenos Aires, 1944.

Schmitt, Karl M., and David D. Burks. *Evolution or Chaos: Dynamics of Latin American Government and Politics.* New York: Praeger, 1963.

Seoane, Manuel. *Rumbo argentino.* Santiago de Chile: Ediciones Ercilla, 1935.

Silvert, Kalman H. *The Annual Political Cycle in Argentina: A Jaundiced Retrospective.* [KHS-6-'61]. American Universities Field Staff Reports Service, East Coast South American Series, vol. VIII, no. 6. Hanover, N.H., 1961.

————. *Economics, Democracy, and Honesty: An Assessment of the Frondizi Regime.* [KHS-1-'60]. American Universities Field Staff Reports Service, East Coast South American Series, vol. VII, no. 1. Hanover, N.H., 1960.

Snow, Peter G. *Political Forces in Argentina.* Boston: Allyn and Bacon, 1971.

Snyder, Louis L. *The Meaning of Nationalism.* New Brunswick, N.J.: Rutgers University Press, 1954.

Spangenberg Leguizamón, Enrique J. *Los responsables: El ejército y la Unión Cívica Radical ante la democracia argentina.* Buenos Aires: Librería "El Ateneo," 1936.

Szulc, Tad. *Twilight of the Tyrants.* New York: Henry Holt and Co., 1959.

Torre, Lisandro de la. *Obras.* 2d ed. 6 vols. Buenos Aires: Editorial Hemisferio, 1952–1954.

Troncoso, Oscar. *Los nacionalistas argentinos.* Buenos Aires: Editorial S.A.G.A., 1957.

Universidad Nacional de La Plata. *Curso de cultura superior universitaria: Cátedra de defensa nacional.* La Plata, Argentina, 1945.

Uriburu, José F. *La palabra del General Uriburu*. Buenos Aires: Roldán, 1933.

Villafañe, Benjamín. *La tragedia argentina*. Buenos Aires: Casa J. Peuser, 1943.

Viñas, Ismael. *Orden y progreso: La era del frondizismo*. Buenos Aires: Editorial Palestra, 1960.

Whitaker, Arthur P. *Argentina*. Englewood Cliffs, N.J.: Prentice-Hall, 1964.

———. *Argentine Upheaval*. New York: Praeger, 1956.

———. *The United States and Argentina*. Cambridge, Mass.: Harvard University Press, 1954.

White, John W. *Argentina: The Life Story of a Nation*. New York: Viking Press, 1942.

Yacimientos Petrolíferos Fiscales. *Desarrollo de la industria petrolífera fiscal, 1907–1932*. Buenos Aires, 1932.

Ybarra, T. R. *America Faces South*. New York: Dodd, Mead and Co., 1939.

Zabala, Arturo J. *La revolución del 16 de septiembre*. Buenos Aires: Ediciones Debate, 1955.

ARTICLES AND MANUSCRIPTS

Abarca, Mariano. "La industria y la independencia nacional." *Revista de Economía* 43 (May, 1944): 66–67.

Alexander, Robert J. "Argentine Socialism after Perón." *Socialist Call* 26 (October, 1958): 12–14.

———. "Peronism and Argentina's Quest for Leadership in Latin America." *Journal of International Affairs* 9 (1955): 47–55.

"Argentina Two Years after Perón." *World Today* 14 (December–January, 1958): 18–26.

Bagú, Sergio. "Diagrama político de la Argentina de hoy." *Cuadernos Americanos* 90 (November–December, 1956): 38–57.

Becke, Carlos von der. "La République Argentine et l'armee argentine." *Revue Militaire Génèrale* 4, ser. 2 (1948): 443–468.

"Behind the Scenes in Argentina." *America*, August 6, 1955, p. 441.

Benítez, Hernán. "La iglesia y el justicialismo." *Revista de la Universidad de Buenos Aires*, no. 24 (1952): 313–360.

Botsford, Keith. "Paralysis in Argentina." *New Leader*, October 15, 1962, pp. 15–16.

Bristol, William B. "Hispanidad in Argentina, 1936–1945." Ph.D. dissertation, University of Pennsylvania. 1947.

Bunge, Alejandro E. "La república argentina define su politica economía nacional." *Revista de Economía Argentina* 28, no. 163 (1932): 3–4.

Bunkley, A. W. "Peronist Crisis." *Yale Review* 39 (Spring, 1950): 402–413.

"Church and State in Argentina." *World Today* 12 (February, 1956): 58–66.

Cuesta, Rafael. "Normas integrantes del derecho de guerra aplicables para casos de acción subversiva." *Revista de la Escuela Superior de Guerra*, 38 (July–September, 1960): 364–390.

"Curso de orientación para jefes de unidad." *Revista Militar*, no. 622 (November–December, 1953): 7–26.

Epstein, Fritz T. "Argentinien und das Deutsche Heer." In *Geschichtliche Kräfte und Entscheidungen*. Wiesbaden, Germany: F. Steiner, 1954.

———. "European Military Influences in Latin America." Unpublished manuscript, Library of Congress, Washington, D.C. 1941.

"Escuela Superior de Guerra." *Revista Universitaria* 6 (1935): 135–138.

Etchepareborda, Roberto. "Aspectos políticos de la crisis de 1930." *Revista de Historia*, no. 3 (1958): 7–40.

———. "Cronología nacional." *Revista de Historia*, no. 3 (1958): 144–155.

Fisk [Rennie], Ysabel. "Argentina: The Thirteen-Year Crisis." *Foreign Affairs* 22 (January, 1944): 256–266.

Fitzgibbon, Russell H. "Argentina after Eva Perón." *Yale Review* 43 (Autumn, 1952): 32–45.

Gollán, José Santos. "Argentine Interregnum." *Foreign Affairs* 35 (October, 1956): 84–94.

González, Luis Rodolfo. "Ideas Contrary to the Spirit of May and Their Repercussion in Argentine Life: A Military Opinion at the Service of Definitive Pacification." Translated by K. H. Silvert, and titled "The Military: A Handbook for Their Control." In *Letters and Reports Written for the American Universities Field Staff, 1955–1958*. Buenos Aires, 1958.

"Green Dragons and Gorillas." *The Economist*, September 26, 1959, pp. 1031–1032.

Horowitz, Irving L. "Modern Argentina: The Politics of Power." *Political Quarterly* 30 (1959): 400–410.

Horowitz, Morris A. "The Legacy of Juan Perón." *Challenge* 12 (October, 1963): 27–30.

Huelin, David. "Conflicting Forces in Argentina." *World Today* 18 (April, 1962): 142–152.

Imaz, José Luis de. "Los que mandan: Las fuerzas armadas en Argentina" *América Latina* 7 (October–December, 1964): 35–69.

Jordan, David C. "Argentina's New Military Government." *Current History* 58 (February, 1970): 85–90, 116–117.

Kennedy, John J. "Accountable Government in Argentina." *Foreign Affairs* 37 (April, 1959): 453–461.

Kuebler, Jeanne. "Argentina and Peronism." *Editorial Research Reports*, May 15, 1963, pp. 367–383.

"La escuadra y la escuela naval: Breve reseña histórico." In *Los viajes de la "Sarmiento."* Buenos Aires: Ediciones Argentinas, 1931.

Loughran, J. A. "Some Reflections on the Argentine Problem." *Inter-American Economic Affairs* 18 (Summer, 1964): 29–43.

Maligne, Augusto A. "El ejército en octubre de 1910." *Revista de Derecho, Historia y Letras* 39 (1911): 397–425.

Marvin, George. "Universal Military Service in Argentina." *World's Week* 33 (1916–1917): 381–392.

Matthews, H. L. "Juan Perón's War with the Catholic Church." *Reporter*, June 16, 1955, pp. 19–22.

Millington, Thomas M. "President Arturo Illía and the Argentine Military." *Journal of Inter-American Studies* 6 (July, 1964): 405–424.

Molina, Ramón. "La subversión institucional de la república de los últimos años transcurridos—causas y remedios." In his *Defendamos nuestro país.* Buenos Aires: Levante, Dept. Editorial de Proventes, 1940.

Murray, John, S.J. "Perón and the Church." *Studies* 44 (Autumn, 1955): 257–270.

Onís, Juan de. "Argentina Tested by Economic Realities," *Foreign Policy Bulletin*, July 15, 1959, pp. 161–162, 168.

Orona, Juan V. "Una logia poco conocida y la revolución del 6 de septiembre." *Revista de Historia*, no. 3 (1958): 73–94.

Pascal, Vicente de. "Argentina's Man of Destiny?" *Inter-American Monthly* 1 (1942): 15–19.

Pendle, George. "Perón and Vargas." *Fortnightly Review* 176 (November, 1951): 723–728.

———. "The Revolution in Argentina." *International Affairs* 32 (April, 1956): 166–172.

Pérez Aznar, Ataúlfo. "Esquema de las fuerzas políticas actuantes hasta 1890." *Revista de Historia,* no. 1 (1957): 36–51.

Popper, David H. "The Argentine Way." *Inter-American Monthly* 1 (1942): 10–11, 45.

Potash, Robert A. "Argentine Political Parties." *Journal of Inter-American Studies* 1 (October, 1959): 515–524.

Ranis, Peter. "Background to the 1965 Argentine Elections." *World Today* 21 (May, 1965): 198–209.

———. "Peronismo without Perón: Ten Years after the Fall (1955–1965)." *Journal of Inter-American Studies* 8 (January, 1966): 112–128.

Rennie, Robert A. "Argentine Fiscal Policy." *Inter-American Economic Affairs* 1 (June, 1947): 51–76.

Reynal, Arnaldo Orfila. "Breve historia y examen del peronismo." *Cuadernos Americanos* 84 (November–December, 1955): 7–37.

Rowe, James W. "Argentina: Reds, Blues and the New Year, II." Mimeographed Report. Institute of Current World Affairs, Buenos Aires. 1962.

———. "The Argentine Elections. II: The Votes." Mimeographed Report, Institute of Current World Affairs, Buenos Aires. 1962.

———. "The Argentine Elections. III: The Reluctant Coup." Mimeographed Report. Institute of Current World Affairs, Buenos Aires. 1962.

———. "Election Eve Again." Mimeographed Report. Institute of Current World Affairs, Buenos Aires. 1963.

"Show of Strength." *Business Week,* July 1, 1944, pp. 114–116.

Silvert, Kalman H. "The Military: A Handbook for Their Control." In *Letters and Reports Written for the American Universities Field Staff, 1955–1958.* Hanover, N.H., 1958.

Springer, Philip B. "Disunity and Disorder: Factional Politics in the Argentine Military." In *The Military Intervenes: Case Studies in Political Development* edited by Henry Bienen. New York: Russell Sage Foundation, 1968.

Teisseire, Germán R. "Influencia del ejército en el desarrollo de los volares materiales y morales del pueblo argentino." *Revista Militar* 99 (January–February, 1953): 33–39.

Valle, Delfor del. "La unión cívica radical y el ejército." *Hechos e Ideas* 1 (1935): 122–126.

Whitaker, Arthur P. "Left and Right Extremism in Argentina." *Current History* 44 (February, 1963): 84–88.

PERIODICALS

America (New York, weekly), August 6, 1955.
América Latina (Rio de Janeiro, quarterly), October–December, 1964.
Business Week (New York, weekly), July 1, 1944.
Challenge (New York, bimonthly), October, 1963.
Cuadernos Americanos (Mexico City, bimonthly), November–December, 1956.
Current History (New York, monthly), November, 1967, February, 1970.
Economist (London, weekly), June, 1956, September, 1959.
Editorial Research Reports (Washington, D.C., weekly), May 15, 1963.
Encounter (London, monthly), September, 1965.
Foreign Affairs (New York, quarterly), January, 1944, April, 1959.
Foreign Policy Bulletin (New York, weekly), July, 1959.
Fortnightly Review (London, monthly), November, 1951.
Hispanic American Report (Stanford University, monthly), September, 1951.
Hispanic World Report (Stanford University; later changed to *Hispanic American Report*, monthly), April, 1949.
Hispanic American Historical Review (Duke University Press, quarterly), May, 1968.
Inter-American Economic Affairs (Washington, D.C., quarterly), June, 1947.
Inter-American Monthly (Silver Spring, Md., monthly), 1942.
International Affairs (London, monthly), April, 1, 1956.
Journal of Inter-American Studies (Gainesville, Florida, quarterly), October, 1959, July, 1964, January, 1966.
Journal of International Affairs (New York, semiannual), 1955.
New Leader (New York, biweekly), October 15, 1962.
Orbis (Philadelphia, quarterly), Fall, 1966.
Political Quarterly (London, quarterly), 1959.
Reporter (New York, biweekly), June 16, 1955.
Revista de Derecho, Historia y Letras (Buenos Aires, monthly), 1910 and 1911.
Revista de Economía Argentina (Buenos Aires, monthly), 1932 and 1944.
Revista de Historia (Buenos Aires, quarterly), 1957 and 1958.
Revista de la Escuela Superior de Guerra (Buenos Aires, quarterly), July–September, 1960.

Revista Militar (Buenos Aires, bimonthly), January–February, 1953, November–December, 1953.
Revista de la Universidad de Buenos Aires (Buenos Aires, quarterly), 1952.
Revista Universitaria (Buenos Aires, quarterly), 1935.
Revue Militaire Générale (Paris, monthly), ser. 2, 1948.
Socialist Call (New York, quarterly), October, 1958.
Studies (Dublin, quarterly), Autumn, 1955.
Time (New York, weekly), March 24, 1952.
U.S. News and World Report (Washington, D.C., weekly), July 11, 1966.
World Today (London, monthly), February, 1956, October, 1958, May, 1965.
World's Week (New York, weekly), 1916–1917.
Yale Review (New Haven, Conn., quarterly), Spring, 1950, Autumn, 1952.

NEWSPAPERS

Azul y Blanco (Buenos Aires), April 3, 1957.
Buenos Aires Herald, November 14, 1955, April 2, 1961.
Christian Science Monitor (Boston), August 11, 1970, June 12, 1971.
New York Herald Tribune, December 26, 1945, July 3, 1948.
New York Times, August 22, 1940; August 26, 1940; September 10, 1941; September 25, 1941; September 22, 1948; June 11, 1956; June 12, 1956; January 26, 1957; July 9, 1958; October 23, 1958; November 12, 1958; June 10, 1970; June 24, 1970; March 25, 1971; March 28, 1971; March 19, 1971; February 19, 1971; March 24, 1971; March 26, 1971.
Noticias Gráficas (Buenos Aires), November 30, 1955, December 1, 1955.
La Nación (Buenos Aires), September 17, 1921; February 21, 1928; September 4, 1930; May 3, 1932; July 7, 1951; February 14, 1952.
La Prensa (Buenos Aires), August 23, 1930; July 6, 1932; January 11, 1943; June 21, 1943; June 24, 1943; November 12, 1943; December 12, 1943; July 6, 1950.
La Vanguardia (Buenos Aires), July 17, 1945; September 18, 1945; October 2, 1945; October 9, 1945.
Ultima Hora (Buenos Aires), December 9, 1928.

INTERVIEWS

Juan D. Perón to Robert Alexander in personal interview, Madrid, September 1, 1960. Used by permission of Professor Alexander, and on file in his office at Rutgers University.

José M. Argana to Robert Alexander in personal interview, Buenos Aires, October 30, 1949. Used by permission of Professor Alexander, and on file in his office at Rutgers University.

Luis Gay, Secretary General of CGT, to Robert Alexander in personal interview, Buenos Aires, November 22, 1946. Used by permission of Professor Alexander, and on file in his office at Rutgers University.

Francisco Pérez Leiros, Secretary General of Unión Obreros y Empleados Municipales, to Robert Alexander in personal interview, Buenos Aires, May 19, 1956. Used by permission of Professor Alexander, and on file in his office at Rutgers University.

David Belnap, United Press International, to Marvin Goldwert in personal interview, Buenos Aires, February 3, 1961.

William Horsey, United Press International, to Marvin Goldwert in personal interview, Buenos Aires, February 17, 1961.

INDEX

Abrahim, Brigadier Ramón: 178
Achával, Clemente Villada. SEE Villada Achával, Clemente
Achával, Mercedes Villada. SEE Villada Achával, Mercedes
Action Française: 17
Adalid, Lt. Col. Sabino: 40
agriculture: 108, 115, 123, 151, 154
Aguirre, Capt. Julio: 189
air force: and revolution of 1930, 28; under Perón, 102–103, 112, 129, 130; and 1951 conspiracy, 112; anti-Peronist stand of, 142; in five-man junta, 162; supports *azules*, 191; and Little Revolution of April, 1963, 193. SEE ALSO armed forces
airplanes: 102
Alende, Oscar: 196
Alliance for Progress: 175
Alsogaray, Lt. Col. Alvaro: and revolution of 1930, 25; and Carlos Toranzo Montero, 180–181; mentioned, 145
Alsogaray, Gen. Julio: 189, 205
Alvear, Marcelo T. de: elected to presidency, 13; and Gen. Justo, 13, 16, 46; and Yrigoyen, 13; taken into custody, 46; and Radical party (after 1924), 47, 68; and the army, 66, 68; mentioned, 14, 15, 23, 44
Amadeo, Mario: 85, 125, 158, 159
Anaya, Gen. Elbio C.: 117, 180
Antipersonalists: formation of (1924), 13; and oligarchy, 16; and Gen. Justo, 20, 50, 66; and liberal nationalism, 20, 66; and the 1928 election, 20; and nationalization of the petroleum industry, 21; alliance of, with Conservatives, 20, 21, 25, 66; alliance of, with Independent Socialists, 25; mentioned, 21, 23, 54, 76
Aramburu, Gen. Pedro Eugenio: revolutionary activities of, 133–135; and Lonardi, 134, 135, 142, 160; and Gori-

llas, 142, 166, 169, 170; and Democratic party, 144; and Popular Radicals, 146; provisional presidency of, 142, 147, 162, 163–166, 167; and the Peronists, 147, 163, 164, 169; economic measures of, 152, 153, 163; and army, 160, 165, 166, 167, 183; career of, 162–163; and Prebisch, 163; uprising against, 165–166; transfers power, 167–168; and Frondizi, 170, 186; kidnapping of, 207, 209; mentioned, 148, 150, 152, 177
Arana, Col. Arturo Ossorio. SEE Ossorio Arana, Col. Arturo
Arendt, Col. Alfred: 6
Argana, José M.: 87
Argentine Institute for the Promotion of Trade (IAPI): 102, 107–108
Argentine Socialist Party: and Radicals (after 1924), 21; and labor, 33; policies of, 33, 167; and Unión Democrática, 92; and Peronism, 125, 146; fragmentation of, after Perón, 143; and Lonardi, 159; and Frondizi, 176; mentioned, 42, 77
armaments: 39, 84, 102
armed forces: and anti-Peronism, xx, 110, 142, 147, 186–187, 193, 195; policies and power of, since Perón's exile, xx, 141–144; fear of, for *descamisados*, 100–101, 113–114, 117–118, 132; manipulation of, by Perón, 100–101, 103–105, 112–114, 116, 117, 118–119, 126, 130; resistance of, against Perón, 110, 111, 112, 116–117, 131, 133–138; under Aramburu, 142, 163, 164–165, 166–167; under Frondizi, 170, 175, 176–184, 185, 186; and Green Dragons, 176–177, 179; and *azul-colorado* power struggle, 190–192, 193–194; and Illía regime, 201, 202; and Onganía regime, 205, 207; and Levingston, 207, 209; and present